818.20809896073 F138z 2002
"Face Zion forward" : first
writers of the Black
Atlantic, 1785-1798

"FACE ZION FORWARD"

D1711498

WITHDRAWN

Other titles in
The Northeastern Library of Black Literature
edited by Richard Yarborough

"FACE ZION FORWARD"

First Writers of the Black Atlantic, 1785–1798

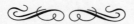

EDITED AND INTRODUCED BY
Joanna Brooks & John Saillant

818.208
F138z

7/07

Northeastern University Press

BOSTON

CUYAHOGA COMMUNITY COLLEGE
EASTERN CAMPUS LIBRARY   SEP 4 2007

Northeastern University Press

Copyright 2002 by Joanna Brooks and John Saillant

All rights reserved. Except for the quotation of short passages for the purposes of
criticism and review, no part of this book may be reproduced in any form or by any
means, electronic or mechanical, including photocopying, recording, or any
information storage and retrieval system now known or to be invented,
without written permission of the publisher.

Library of Congress Cataloging-in-Publication Data
"Face Zion Forward":
First writers of the Black Atlantic, 1785–1798 / edited and introduced
by Joanna Brooks and John Saillant.
p. cm.
Includes bibliographical references.
ISBN 1-55553-540-2 (acid-free paper)—ISBN 1-55553-539-9 (pbk. :
acid-free paper)
1. American prose literature—African American authors. 2. American
prose literature—Colonial period, ca. 1600–1775. 3. African
Americans—History—To 1863—Sources. 4. African Americans—Literary
collections. I. Brooks, Joanna, 1971– II. Saillant, John.
PS647 .A35 .F47 2002
818'.20809896073—dc21   2002007482

Designed by Ann Twombly

Composed in Centaur by Binghamton Valley Composition, Binghamton, New York.
Printed and bound by Maple Press, York, Pennsylvania. The paper is Sebago Antique,
an acid-free stock.

MANUFACTURED IN THE UNITED STATES OF AMERICA
06   05   04   03   02   5   4   3   2   1

Contents

JOHN MARRANT

A Narrative of the Lord's wonderful Dealings with John Marrant, a Black, (Now Going to Preach the Gospel in Nova-Scotia) Born in New-York, in North-America. Taken Down from His Own Relation, Arranged, Corrected, and Published by the Rev. Mr. Aldridge. The Fourth Edition, Enlarged by Mr. Marrant, and Printed (with Permission) for His Sole Benefit, with Notes Explanatory (1785)

JOHN MARRANT

A Sermon Preached on the 24th Day of June 1789, Being the Festival of St. John the Baptist, at the Request of the Right Worshipful the Grand Master Prince Hall, and the Rest of the Brethren of the African Lodge of the Honorable Society of Free and Accepted Masons in Boston (1789)

Contents   vi

Illustrations

Acknowledgments

THE SUPPORT OF Richard Yarborough, the series editor for the North-eastern Library of Black Literature, has been essential to *"Face Zion For-ward."* We also thank Northeastern University Press's senior editor, John Weingartner, for his commitment to this volume.

A *Journal of the Rev. John Marrant* appears here courtesy of the Trustees of the Boston Public Library. Roberta Zonghi, Curator and Head of the Rare Books and Manuscripts Department at the library, helped us secure this permission. Tyler Mabry provided invaluable assistance in preparing the text of the *Journal* for publication.

Joanna Brooks thanks members of her Fall 2000 graduate seminar at the University of Texas at Austin—Lynn Makau, Rebecca Valenzuela, Paul Minifee, Julie Sievers, and Tyler Mabry—for their encouraging responses to John Marrant's *Journal.* The University of Texas at Austin supported the completion of this project with a Special Research Grant, a Ransom Summer Research Grant, and a Dean's Fellowship. Invaluable assistance also came from librarians and staff members at the State Library of Pennsylvania; the Armstrong-Browning Library, Baylor University; the Harry Ransom Center, University of Texas at Austin; and the Shelburne County Historical Society, Shelburne, Nova Scotia. The work of the late Dorothy Porter, an unsung hero of early African American literary research, has been a source of direction and inspiration. Michele Brooks—an exemplary historian in her own right—came through in a clinch with ace genealogical research. John Saillant has kept the faith from beginning to end; as coeditor, he has been stalwart, generous, and true. Finally, thanks to David Kamper for frybread, basketball, and love.

John Saillant acknowledges and thanks these institutions and individuals. The American Antiquarian Society, the Boston Athenæum, the Boston Public Library, Glasgow University Library, and the University of Aberdeen—all places where he read rare documents concerning the eighteenth-century black Atlantic. The United States Department of Education, in a grant to Western Michigan University, "Preparing Tomorrow's Teachers to Use Technology," faculty liaison Allen Webb, provided funding for instructional Web sites that allowed the use of rare documents of the first black Atlantic in undergraduate courses. Sara Bearss, Joanna Brooks, Randall Burkett, Moira Ferguson, Roy Finkenbine, Michael S. Harper, Nelson Lankford, Paul Lovejoy, Joanne Pope Melish, Richard Newman, Phillip M. Richards, John Wood Sweet, Judith Weisenfeld, and Rafia Zafar—all of them understand the importance of preserving the texts of the first African American authors. Kevin Griffin is the one who let it be known that Zion is neither Africa nor South Carolina nor Chicago (all of them his ancestral homes), but rather the heavenly city.

A portion of the proceeds generated by *"Face Zion Forward"* will be donated by the editors to the United Negro College Fund.

"FACE ZION FORWARD"

Introduction

THE "BLACK ATLANTIC" is a phrase coined in the late twentieth century, but the notion was implicit in the late-eighteenth-century African diaspora.[1] Black authors, along with many of their less literary counterparts, assumed a transatlantic perspective beginning in the late eighteenth century—an age of revolution in America, France, and Haiti; of high imports of African slaves into the New World; and of political and military conflict between Christian and Muslim nations.[2] This age of revolution eradicated neither the slave trade nor slavery from the Atlantic littoral, but it did encompass both agitation against the trade and many protests against the enslavement of blacks. Slavery began to end piecemeal in the 1770s, through individual manumissions and state laws against holding men and women in bondage. Wide-scale legislation against the traffic in African slaves and slavery would first be enacted in the nineteenth century.[3] Hostility to Islam, as seemingly a despotic religion that encouraged slavery, became a part of abolitionism in the late eighteenth century. In this momentous age, a transatlantic perspective allowed black men and black women to analyze the origins and persistence of the slave trade and slavery, to argue against slavery in an idiom comprehensible to both whites and blacks, and to envision a free future for blacks, whether in Africa, Europe, or the Americas.

"Face Zion Forward" collects a number of remarkable documents of the 1780s and 1790s in which black authors envisioned the role of Africa and

African American communities in the African diaspora. Several of these documents justified—sometimes explicitly, sometimes allusively—the resettlement of African Americans in West Africa. Others cast Africa as a spiritual environment into which blacks anywhere could enter if they attained the proper consciousness. Black men and black women literate in English were found by the mid-eighteenth century in North America, the West Indies, England, and West Africa, and "back-to-Africa" plans were discussed in writing and, one assumes, in conversation from the 1770s to the twentieth century. Some of the documents collected here were inspired by the experiences of a particular set of African Americans—the black Loyalists, who had joined the British in the American War of Independence and almost 3,000 of whom became refugees to Nova Scotia in the 1780s after the patriot victory. About 1,200 of the black Loyalist refugees gathered in 1791 to sail from Nova Scotia to Sierra Leone. They embarked in January 1792.[4] A desire for freedom, both individual and community, and an understanding of the history of the slave trade and slavery informed this transatlantic migration.

The spokesmen and spokeswomen of the first black Atlantic understood the slave trade and slavery to have originated in the ancient cultures described in the Old Testament and to have continued, more or less in their traditional forms, in West African societies. The slave trade and slavery seemed to have been at one time guided and moderated by the strictures of the Old Testament or the Quran, both of which legitimized property and commerce in men and women but mandated decent treatment of at least some of the unfree. Yet, it seemed to eighteenth-century abolitionists, such traditional systems of unfreedom had been distended into the horrors of the Atlantic slave trade and New World slavery. No ancient justifications of bondage could ever apply to the slave trade and slavery as they were known in the eighteenth-century Atlantic littoral. Moreover, abolitionists were certain that the New Testament, properly understood, barred the slave trade and slavery. Indeed, belief in an antislavery Christianity versus a proslavery Judaism and Islam became in the eighteenth century another chapter in the long history of European and American hostility to the Jewish and Islamic worlds.[5]

To those who argued that slavery was authorized in the New Testament, two Christian arguments were possible and, indeed, were made, by white as well as black enemies of slave trading and slaveholding: that Christian texts had been misinterpreted by those under the sway of the greed and lust that slave trading and slaveholding could satisfy, and that new revelations of God's will were always possible. The interpretive schemes of the first black Atlantic thus spanned the sea and delved into the culture and history of different societies of the Atlantic world. The idiom of black abolitionism was African in recalling events like sale by slave traders in Africa, many of whom were Muslim in areas with heavy exports of slaves in the late eighteenth century.[6] Yet this idiom also adopted Euro-American conventions in insisting on the friendliness of Christianity and the hostility of Islam to the antislavery cause. An idiom that could appeal not only to black slaves but also to the white people who held the power to legislate against the slave trade and slavery could hardly have been better devised.

The free future for blacks was to be the black Atlantic, whether understood as a new black nation forged in the eighteenth century or as black culture imbricated with other traditions and innovations of the Atlantic littoral yet still somehow within the purview of African diasporans. This latter understanding is explored and elaborated by Paul Gilroy in his influential book *The Black Atlantic: Modernity and Double-Consciousness* (1993). According to Gilroy, writings by African Americans and Afro-Britons from the eighteenth century onward constitute a "counterculture of modernity" characterized by a "politics of transfiguration" not "rooted" in the modern nation-state but rather "routed" through black communities, political movements, and migrations around the Atlantic world.[7] Yet, for some blacks in the eighteenth-century age of revolution, a new black nation still seemed possible. Beginning in 1791, slave revolts and a civil war in St. Domingue led eventually to the creation of the independent republic of Haiti in 1804.[8] Around 1790, too, Anglophone blacks came to envision a free black nation in Sierra Leone.

Although the prospect of removal to Sierra Leone generated discussion throughout the British black Atlantic, in London, Boston, Philadelphia, and elsewhere, it generated the greatest response among the black Loyalist population of Nova Scotia. The British Canadian province was home to more than 3,000 African American exiles, many of whom had joined the Loyalists in the American War of Independence because they believed Great Britain to be more friendly to the prospect of black freedom. This belief was in part substantiated by the antislavery stance of the British courts. In 1772, Lord Mansfield, the Chief Justice of the King's Bench, had ruled in the Somerset case that a slave transported to England could not be compelled to return to a slave colony. Although the Mansfield decision did not prohibit slavery or the slave trade in British colonies, it was broadly interpreted to mean the end of slavery in England itself.[9] British military officers capitalized upon England's antislavery reputation to recruit African American soldiers. Twice during wartime, with the "Dunmore Proclamation" of November 1775 and the "Philipsburg Proclamation" of June 1779, the British promised that enslaved and indentured blacks who left patriot owners and joined Loyalist forces would be emancipated. This appeal to black slaves was designed not only to enlarge British ranks but also to disrupt the heavily contested slaveholding American South. It was a successful strategy. Men and women, slave and free, volunteered with black Loyalist military units, and some were issued uniforms emblazoned with the slogan "Liberty to Slaves." Others joined the Loyalist side involuntarily, being impressed into service or taken as plunder by victorious British forces. Still others used the chaos of British raids on Boston, Philadelphia, Savannah, and Charleston to flee their masters and take refuge behind British lines.[10]

At the end of the War of Independence, in 1783, about 3,000 blacks took part in a massive Loyalist evacuation to Nova Scotia. As mandated by the new United States government, every black Loyalist emigrant carried a certificate of passage authorized by high-ranking British military officers, and the emigrants' names, ages, birthplaces, physical descriptions, and status as slave or free persons were officially registered. These passenger lists, known collectively as *The Book of Negroes*, provide a strikingly detailed portrait of the black Loyalist migration. They show a remarkable diversity among the emigrants: males and females; freeborn blacks, former indentured servants, ex-slaves, and slaves; Anglophones and Franco-phones; saltwater and creole emigrants. Reported birthplaces ranged from Massachusetts and Georgia, to Antigua, Grenada, Jamaica, Barbados, and Montserrat, to Guinea. Some wore traditional African "country marks," or scars, on parts of the face, while others bore evidence of the physical cruelties of slavery. *The Book of Negroes* shows that hundreds of black Loyalist women emigrated to Nova Scotia with young children, the youngest born free "within British lines." Two emigrants—Deborah, twenty, and Harry Washington, forty-three—reportedly fled their slavemaster, General George Washington, to find freedom on the Loyalist side.[11]

Once in Nova Scotia, black Loyalists united by their desire for freedom sought also to establish communal independence in separate townships. The largest of these was Birchtown, a settlement of 1,500 free blacks, which was named after the British Brigadier General Samuel Birch, whose signature had authorized the black Loyalists' certificates of passage. From its beginnings in 1783, Birchtown was beset by troubles. Black Loyalist Colonel Stephen Blucke and other founders settled on a rocky shoreline at the heel of an inlet of a larger bay, about three miles from the larger port city of Shelburne. Birchtown mirrored Shelburne in its location—the white settlement was at the head of the inlet and the black settlement on its heel—so the black Loyalists may have thought they could both compete and cooperate with Shelburne. Since Shelburne declined in the 1780s as white settlers fanned out into other points in Nova Scotia, few collateral benefits were enjoyed by Birchtowners. Moreover, it was a poor location for a settlement of craftspeople and subsistence farmers: the coastal land was too rocky or too swampy for farming. The growing season was short, and the winters harsh. Still, despite its endemic disadvantages, Birchtown was then the largest free black settlement in the New World. Significant black Loyalist populations also existed at Shelburne and near the smaller towns of Digby, St. John's, and Preston.[12]

These communities faced harsh conditions. Cold, famine, and small-pox infections persisting from the epidemics of the revolutionary era afflicted their tenuous settlements, as did provincial racism.[13] At Birchtown, black Loyalist settlers had been promised land grants of ten to forty acres; white Shelburne Loyalists plotted to reapportion these lands to themselves until they were discovered and confronted by government surveyor Benjamin Marston. Still, most Birchtowners received only half of the acreage once promised them, and the corruption scandal so delayed the grant process as to leave settlers homeless at the onset of their first Nova Scotian winter. Moreover, because the maritime colonies had always suffered a labor shortage, white settlers viewed the new black immigrants not as potential freeholders but as the agricultural laborers long wanted by the settlement.[14] The hardships of resettlement, exacerbated by the northern winter, led a number of the blacks into tenant farming, perpetual indebtedness, or indenture for the necessities of life. Finally, these economic hardships were compounded by antiblack mob violence, particularly when whites attacked the blacks of Shelburne and Birchtown in July 1784, destroying many newly built black homes during the month-long riot. Black Baptist minister and Shelburne resident David George, whose home was burned down by rioting white soldiers, recorded that white Nova Scotians "had been very cruel to us, and treated many of us as bad as though we had been slaves."[15]

Nova Scotia's black Loyalists also shared in the intensity of their religious belief. Many had participated in the "New Light" evangelical revivals that had stirred parts of Virginia, the Carolinas, and Georgia in the 1760s and 1770s. Some joined or even led pioneering black Christian separatist movements in the colonies. Not surprisingly, these emigrants brought a religious perspective to their commitment to freedom as Loyalists and to their removal to Nova Scotia. They also contributed to a vital and independent black Nova Scotian religious sphere. Finding themselves unwelcome in established congregations, black communities in Birchtown, Shelburne, and Preston established their own churches and miraculously scraped together enough resources to build their own meetinghouses. In addition to attending these congregations, a charismatic cohort of black preachers representing a number of Christian denominations itinerated throughout Nova Scotia, winning audiences and converts among whites, blacks, and Indians alike.[16]

A number of black Loyalists belonged to the Church of England, and they were attended by two black lay preachers, Isaiah Limerick and Joseph Leonard. Limerick, aligned with Blucke, won favor from the Anglican establishment and was sometimes sent to roust more controversial black Anglican and Methodist preachers from Nova Scotian communities. He later joined the Sierra Leone Project, both as an appointed screener of prospective black emigrants and as a migrant. Leonard tended the black Loyalist communities at Digby and nearby Brindley Town. Although he, like Isaiah Limerick, had not been ordained, Leonard independently baptized children and converts, performed marriages, and administered communion. When confronted by the Bishop of Nova Scotia, Charles Inglis, Leonard demanded ordination and asserted that his congregation wanted "to be entirely independent and separate from the whites, and to have a church of their own." In response to this controversial demand, Anglican leaders appointed Limerick to replace him, and the local black community responded by protesting Limerick and boycotting his church. Leonard later joined the migration to Sierra Leone.[17]

The Wesleyan Methodist Society also influenced Nova Scotia's black communities. High-ranking Society officials toured the province and monitored developments at Birchtown, which they viewed as a valuable evangelical prospect. After visiting the region in 1784, John Wesley himself remarked of Birchtown: "The little town they have built is, I suppose, the only town of negroes which has been built in America—nay, perhaps in any part of the world, except only in Africa. I doubt not but some of them can read. When, therefore, we send a preacher or two to Nova Scotia, we will send some books to be distributed among them; and they never need want books while I live." American Methodist itinerants Freeborn Garrettson and John Oliver Cromwell also visited Birchtown, in August 1785, and recommended that the society appoint a resident black exhorter or instructor. The leader they appointed for Birchtown's black Methodists was Moses Wilkinson, a blind and crippled ex-slave who had escaped a Virginia plantation at the onset of the War of Independence. With his fiery preaching style, Wilkinson won many converts to the Wesleyan Methodist Society, including Violet King and her husband, Boston, author of the final narrative in this volume. Most of the black

Methodists, including Wilkinson and the Kings, made the voyage to Sierra Leone, where Wilkinson continued to preach and the black Methodist congregation became a leading voice in protesting the misdeeds of the Sierra Leone Company.[18]

Many black Loyalists adhered to the creed of the Baptists, who preached the necessity of water baptism and eschewed the ritual formalism of Anglicans, Congregationalists, and Methodists. David George, an ex-slave who had pastored a pioneering black church in Silver Bluff, South Carolina, in 1773, reestablished his congregation in the black neighborhoods at the northern end of Shelburne. His account of his conversion, Nova Scotian ministry, and voyage to Sierra Leone appears in this volume. It documents the significance of water baptism to George and his followers. George himself chose for their Shelburne meetinghouse a site "where there was plenty of water, which I had before secretly wished for, as I knew it would be convenient for baptizing at any time." He also recorded the enthusiastic response of black candidates for baptism when he visited the Nova Scotian port city of St. John's: "Some of the people who intended to be baptized were so full of joy that they ran out from waiting at table on their masters, with the knives and forks in their hands, to meet me at the water side." Some historians of religion have suggested that these water-based rituals of rebirth were especially attractive to African Americans because they resembled indigenous West African practices. The experience of David George and the black Baptists of Nova Scotia, then, offers another perspective on the ritual reconstitution of Africanness in the black Atlantic.[19]

Another strain of dissenting Christianity was introduced to black Nova Scotia by an American-born preacher, John Marrant (1755–91). Marrant was one of the early black Atlantic's most prolific authors, and his collected writings appear together here for the first time. He, too, had served with the British as an impressed sailor during the War of Independence. Discharged in London, Marrant resumed his prewar avocation of exhorting, then came to desire the salvation of his "brethren" and "kinsmen, according to the flesh"—the black Nova Scotians, one of whom was his brother, a refugee from Charleston. On May 15, 1785,

Marrant was ordained a member of the Huntingdon Connexion, at the Bath chapel of Connexion founder Selina Hastings, Countess of Huntingdon. The Connexion espoused an evangelical Calvinism made popular by the celebrity preacher George Whitefield, who had died in 1770, shortly after leading a revival meeting in Charleston during which Marrant was converted. It also demonstrated a willingness to educate and ordain black preachers, the first being a black Briton named David Margate, who after his 1774 ordination became notorious for preaching the possibility of liberation to the slaves of the American South. Despite the controversial legacy of David Margate, Marrant sailed to Nova Scotia in August 1785, with the blessing of the Connexion, its trademark clerical band and gown, and full pastoral authority to perform baptisms, marriages, and communions.[20] After establishing a congregation and school at Birchtown, in 1786, he ordained Cato Perkins to serve as his assistant and successor. Illness, impoverishment, and declining communications from the Huntingdon Connexion forced Marrant to leave Nova Scotia in 1789, and so it was Perkins who led the black Huntingdonian congregation to Sierra Leone. There Perkins established a Huntingdonian chapel that continues to operate today, and he also assumed an activist role in redressing the grievances of the Sierra Leone settlers.[21]

By the late 1780s, Nova Scotia was home to a remarkable concentration of black preachers, whose writings document significant contestation among Anglicans, Methodists, Baptists, and Huntingdonians for the theological, ecclesiastical, and political loyalties of their black constituencies. Sometimes these contests led to public battles between rival black preachers, as when Joseph Leonard and Isaiah Limerick clashed over black Anglicans' relationship to the institutional Church in Preston. At Birchtown, Huntingdonian John Marrant and Wesleyan Methodist Moses Wilkinson publicly contended as rivals in a bitter Calvinist-Arminian debate. In 1783, the Huntingdon Connexion formally defended its Calvinist belief in predestination and disavowed the Arminianism of the Wesleyan Methodists. His Huntingdonian ordination also vested Marrant with complete pastoral independence, whereas Wilkinson as a lay preacher was reliant on his Methodist Society superiors and regulated by them. Recounting his story in 1798, Boston King furthered the Calvinist-Arminian paper war by associating predestination with the devil, recalling the motion of his own self-directed will toward God, and noting his connection with the famed Wesleyan itinerant Thomas Coke. Indeed, Coke himself arranged for Methodist missionaries to preach in Nova Scotia and Sierra Leone, even using his own funds to provide those in Nova Scotia with winter supplies.[22]

It is important to recognize that these sectarian contests were not merely matters of personality or local politics. More fundamentally, they concerned how freedom and independence were to be conceptualized and realized in the modern black Atlantic. During the 1780s and 1790s, similar discussions were taking place in black churches around the Atlantic littoral, from the rival black congregations of Nova Scotia, to the black Methodists of Philadelphia organized by Richard Allen and Absalom Jones, to the black Baptists of Kingston, Jamaica, led by George Liele.[23] Theses churches offered postslavery communities unique opportunities for self-governance, mutual assistance, leadership development, and education. They also generated competing understandings of black displacement, enslavement, racism, and emancipation, shaped by their differing theological perspectives on the relationship among God, humankind, and history and on matters such as predestination, providentialism, free will, and human depravity. Finally, different denominations maintained varying degrees of connection with white church leaders and coreligionists, regional and ethnic affiliations, and worship customs. Black churches emerged in the late eighteenth century as a primary venue for black political organization, cultural expression, and consciousness.

Nova Scotia's black churches were instrumental in the organization and mobilization of the removal to Sierra Leone. Sierra Leone was first proposed as a prospective resettlement for the "black poor" of London in 1786. White abolitionists, philanthropists, and businessmen organized the Sierra Leone Company and directed the ill-fated first embarkation of five or six hundred London blacks in 1787. In 1791, when the black Loyalist Thomas Peters sailed from Nova Scotia to London seeking redress for his compatriots, he was recruited by British abolitionists to promote a new emigration to Sierra Leone. By the terms of a compact approved in August 1791, prospective emigrants were to be screened for their "Honesty, Sobriety, and Industry"; every qualified male settler would be granted "not less than Twenty Acres of Land for himself, Ten for his wife, and five for every child"; blacks and whites were to enjoy equal "civil, military, personal, and commercial rights and duties"; and black settlers were to be protected from enslavement by the prohibition of the slave trade in Sierra Leone. Isaiah Limerick, David George, Moses Wilkinson, and Cato Perkins helped organize the 1,200 black Nova Scotian emigrants who embarked from Halifax for Freetown, Sierra Leone, in 1792.[24]

Plans to establish a free black nation in Sierra Leone were unlikely from the onset. The region chosen for settlement was inhabited by slave-trading and slaveholding societies, and the slave trade was heavy in the region around the time of the settlement. Malaria was endemic in the region and would seem to the settlers a plague of biblical dimensions.[25] Black settlers from England or the New World were inevitably outsiders even if a rhetoric of homecoming surrounded their migration, and any moves of the settlers against the slave trade set them in conflict with both indigenous and Euro-American traders. Moreover, the English interests behind the resettlement scheme valued commerce more than black independence.[26] Why did 1,000 to 2,000 free blacks commit themselves to so precarious an enterprise as resettlement in West Africa?[27] The black Atlantic as, in Gilroy's phrase, a "counterculture of modernity" helps to explain this commitment. The move to Sierra Leone occurred just as a crucial link of the modern world was being forged: the creation of nations through democratic revolution and an attack on unfreedom, whether it was the bondage of the colonist, of the citizen without representation, or of the slave.

This move to Sierra Leone was motivated by a form of modernity different from that of the English and American mainstreams. In religion particularly, the free blacks who aimed for Sierra Leone arranged modernity in their own fashion. Their religion was deeply traditional in a liberal age, premised on God's predestining will and providence, the existence of a covenanted community of believers set against the sinners of the world, the importance of crisis conversion and other rituals of transfiguration, and the goal of a racial homeland as promised for the black elect in a covenant with God. Yet this faith was more than simply traditional, since what its adherents wanted was the protection it offered from the corrosive effects of postslavery society—indeed, from the corrosive effects of untrammeled freedom in a society in which the attitudes and actions of many were inevitably influenced by the slaveholding past. By the 1780s, as black freedom was slowly coming into being, it was obvious to free blacks that liberty itself could not protect them from scorn, poverty, and degradation. Liberty was at best a civil status requiring continual defense and negotiation in an inegalitarian and racist society. The black Zionist impulse was to transcend this imperfect liberty and enjoy a secure freedom. It was a utopian impulse, an urge to separate a community of blacks from the political and social relations of the Euro-American sphere.

Religious belief and material circumstances merged in the use of the language of covenants. The language of the black Loyalists indicates that they believed a contract or a covenant mandated their land grants in Nova Scotia. The broken covenant of Nova Scotia bred in the refugees feelings that a new home could be found and broken promises could be mended, if not by those who had betrayed black people, then by God himself. A rapid sequence of events—the black Loyalist emigration to Nova Scotia in 1783, the mid-1780s discussion of the removal of the black poor to Sierra Leone, the gathering of a critical mass of black clergy in Nova Scotia, proposals beginning in 1789 that the black Loyalists migrate to West Africa, a gathering of prospective migrants in 1791, and the embarkation itself in early 1792—suggests that this strand of black Zionism came almost immediately to focus on resettlement in Sierra Leone. A covenanted community resettled in Sierra Leone was to be free as well as shielded from the antiblack forces in the postslavery world. Since the modern world as most of us experience it includes a liberty that must be defended and redefended and is never a secure state in which we can rest, we might consider the beliefs and values of the settlers the quintessence of countercultural modernity—for freedom, but not as the free world is now obliged to understand it.

Establishing spaces where black people could enjoy security from racial violence and exercise their newfound liberties was a major concern for black Atlantic communities in the years after the War of Independence. While black Loyalists sought to realize this hope by immigrating to Birchtown, Nova Scotia, and Freetown, Sierra Leone, many free blacks who remained in the United States emigrated to urban centers such as Boston and Philadelphia. Some white residents in these cities reacted fearfully and violently to the growth of these free black populations and to their increased public presence.

By the late eighteenth century, black New Englanders had forged a tradition of public festivities known as Negro Election Day. African Americans had also participated in training days for militia, in early Fourth of July celebrations, and, in the Middle Colonies, Pinkster (Pentecost) festivals. Such days amounted to only a few a year, but they were moments of celebration and provisional liberty. Beginning in the 1790s, however, white men, often in mobs, harassed and attacked blacks who were utilizing public space, effectively denying them citizens' rights to act and to express themselves in the public sphere.[28]

In the 1780s and 1790s, a black Bostonian named Prince Hall (1738?–1807) defined what was to become a lasting solution for African Americans. Hall and fourteen other free blacks were initiated into the Masonic Order in March 1775 by members of an Irish Military Masonic lodge stationed in Boston on the eve of the War of Independence. Between 1787 and 1797, Hall organized and chartered a network of African American Masonic lodges in Boston, Philadelphia, and Providence, Rhode Island.[29] These lodges, like the black churches emergent in the same era, provided important resources for black political and cultural development. By reinterpreting Masonic traditions and developing their own brand of Masonic brotherhood, Prince Hall and his fellows constructed for postslavery communities new concepts of black history and identity and, importantly, new spaces.

An early proponent of colonization in Africa, Hall quickly understood that American-born blacks considered their native land their home. Prince Hall fiercely criticized the street violence directed against black men and women in a speech delivered to the African Lodge of Freemasons in 1797 (and reprinted in this volume): "Daily insults you meet with in the streets of Boston; much more on public days of recreation, how are you shamefully abus'd, and that at such a degree, that you may truly be said to carry your lives in your hands; and the arrows of death are flying about your heads; helpless old women have their clothes torn off their backs, even to the exposing of their nakedness." He and his fellow black Freemasons adopted a dual strategy for securing black spaces. First, they asserted their civil rights as citizens of the United States to use public spaces by protesting white mob violence and by participating unapologetically in the long-standing Masonic custom of parading through the streets on semiannual holidays. Second, they also established the more private space of the African Lodge, where black men could exercise without molestation their rights to security, dignity, and equality. In a 1792 address to the lodge (also reprinted in this volume), Hall implied that such a policy of racial separation might be necessary to prevent strife, citing from Genesis 13 the example of Abraham: "How did Abraham prevent the storm, or rebellion that was rising between Lot's servants and his? Saith Abraham to Lot, let there be no strife I pray thee between me and thee, for the land is before us, if you will go to the left, then I will go to the right, and if you will go to the right, then I will go to the left. They divided and peace was restored." The members of the African Lodge had created a black space for themselves both in their society and in their building: this creation was a domestication of the Freetown ideal. But they refused to relinquish public space to their opponents without a struggle. For their bold establishment and defense of black spaces—actions viewed with hostility by some whites—Prince Hall and his lodge members were lampooned in newspaper reports and caricatured in cartoons well into the nineteenth century. Many African Americans of the nineteenth and twentieth centuries would follow in their footsteps, securing safe places (both figuratively and literally) yet trying to expand the sphere of black people further and further into the public world.[30]

Within the space of the African Lodge, Prince Hall redeveloped the content of Freemasonry to promote the equality, honor, and dignity of black people. According to Masonic teachings, the implements of practical masonry—the compass, square, and plumbline—represented the principles of equality, benevolence, love, mutual assistance, and moral rectitude essential to the building of a new humankind. Freemasons also celebrated the secrecy and ancientness of their rituals, which they believed descended from ancient Egyptians through Abraham to the builders of Solomon's Temple and then to a worldwide order of practitioners identifiable only by their knowledge of certain passwords and hand signals. Masonic rituals of rebirth and rebuilding were reinterpreted by Prince Hall and the African Lodge to pertain to the construction of postslavery black identities and communities. Moreover, the celebrated ancient Egyptian roots of the order were claimed by Hall and his fellows as a noble legacy belonging to Africans worldwide, including African Americans. Freemasonry thus became an important if unlikely source of modern black thought about Africa, and Prince Hall inaugurated in the late eighteenth century discursive traditions of Ethiopianism and Egyptophilia important to black liberation, black nationalist, and Afrocentric movements to the present day. Indeed, with the exception of Frederick Douglass, many black political leaders of the eighteenth and nineteenth centuries—including African Methodist Episcopal Church founders Richard Allen and Absalom Jones, Haitian Attorney General Prince Saunders, Liberian President Joseph Jenkins Roberts, James Forten, David Walker, Henry Highland Garnet, William Wells Brown, Josiah Henson, and Martin Delaney—were Prince Hall Freemasons.[31]

John Marrant also became a Prince Hall Freemason when he traveled from Nova Scotia to Boston in 1788. Invited by Prince Hall to serve as African Lodge chaplain, Marrant delivered a ceremonial speech on the customary Masonic feast day of June 24, 1789. This *Sermon to the African Lodge*, included in this volume, articulates the key themes of Prince Hall

Freemasonry: it criticizes racism as antithetical to the egalitarian and humanitarian principles of the Masonic order, it promotes universal brotherly love and acceptance, it calls for greater consciousness among African Americans of their noble history and potential, and it claims biblical and Masonic ancient history as African history, positioning black peoples from Egypt and Ethiopia to Boston as the true subjects of civilization. Although it is likely that Prince Hall assisted Marrant in composing portions of the *Sermon* most concerned with Masonic history, the text also reflects Marrant's preacherly concern with the gathering and redemption of postslavery black communities. The beliefs that motivated his black Loyalist congregants to emigrate to Sierra Leone were shared by the black Freemasons of Boston, in ritual if not in a physical return to Africa. The career of John Marrant thus combined two powerful and distinctive modes of early black emancipationist thought, and it exemplified the remarkable movement of persons and ideas characteristic of the black Atlantic experience.

"Face Zion Forward" is the first publication of the collected works of John Marrant, with contemporary writings by his fellow black Loyalists and Prince Hall Freemasons. These texts document the remarkable vitality and interconnectedness of early black intellectual life, demonstrating that pioneering writers such as Marrant, Prince Hall, David George, and Boston King were not the accidental authorities they are sometimes made out to be.[32] Rather, these men were collaborators and sometimes contestants in the negotiation of a modern postslavery blackness. Marrant, George, and King shared the hardships of the black Loyalist experience in Nova Scotia, and they crossed paths as itinerants of different Christian denominations and theologies; Hall personally guided Marrant through the intimate initiatory rites of Freemasonry and joined with him in the construction of a specifically black interpretation of Masonic principles, symbology, and lore. Taken together, these late-eighteenth-century writings represent a foundational moment in black Atlantic intellectual history, a moment that generated two essential modes of black thought about Africa. The first imagined Africa as a place to be redeemed through emigration, colonization, and proselytization by once-enslaved Christian

blacks, and the second conceived of Africa as a recollected group consciousness among the members of the modern black diaspora.

The earliest of the documents collected here is *A Narrative of the Lord's Wonderful Dealings with John Marrant, a Black, (Now Going to Preach the Gospel in Nova-Scotia)* (1785). This conversion and captivity narrative is based on remarks delivered by Marrant at his Huntingdon Connexion ordination. Attending the ordination was a minor British poet named Samuel Whitchurch, who transcribed, versified, and then published Marrant's story as *The Negro Convert, a Poem; Being the Substance of the Experience of Mr. John Marrant, A Negro* in 1785. Also in attendance was the Methodist minister William Aldridge, whose notes from the ordination probably formed the basis for the published *Narrative*, and who also composed the preface to the work. London's *Monthly Review* scoffed that the *Narrative* was "embellished with a good deal of *adventure*, enlivened by the *marvellous*, and a little touch of the MIRACULOUS; all which, no doubt, will go down, glibly enough, with those readers for whom this publication is chiefly calculated."[33] Still, Marrant's account of his wayward youth, dramatic conversion, Indian captivity, and Loyalist military service won broad popularity among audiences in England, the United States, and Canada, and new editions appeared regularly into the nineteenth century. Only one of these more than twenty editions can be considered authoritative: this is the fourth edition of August 1785, which was, as its title page announces, "enlarged by Mr. Marrant, and printed (with permission) for his sole benefit, with notes explanatory." Significantly, this edition reports the brutal punishment of slaves found to be worshiping God that Marrant witnessed when he attempted to proselytize on a South Carolina plantation. These scenes were excised from most versions of the *Narrative*, except for the authorized fourth edition, the only one that survived the whitewashing by Marrant's publishers, particularly the posthumous ones.

The *Narrative* must be understood not simply as autobiography but also as commentary on the situation of blacks in 1785. In addition to documenting the cruelties of slavery, it conveys the sense of uncertainty and homelessness faced by the free black Loyalists, whether evacuated to Nova Scotia or discharged in London. Marrant opens his account with an announcement that his early wanderings in life, as his family moved from New York to St. Augustine to Georgia to South Carolina, prophesied a fact of life for African Americans, here addressed as "we": "Here we have no continuing city." Subsequent sojourns in the wilderness and among southeastern Indian tribes, impressment into the British navy, and relocation to London extended this pattern of wandering. By 1785, Marrant had traveled extensively around the Atlantic littoral and seems hardly to have had a home himself in the previous ten years.

However much migration was geographical, it was also spiritual for Marrant, for whom the regeneration of black communities required conversion or personal transfiguration, a theme appearing throughout the *Narrative*. Marrant himself had been converted as a teenager, under the influence of George Whitefield. Soon he was transfigured into a more profound believer by faith and by lack of food and water in a pilgrimage in the woods. His ultimate transfiguration in this world occurred as, under threat of Indian torture and execution "in the wilderness," he put his life entirely in God's hands and was rewarded with the ability to preach to the Indians in their own language, a skill that redeemed his life. After his captivity, he appeared in Charleston, unrecognized in Indian garb save by his youngest sister, then rose again as a black man from the strange outfit. As he noted, "Thus the dead was brought to life again; thus the lost was found." Joseph, Lazarus, Jesus, and the apostles were Marrant's models for such transfigurations, particularly in that Marrant's trials often lasted three days and then were succeeded by his salvation and renewal.[34]

The transfiguration of Mary Scott complemented Marrant's experience and suggested the goal of the blacks partaking of such experiences. Mary Scott was a young girl living in Charleston. Her race was not mentioned, but since she was described as Marrant's neighbor and since he associated closely with her and her family, he seems to have implied either that she was black or that her experience had some relevance for black people. Taken with Revelation 20:12, which describes the separation of the good and the evil—the latter including some of the great of the earth—before the opening of "a new heaven and a new earth," "the holy city, new

Jerusalem" (21:1–2), Mary began to contemplate the graves of children in the local cemetery and predict her own demise. Her prediction proved accurate, and, before she died, Mary had a vision of the holy city, which in a traditional sense was heaven, but in Marrant's sense seems to have been a land on earth to which African Americans could aspire. Marrant found Mary "on the bed, with her eyes fixed up to heaven; when turning herself and seeing me, she said, 'Mr. Marrant, don't you see that pretty town, and those fine people, how they shine like gold?—O how I long to be with my Lord and his redeemed Children in Glory!' " Moments later, transfigured at the last, Mary died. Thus, the *Narrative*, which begins in physical and spiritual homelessness, concludes with a final vision of a holy city, a vision that certainly appealed to the black men and women then struggling in the maritime colonies and elsewhere to build post-slavery black communities. That this arc from homelessness to the heavenly city paralleled Marrant's own conversion narrative underscores the importance Marrant assigned to spiritual rebirth as an element of black emancipation. Did he also envision that the heavenly city might be realized on the African continent? Was Mary Scott's prophetic vision of heaven a vision of Africa as well? Marrant does not say, but he does include in her vision one element that had long been associated with West Africa—gold. Gold was mined there, and Marrant may have been invoking that association.

In 1785, Marrant sailed not to Africa but to Birchtown, Nova Scotia, where he established a Huntingdonian congregation, a school, and a home base for his three-year mission. *A Journal of the Rev. John Marrant*, published by Marrant upon his return to London in 1790, records his experiences and documents the unique black Atlantic theology he had developed. The most extensive account of a black man preaching in black communities before the American Civil War, the *Journal* is remarkable for its detailed depiction of life in the black Loyalist settlements and for its revelation of the complexity and diversity of black religious thought in the late eighteenth century. It is an essential albeit long-ignored component of early black Atlantic literature. This volume republishes the *Journal* for the first time since its original 1790 imprint.

In his preface to the *Journal*, Marrant justifies the publication as an attempt to defend himself in a deepening dispute with the Huntingdon Connexion. The text accounts for his time, expenditures, and preaching successes in Nova Scotia. It also describes the hardships and harsh conditions under which he operated. In accordance with the Huntingdon Connexion's mandate that its ministers preach continually and itinerantly, he visited small settlements of impoverished blacks, Indians, and whites scattered along the southeastern coast between Shelburne and Liverpool. Like Birchtown, these small villages—Green Harbor, Ragged Island, Sable River, Cape Negro, and Jordan River—were populated by subsistence farmers and fishermen, who struggled for survival against long winters, short growing seasons, deep snows, rocky soils, and rough seas. Famines and smallpox afflicted the region. Although he attempted to organize community relief efforts, Marrant also found himself in increasingly dire circumstances. He was exhausted from his travels through swamps, snows, icy rivers, and stormy ports, stricken with smallpox, malnourished, and impoverished. Moreover, the Huntingdon Connexion—which was struggling with its own internal crises—failed to respond to his pleadings for financial support. Still, the *Journal* portrays Marrant as a staunch defender of Huntingdonian Calvinism against the machinations of local Wesleyan Methodists, whom he scornfully calls "the Arminians."

While the *Journal* closely details these ecclesiastical disputes, it offers scant information about Marrant's personal and family life. Rarely did eighteenth-century religious autobiographers record with any emphasis major life events such as marriage or the birth of a child. Marrant did not diverge from convention in this respect, and, consequently, his *Journal* provides few answers to some intriguing biographical questions. One of these questions concerns Marrant's relationship to three emigrants documented in *The Book of Negroes*: Mellia Marrant, thirty years old, her six-year-old daughter, Amelia Marrant, and her four-year-old son, Ben Marrant. On June 13, 1783, as she boarded the ship *William and Mary* bound for Annapolis Royal, Nova Scotia, Mellia Marrant reported that she was "formerly the property of John Marrant near Santee, Carolina" but that she "left him at the siege of Charlestown." The *Journal* makes no mention of Mellia, Amelia, or Ben, though it does relate that Marrant enjoyed a tearful reunion with old friends and possibly family members upon his arrival in Birchtown. The historian Margaret Washington has suggested that John was the brother, husband, or ex-husband of Mellia, while Vincent Carretta has argued that he was in fact her owner.[35] Although there were indeed a few free black slave owners in South Carolina before the War of Independence, there is no evidence to show that the author John Marrant and the slave owner "John Marrant" are the same person. In fact, genealogical records document two possible owners of Mellia Marrant in the Charleston area in the late eighteenth century. John Mayrant (1725/6–67) was a prominent planter of St. James, Santee Parish, South Carolina; his son John Mayrant (1762–1836) served in the War of Independence as a lieutenant in the South Carolina navy, then moved from the Santee-Charleston area to Camden District, Claremont County, South Carolina, where United States census records from 1790 show him owning sixty-five slaves. Orthography also suggests that Mellia belonged to the patrician Mayrant family rather than to the black evangelist Marrant. It seems that the evangelist Marrant pronounced his name "Morant," for so it appeared in letters written by Freeborn Garrettson and other Methodist ministers, as well as in Shelburne County land records. Had Mellia Marrant reported the black evangelist Marrant to British officials, it follows that his name would have been transcribed as "Morant" on her freedom certificate and in *The Book of Negroes*. The fact that her former owner was represented as "Marrant" further points to the Mayrant family of Santee.[36]

What other family connections did Marrant have or make in Nova Scotia? Marrant told the audiences at his ordination that his black Loyalist brother had invited him to come to Nova Scotia as a preacher, but the *Journal* does not specifically mention such an individual. The *Journal* does suggest that Marrant had biological or adoptive children in Nova Scotia, as an appended letter from his black Loyalist friend Margaret Blucke inquires, "Let me know how your children and yourself does." It also relates that an unnamed "boy" sometimes accompanied him in his itinerancy. Perhaps this youngster was one of Marrant's children;

perhaps it was Anthony Elliot, a young pastoral assistant from Birchtown. Similarly mysterious are the circumstances of Marrant's marriage on August 15, 1788, to a black woman named Elizabeth Herries (or Harries), an event recorded in the Shelburne County *Register of Marriages* but not in the *Journal* itself.[37] What became of these family relationships after Marrant left Nova Scotia is unknown. A note inscribed in one of the surviving copies of the *Journal* reports that Marrant died in April 1791 and was buried at Church Street in Islington, England.

Ultimately, the *Journal* is more than a missionary's autobiography. Behind the traditional genre lurks a hidden transcript that shows that John Marrant went to Nova Scotia not only to further the work of the Huntingdon Connexion but to deliver a message of specific import to its black Loyalist communities. This message is encoded in the *Journal's* numerous biblical citations, which refer the reader to the chapters and verses that formed the bases for Marrant's sermons. For example, the *Journal* records that for his first sermon at Birchtown, on Sunday morning, December 20, 1785, Marrant chose as his text Acts 3:22–23. It does not reprint the full text of these verses, which reads: "For Moses truly said unto the fathers, A prophet shall the Lord your God raise up unto you of your brethren, like unto me; him shall ye hear in all things whatsoever he shall say unto you. And it shall come to pass, that every soul, which will not hear that prophet, shall be destroyed from among the people." This text bore several powerful implications for his ministry and for Birchtown. It suggested that Marrant believed himself to be a prophet called of God to deliver a message to the black Loyalists, and it positioned the community as a covenanted people or a new Israel. Marrant also claimed the prophetic authority to promulgate a new theology specifically relevant to the conditions and needs of his black congregants, and this theology took shape in subsequent biblical citations. It is important to notice that the *Journal* provides references but not texts, because this method of encoding disguised the specifically black content of his preaching from the Huntingdon Connexion and other potentially hostile or dangerous readers. Marrant would not have been the first black Huntingdonian to upset the Connexion with his ministrations to black audiences: David Margate was summarily recalled from South Carolina in 1774, after declaring himself a black Moses and preaching rebellion to local slaves. Nor was Marrant alone in his use of Scripture for covert communication to black audiences, as many early African American orators and writers relied upon their target audiences' knowledge of the Bible to convey sentiments considered dangerous by the white public.[38]

Marrant used Scripture references to contextualize the sufferings of black Nova Scotians within a redemptionist design. The fundamental doctrine of his theology was that an overruling God worked a design in the universe by countering human sin with beneficent provisions. Theodicy was thus of the first importance in the theology Marrant articulated in the *Journal* and in sermons delivered in Nova Scotia. Enacting a "grand design," God "overruled all things for his glory," Marrant assured the Nova Scotians. Describing for his audience the "proportion of one dispensation with another, in the divine government," Marrant promised that there would be a "harmony and correspondence" of the "dispensations." The proportionality of the dispensations of a benevolent, omnipotent God—the notion that God countered evil with an overruling good, as with the Crucifixion and the Resurrection—was a central doctrine of predestinarian Christianity. Using a key word of the Calvinist tradition, Marrant urged onto his audience "a relish of those divine provisions." Still, acknowledging the suffering of his audience, Marrant conceded the difficulty that "sometimes things are so variable, or mixed in providence, that we are ready to say, 'wherein does the holiness and glory of God appear in them?'" "God often hides the sensible signs of his favour from his dearest friends," Marrant further conceded, yet "real Christians, whilst they are among fiery serpents are awaiting with desire, and holy expectations, for the good of the promise." He assured black Nova Scotians that "the judge of all the earth does right."

A fuller sense of Marrant's preaching style can be gleaned from his *Funeral Sermon Preached by the Desire of the Deceased, John Lock; the Text Chosen by Himself, from the Epistle of St. Paul to the Philippians, Chap. i., Ver. 21*, which was published with the *Journal* in 1790 and also appears in this book. The *Journal* remembers John Lock, Jr., as a convert of exceptional piety and a victim of the smallpox epidemic; local Nova Scotian historians believe he was a member of the Locke family who came from New England and settled Ragged Island in the late 1750s. Before his death, Lock requested that Marrant preach from Philippians 1:21, "For me to live, is Christ; and to die, is gain"; Marrant complied on October 27, 1787, at Ragged Island. For the immiserated Nova Scotians, death was an ever-present threat, and in the *Funeral Sermon* Marrant exhorts his audience to face it fearlessly. He charges his audience to wean themselves from the things of this world, an essential Calvinist theme, and to place full faith in God's redemptionist design. Doing so will prepare them for their own deaths as well as for conversion and for facing worldly trials. Marrant preaches, "We are not to let drop the interest of Christ, though its defence requires the greatest application of mind, the severest self-denial, and the most evident danger, of parting with dear friends, or feeling the resentment of cruel enemies." Teachings such as this also prepared black Nova Scotians to undertake the hazardous and uncertain emigration to Sierra Leone in 1792 and seemed to portray the migration to Africa as a transfiguration accomplished by dying to the racist and slaveholding New World and being reborn in Zion.

One of the uniquely Africanist elements of Marrant's theology was his merger of an orthodox definition of conversion with a notion of the covenanted community, which had faded out of late-eighteenth-century Calvinism but was still convincing to the dispossessed blacks of Nova Scotia.[39] Had Marrant merely used Christian sentimentalist language— affection, benevolence, charity, and the like—he would have established himself as a major theologian of black community, a theoretician of the way in which conversion integrated blacks into a community of believers. But Marrant adds to Christian sentimentalism an ancient notion of the covenanted community—in his formulation, a black community in a particular covenant with God to pass through suffering into Zion. He promises that God will lead the covenanted community to "mount Sion," where those with his "Father's name written in their foreheads" will live with the Lamb, who "shall feed them, and shall lead them unto living fountains of waters: and God shall wipe away all tears from their eyes"

(Revelation 7). In one of his few uses of an entire chapter, instead of a few verses, Marrant preaches from Isaiah 60, which begins, "Arise, shine; for thy light is come," and ends, "A little one shall become a thousand, and a small one a strong nation: I the Lord will hasten it in his heart." Marrant preaches that this postslavery reconstruction of the black community is premised on conversion, or the new birth, when he states that one who feels "the sweet workings of the spirit" has "a sympathetic feeling for those of his fellow-creatures, who has [sic] their face Zion forward."

The Sierra Leone emigration experience is represented by two texts in this volume: *An Account of the Life of Mr. David George, from Sierra Leone in Africa* (1793) and *Memoirs of the Life of Boston King, a Black Preacher. Written by Himself, during His Residence at Kingswood-School* (1798). David George delivered his life narrative to the Baptist ministers John Rippon and Samuel Pearce, during a visit to England in summer 1793; Rippon, the editor of *The Annual Baptist Register*, a serial compilation of reports from Baptist congregations worldwide, published George's *Account* in the 1793 edition. Boston King left his post as a teacher of native Africans to study at the Methodist Kingswood School near Bristol, England, from May 1794 to August 1796. There he wrote his *Memoirs,* which were published serially in the *Methodist Magazine,* March through June 1798. Both men were exslaves, and their narratives relate the cruelties of slavery, the tenuous transition from slave to free, and the fragility of postslavery freedom. They also provide eyewitness accounts of the Nova Scotian emigrants' initial struggle against tropical conditions and endemic fevers to establish homes and churches in Freetown, Sierra Leone. King, whose father was African born, viewed the Christianization of native Africans as a key objective of the Sierra Leone emigration. After attending Kingswood School to improve his abilities as a teacher, he returned to his school and Methodist church in Sierra Leone, where he died in 1802. George also died in Sierra Leone, in 1810, leaving behind a vigorous Baptist congregation.

The writings of John Marrant, Boston King, and David George record black people in pursuit of a space they could control. These texts convey a sense that many blacks felt at home only in precarious or marginal spaces: worshiping outdoors, in Indian towns, seeking refuge in British camps, being at sea, and migrating to the Maritimes. John Marrant's young convert Mary Scott seems to have been comfortable wandering in a graveyard, and Marrant himself seems never to have settled anywhere. Sierra Leone, however, was to be a place where black men and women were to be "free and happy."[40] Its political space was to be defined by suffrage for black men only, while its religious space was to be defined by churches for the settlers, with black ministers. These ideals for Freetown were quickly crushed as the Sierra Leone Company, followed by the royal governors, placed white Britons in authority and ultimately razed the largest church the settlers had built. The congregation was dismembered and placed in groups under the supervision of Anglican missionaries. Malaria, too, made Sierra Leone an unsafe location.[41]

For most African Americans, slave and free, the prospect of emigration to Africa was exceedingly remote. Although plans for the removal of blacks to locations outside the United States were promoted in the late eighteenth century by prominent white Americans, including Thomas Jefferson, the Reverend Samuel Hopkins, and Philadelphia publisher Matthew Carey, many black intellectuals came to question their premises and purposes. Moreover, the end of the War of Independence and the founding of the United States gave black people reason to wonder whether the patriot rhetoric of liberty and justice might not apply to them as well. Indeed, in a handful of northern states, this rhetoric found a juridical and legal articulation as courts and legislatures in Massachusetts, Vermont, and Pennsylvania mandated slave emancipation, albeit on very limited and gradual terms.[42] As thousands of newly emancipated ex-slaves migrated to northern cities, they formed their own social and political institutions. The names of these pioneering institutions—for example, the African Lodge of Freemasons and the African Methodist Episcopal Church—signified that black people intended to live freely and prosper as Americans while also maintaining in memory, thought, and practice their place within the African diaspora.

In January 1787, African Lodge founder Prince Hall petitioned the

Massachusetts legislature to assist black Bostonians in removing to Africa, but he changed course after news of the problems afflicting the first Sierra Leone Company expedition reached Boston that summer. A new petition presented to the legislature by Hall in October 1787 demanded state funding for the education of black children, and it signaled his new focus on advancing the rights and concerns of black people in the American political arena. His ongoing promotion of black Freemasonry fostered a complementary social and cultural space for the development of African American identity, leadership, and consciousness. The lessons of the African Lodge of Freemasons are represented in three speeches published here: John Marrant, *A Sermon Preached on the 24th Day of June 1789, Being the Festival of St. John the Baptist, at the Request of the Right Worshipful the Grand Master Prince Hall, and the Rest of the Brethren of the African Lodge of the Honorable Society of Free and Accepted Masons in Boston* (1789); Prince Hall, *A Charge, Delivered to the Brethren of the African Lodge on the 25th of June, 1792* (1792); and Hall, *A Charge, Delivered to the African Lodge, June 24, 1797, at Menotomy* (1797). These three speeches were designed to provide lodge members a systematic education—or, using the architectural tropes of Freemasonry, a "foundation" laid by Marrant and two "pillars" of "superstructure" erected by Hall—for advancement within Freemasonry. They were published by special arrangement so that lodge members not in attendance at the ceremonial feast days in Boston, including members in Philadelphia and Providence, Rhode Island, would have access to these valuable lessons.

The modernity characteristic of the black Atlantic appears in all three speeches, which criticize the slave trade, slavery, and racism and posit a countercultural legacy for American blacks as the heirs of Africa. Both Marrant and Hall encouraged African Lodge members to know themselves as black people. Adapting the Masonic lore celebrating the builders of ancient Egypt, they taught that Africa—not Europe—had been since the world's beginnings the center of human advancement. Marrant pointed out that the Bible and biblical commentators located the Garden of Eden, or "Paradise," as bordering on "Egypt, which is the principal part of African Ethiopia," and that by implication Africa—not Europe—

was a land chosen by God as the scene of biblical history. The slave trade as well as slavery and antiblack racism were, then, an assault against a holy land and holy people. Marrant and Hall suggested to their audiences that "African kings" and Islamic traders had betrayed their fellow Africans in the slave trade, and that as the descendants of these enslaved peoples, they themselves could rehabilitate a black spiritual brotherhood through the teachings of Christianity and Freemasonry. They also taught that African men and women from the Queen of Sheba to the early Church fathers Augustine and Tertullian had attained exalted levels of knowledge and distinction and that African Americans must also value their potential for similar achievements.

Most fundamentally, Marrant and Hall emphasized that blacks deserved not only freedom from slavery but also the freedom to love and to be loved. Race and sentiment were often linked in eighteenth-century thought on slavery and freedom. The Masonic fraternity provided an opportunity for the exercise of equality and fraternity among black men and among Masons worldwide. The Masons of history had enjoyed, Marrant wrote, "a free intercourse with all Lodges over the terrestrial globe; wherever arts flourish, a man hath a free right (having a recommendation) to visit his brethren, and they are bound to accept him; these are the laudable bonds that unite Free Masons together in one indissoluble fraternity—thus in every nation he finds a friend, and in every climate he may find a house—this it is to be kindly affectioned one to another, with brotherly love, in honour preferring one another." Hall used this sentimental concept of affectionate fraternity as a basis for claiming that black people should enjoy equal treatment as citizens of the United States. He reminded his audiences that black men had fought with white men "shoulder to shoulder, brother soldier to brother soldier" in the War of Independence and that they had remained loyal to the United States even as a series of small postwar rebellions, some led by Freemasons, embroiled western New England. But in his 1797 *Charge*, Hall also pointed to the ongoing revolution in St. Domingue (soon to be renamed Haiti) as evidence that black people could rise up to seize for themselves unfulfilled promises of freedom, equality, and fraternity.

Might not African Americans do likewise? Hall's 1797 *Charge* suggested in sometimes coded language that black people should avoid "the slavish fear of man" and be prepared to actively defend and advance their own interests. If America was to be their physical home, then they could create their own Africanist social, cultural, and spiritual home within spaces such as the African Lodge and the black church.

The writings collected in *"Face Zion Forward"* represent the vanguard of black religious and political thought at the end of the eighteenth century. To their original audiences as well as to contemporary readers, they documented sophistication and diversity of opinion among the writers of the early black Atlantic on subjects such as the role of Africa in black liberation, and they demonstrated the value of Christian theology and Freemasonry as frameworks for developing countercultural and emancipationist ideas and movements. Given their frequent references to scripture and Masonic lore and their sometimes unfamiliar eighteenth-century usages of language, these texts may present an interpretive challenge even to readers familiar with the black Atlantic tradition. Moreover, because they do not conform to more familiar genres and styles of early African American writing such as the slave narrative, these texts challenge us to deepen and complicate our understanding of black intellectual and literary history.

We encourage readers to be alert to the rich intertextuality of the writings collected in *"Face Zion Forward."* None of them, not even an apparently straightforward autobiographical narrative, stands independent of its historical context or of the beliefs and denominational loyalties of its author. These writings refer to the Bible and quote it, sometimes without attribution. They frequently quote from eighteenth-century evangelical hymnody, especially the works of Isaac Watts, and invoke contemporary theological and ecclesiastical controversies. Finally, as documents of a particularly charged and coherent moment in eighteenth-century black history, these texts refer to the actors, places, events, racial theories, and policies of that era. This complex interweaving of biblical, hymnological, theological, ecclesiastical, biographical, and historical texts requires special consideration. We encourage readers to cultivate an awareness of the polysemism of these writings and to participate actively in their interpretation by complementing primary text close readings with explorations of secondary resources. It is especially important that readers follow in-text Scripture references to their sources in the King James Version of the Bible so as to assess the full relevance of these Scriptures.

FOR FURTHER READING

Blakeley, Phyllis R., and John N. Grant, eds. *Eleven Exiles: Accounts of Loyalists in the American Revolution.* Toronto: Dundurn Press, 1982.

Brooks, Joanna. "Prince Hall, Freemasonry, and Genealogy." *African American Review* 34 (summer 2000): 197–216.

Clifford, Mary Louise. *From Slavery to Freetown: Black Loyalists after the American Revolution.* Jefferson, N.C.: McFarland, 1999.

Frey, Sylvia. *Water from the Rock: Black Resistance in a Revolutionary Age.* Princeton: Princeton University Press, 1991.

Frey, Sylvia, and Betty Wood. *Come Shouting to Zion: African American Protestantism in the American South and British Caribbean to 1830.* Chapel Hill: University of North Carolina Press, 1998.

Fyfe, Christopher. *A History of Sierra Leone.* New York: Oxford University Press, 1962.

Fyfe, Christopher, ed. *"Our Children Free and Happy": Letters from Black Settlers in Africa in the 1790s.* Edinburgh: Edinburgh University Press, 1991.

Gilroy, Paul. *The Black Atlantic: Modernity and Double-Consciousness.* Cambridge: Harvard University Press, 1993.

Hodges, Graham Russell. *The Black Loyalists Directory.* New York: Garland, 1996.

McKerrow, P. E. *A Brief History of the Coloured Baptists of Nova Scotia, 1783–1895.* Ed. Frank Stanley Boyd, Jr. Halifax: Afro Nova Scotian Enterprises, 1975.

Pulis, John, ed. *Moving On: Black Loyalists in the Afro-Atlantic World.* New York: Garland, 1999.

Saillant, John. "Hymnody and the Persistence of an African-American Faith in Sierra Leone." *The Hymn* 48 (January 1997): 8–17.

———. "'Wipe Away All Tears from Their Eyes': John Marrant's Theology in the Black Atlantic, 1785–1808." *Journal of Millennial Studies* 1 (winter 1999); <http://www.mille.org/publications/journal.html>

Walker, James W. St. George. *The Black Loyalists: The Search for a Promised Land in*

Nova Scotia and Sierra Leone. Dalhousie African Studies Series. New York: Africana Press and Dalhousie University Press, 1976.

Walkes, Joseph A., Jr. *Black Square and Compass: 200 Years of Prince Hall Freemasonry*. Richmond: Macoy Publishing and Masonic Supply, 1979.

Wesley, Charles H. *Prince Hall: Life and Legacy*. Philadelphia: Afro-American Historical and Cultural Museum, and Washington, D.C.: United Supreme Council, Prince Hall Affiliation, 1977.

Wilson, Ellen Gibson. *The Loyal Blacks*. New York: G. P. Putnam's Sons, 1976.

Winks, Robin W. *The Blacks in Canada: A History*, 2d ed. Montreal: McGill-Queens University Press, 1997.

A Note on the Texts

"Face Zion Forward" presents texts written by black authors and published in England or America between 1785 and 1798. The authors selected for inclusion in this volume represent a strikingly coherent and articulate moment in the early history of the black Atlantic, when the first post-slavery communities gathered and established themselves in the newly formed United States of America, the British Canadian province of Nova Scotia, and Freetown, Sierra Leone. The individual experiences of John Marrant, Boston King, Prince Hall, and David George—as Africans, African Americans, Afro-Canadians, and Afro-Britons; as slaves, ex-slaves, and freeborn men; as Indian captives, impressed sailors, and Loyalist volunteers; as Huntingdonian Calvinists, Methodists, Baptists, and Free-masons; as converts, exhorters, itinerants, pastors, chaplains, and institutional founders; and as exiles, emigrants, and citizens—reflect the mobility and diversity of the early black Atlantic. The texts published here record collaboration and competition among authors striving to influence the shape of modern blackness. In gathering the writings of Marrant, King, Hall, and George, *"Face Zion Forward"* offers an unprece-dented firsthand view of the beginnings of the modern black Atlantic not only as a consequence of the slave trade and the scattering of African peoples but also as a self-determining enterprise, at once political, spir-itual, and cultural.

The centerpiece of *"Face Zion Forward"* is *A Journal of the Rev. John Marrant*.

This record of Marrant's missionary efforts at Birchtown, Nova Scotia, and Boston, Massachusetts, is the most extensive account of a black man preaching in black communities before the mid-nineteenth century. Originally published in London in 1790 and surviving in only a few copies, it is reprinted here for the first time. Although Marrant has been reintroduced to contemporary audiences through twentieth-century republications of his popular 1785 *Narrative*, without a modern edition of the *Journal* the full extent of his literary career has not been apparent. This volume presents the four extant works of John Marrant—the 1785 *Narrative*, the 1789 *Sermon* to the African Lodge of Freemasons, and the 1790 *Journal of the Rev. John Marrant*, which was copublished with the 1787 *Funeral Sermon . . . from the Epistle of St. Paul to the Philippians*. These works established him as one of the most prolific black authors of his era. They also established him as a theologian of black Atlantic experience, who composed from elements of Calvinist theology and theodicy and Masonic lore and practices a rich and prophetic vision of black history and destiny. This John Marrant is very different from the hapless Indian captive and theatrical convert we find in his *Narrative*. It is our hope that this volume will encourage a new appreciation of his literary career and of the dimensions of black Atlantic thought it represents.

We encourage readers to be alert to the rich intertextual quality of the writings presented in *"Face Zion Forward."* Recovering early African American texts in the late twentieth and the early twenty-first centuries has required an awareness that the authors of the first black Atlantic related their writings to the texts and events of ancient civilizations, European and American Christianity, and contemporary events, particularly those concerning the slave trade and slavery and the efforts to abolish them. Moreover, these writings frequently culled lines from eighteenth-century evangelical hymnody, most commonly the works of Isaac Watts, and they invoked contemporary theological and ecclesiastical controversies. (A contemporary of Marrant remembered him as an inspired singer in a poem inscribed in a copy of Marrant's 1789 *Sermon* to the African Lodge; see pages 40–41.) As documents of a particularly charged and coherent moment in eighteenth-century black history, these texts referred to the actors, places, events, racial theories, and policies of that era. This complex interweaving of biblical, hymnological, theological, ecclesiastical, biographical, and historical texts requires special consideration.

Readers can participate actively in the interpretation of these texts by supplementing close readings with explorations of other resources. It is especially important that in-text Scripture references be followed to their sources in the King James Version of the Bible, so as to assess the full extent and significance of allusions to Scripture. The Bible was one of the few books that black authors could assume a black audience would know, either through reading or through listening to prayers, hymns, and sermons. Allusions to the Bible were probably meant to be bursting with significance to black readers as well as appealing to white readers. *A Journal of the Rev. John Marrant*, for instance, refers to over one hundred passages of Scripture. It is unlikely that Marrant believed readers would consider his account without being mindful of the biblical passages to which he referred. Another example comes from Marrant's *Narrative*. In its account of the South Carolina backcountry as well as of Marrant's experiences as a young musician, then convert, it echoes accounts of earlier events in the eighteenth-century colony. As with the *Journal*, this intertextual relationship was almost certainly strategic, allowing the author to situate himself squarely in settler history in South Carolina. He shared an awareness of settler history with the white population, while he shared his race and his hatred of slavery with South Carolina's majority population. Furthermore, these texts sometimes refer to one another, as when Prince Hall's 1792 *Charge* describes Marrant's 1789 *Sermon* as the "foundation" and itself accordingly as a "superstructure." Here we seek not to set the documents definitively in matrices of other texts, but to inform readers that they can pursue valuable research in the intertextual quality of early black writing.

Another relevant editorial concern is the involvement of amanuenses in the texts collected here. There is a tendency to imagine early black narratives as testimony snatched from the lips of illiterate and passive slave witnesses by more powerful and authoritative white amanuenses.

This model may reflect the historical imbalance of power between black authors and white editors and printers, but it does not accurately represent the conditions of production for most eighteenth-century and nineteenth-century black texts. Each text has its own unique production history, a history that reflects the macropolitics and micropolitics of its time and place. Even when the title page or prefatory documents indicate that a white transcriber, editor, or printer was involved in the production of a black text, it is difficult, if not impossible, to ascertain exactly the nature and intensity of their intervention. Manuscripts for most early black texts have not survived. The absence of these manuscripts reflects more on the scattered, difficult, and even destitute conditions in which black authors concluded their lives, on their lack of connection to major religious institutions, universities, or libraries, and on the value these institutions have historically assigned to black culture than it does on the authenticity or value of the texts themselves. Finally, it is important to recognize that editors' and amanuenses' practices were not exercised on black texts alone: many seventeenth-century and eighteenth-century sermons and narratives by whites were also transcribed, edited, and printed by persons other than the author. To assume that early black texts are always compromised by editorial activity is not only a misapprehension of historical literary practices but an unfair diminution of black authority. "Author" in African American literary history implies authority and origination, but not necessarily literacy.

Even without surviving manuscripts, we can glean some insights into the production of early black writings from the place and manner of their publication, from the title pages, prefaces, and editorial comments that accompanied them, and sometimes from notes penned into surviving copies of the original editions. *A Narrative of the Lord's Wonderful Dealings with John Marrant* was based on remarks Marrant delivered in England at his ordination in the Huntingdon Connexion. It was, according to the title pages of its first edition, "arranged, corrected, and published" by the Reverend William Aldridge. His preface relates that Aldridge attended the ordination ceremony and "observed" Marrant, who "appeared" "to pay a conscientious regard to his word." Aldridge also explained his own handling of the text: "I have always preserved Mr. Marrant's ideas, tho' I could not his language; no more alterations, however, have been made, than were thought necessary." In comparing the version of the *Narrative* supervised by William Aldridge with a unique fourth edition published under the direct supervision of Marrant himself, we see clearly that the first edition was not a reliable account of the black man's experience.

This unique fourth edition, which, according to the title page, was "Enlarged by Mr. MARRANT, and Printed (with Permission) for his Sole Benefit, WITH NOTES EXPLANATORY" by "R. Hawes of No. 40, Dorset Street," detailed the cruelty and brutal violence of white South Carolina masters toward slaves seeking religious education. It also described some violence between siblings within the Marrant household, and it linked Indian raids against white settlers to colonization and the usurpation of tribal lands. Only in the fourth edition, supervised by John Marrant, do these scenes of violence and these antislavery sentiments appear. Aldridge may have condensed Marrant's account to make it more palatable to a white audience, or Marrant may have had information he wanted to add to a new edition. Since Marrant's new material was strongly critical of slaveholding, and since posthumous editions printed nothing revealing antislavery sentiments and, sometimes, nothing suggesting the author's race, we can infer that the *Narrative* was whitewashed to make it an acceptable captivity and conversion memoir instead of a challenging antislavery work. What role Aldridge played in the whitewashing process is unclear, since we do not know how much control he exerted over later editions. We have used as the basis for our transcription a Boston Public Library microfilm of Marrant's unique and unexpurgated fourth edition, and our text has been checked against a physical copy of this text at the Harry Ransom Humanities Research Center at the University of Texas at Austin.

John Marrant and Prince Hall may have collaborated in the composition of *A Sermon Preached on the 24th Day of June 1789, Being the Festival of St. John the Baptist, at the Request of the Right Worshipful the Grand Master Prince Hall, and the Rest of the Brethren of the African Lodge of the Honorable Society of*

Free and Accepted Masons in Boston. Prince Hall supervised the printing and sale of the *Sermon,* which was published in 1789 by Thomas and John Fleet at the Bible and Heart in Boston. It was republished in London in 1790 as an appendix to *A Journal of the Rev. John Marrant.* A third imprint appeared in 1920, when Arthur Alfonso Schomburg (1874–1938)—the originator of the Schomburg Center for Research in Black Culture at the New York Public Library and Grand Secretary of the New York Grand Lodge of Prince Hall Freemasons—sponsored a limited edition of the *Sermon* to circulate among friends and fellow Freemasons. (The title page of the Schomburg edition incorrectly gives 1784 as the date of Marrant's *Sermon.*) The New York Public Library produced a microfilm of the Schomburg edition of the *Sermon* in 1969; Bell and Howell MicroPhoto Division of Wooster, Ohio, microfilmed the original for the *Black Culture Collection* (reel 368, number 9); and the Readex Microprint Corporation of New York, New York, microfilmed the original 1789 edition for *Early American Imprints* (first series, number 21931). Our transcription is based on the *Early American Imprints* microform, and we have relied upon physical copies of the 1789 edition belonging to the American Antiquarian Society and the Boston Athenaeum for checking. The latter lacks several pages; the former is integral. The overleaf at the end of the American Antiquarian Society copy bears a noteworthy inscription: a poem or hymn written in honor of Marrant, George Whitefield, and the Countess of Huntingdon:

> Ecce spectaculum!
> Whitfield, Marrant and many others,
> Come here to preach th' [several letters crossed out] eternal son,
> Let then the race of Christian brothers,
> Exalt the name of Huntingdon!
> She, holy woman sent them oer,
> To beg and pray, to sing weep.—
> She thot religion on this shore,
> For want of [word crossed out] friends had gone to sleep—
> So thinking men of brazen lungs,

With holy feelings, faith, quite strong,
She sent, that they with noisy tongues,
Might wake her, with Devotion's song.

Additional surviving copies are located at Atlanta University, the College of William and Mary, the Houghton Library of Harvard University, the New-York Historical Society Archive, the New York Public Library, Stanford University, the University of Chicago, the University of Connecticut, and Yale University.

A Journal of the Rev. John Marrant, from August the 18th, 1785, to the 16th of March, 1790. To Which Are Added, Two Sermons; One Preached on Ragged Island on Sabbath Day, the 27th Day of October, 1787; The Other at Boston in New England, on Thursday, the 24th of June 1789 was published "for the author" in London in 1790. Its title page stated that the *Journal* was sold "by J. Taylor and Co. at the Royal Exchange" and by Marrant himself, from his home at "No. 2, Black Horse Court, in Aldersgate-street." We believe that the *Journal* is an authoritative text, because, like the unique fourth edition of the *Narrative,* it was supervised and sold by Marrant himself. The original printing of the *Journal* included both *A Sermon Preached on the 24th Day of June 1789* and *A Funeral Sermon Preached by the Desire of the Deceased, John Lock; The Text Chosen by Himself, from the Epistle of St. Paul to the Philippians, Chap. i., Ver. 21. And Was Preached According to Promise, before His Father and Mother, Brothers and Sisters, and All the Inhabitants round the Neighbouring Village, by the Rev. John Marrant.* The *Journal* is now held at the Boston Public Library and the State Library of Pennsylvania. *"Face Zion Forward"* presents the first republication of the *Journal* and the *Funeral Sermon.* Our text is transcribed from a Boston Public Library microfilm and has been checked against the physical text housed at the State Library of Pennsylvania. A signature dated "Feby 5th 1837" on the inside cover of the Boston Public Library copy indicates that the text was owned by Maria and John Flem[m]ing. A second inscription at the top of the first page of the *Journal*'s "Preface" provides biographical information about Marrant: "This Man died in April 1791 and [was] buried in the Burial Ground in Church Street, Islington." Several words were marked out on page 4 of the *Journal*, as well as in a footnote to the first page of the *Funeral Sermon*. These missing words have been supplied by the State Library of Pennsylvania copy of the *Journal*, and we have restored them to this transcription in square brackets.

An Account of the Life of Mr. David George, from Sierra Leone in Africa; Given by Himself in a Conversation with Brother Rippon of London, and Brother Pearce of Birmingham was first published in *The Baptist Annual Register for 1790, 1791, 1792, and Part of 1793*, pages 473–84. Our transcription is based on a microfilm produced by the Historical Commission of the Southern Baptist Convention, in Nashville, Tennessee, and loaned from Shorter College, Rome, Georgia. A physical copy of the *Register* at Baylor University has served as the basis for our checking. Additional physical and microfilm copies of the *Register* are available at libraries throughout the United States.

Prince Hall's *Charge Delivered to the Brethren of the African Lodge on the 25th of June, 1792. At the Hall of Brother William Smith, in Charlestown* was published in 1792 at Cornhill, in Boston, Massachusetts, by Thomas and John Fleet and sold at their store, the Bible and Heart. In 1866, the *Charge* was republished as an appendix to Lewis Hayden, *Caste Among Masons: An Address before the Prince Hall Grand Lodge of Free and Accepted Masons of the State of Massachusetts, at the Festival of St. John the Evangelist, December 27, 1865* (Boston: Edwards S. Coombs and Co.). Hayden was then Grand Master of the Massachusetts Grand Lodge, and his republication of the 1792 *Charge* indicates that Hall remained an important figure to black Freemasons well into the nineteenth century. A microform edition of this text has been produced for *Early American Imprints* by the Readex Microprint Corporation of New York, New York. Our transcription is based on the *Early American Imprints* microform, and we have used an original belonging to the American Antiquarian Society for checking. Other first-edition copies of the 1792 *Charge* are located at the New York Public Library and at the College of William and Mary.

A Charge, Delivered to the African Lodge, June 24, 1797, at Menotomy. By the Right Worshipful Prince Hall was printed in 1797 at the Boston press of Benjamin Edes and sold at "Prince Hall's shop, opposite the Quaker meeting-house, Quaker-lane." As he did with John Marrant's 1789 *Sermon* and his own 1792 *Charge*, Hall closely monitored the publication and sales of the 1797 publication. Decades after his death, it was republished with the 1792 *Charge* in the appendix to Hayden's *Caste Among Masons* (1866). More than five decades later, Schomburg sponsored yet another edition of the 1797 *Charge*, which he had "obtained through the courtesy of Bro. Augustus Fleet from H. E. Pickersgill"; the publication date of the Schomburg edition is not precisely known but has been placed between 1920 and 1929. A microfiche of the Schomburg edition was produced by the New York Public Library in 1976. A microform edition of the 1797 imprint was produced for *Early American Imprints* by the Readex Microprint Corporation of New York, New York. Our transcription is based on the *Early American Imprints* microform, and we have checked the transcription against a physical copy belonging to the American Antiquarian Society. That copy once belonged to the Reverend William Bentley (1759–1819) of Salem, Massachusetts, who inscribed the following eulogy on the overleaf of the title page: "This Prince Hall was a worthy African, whom I well knew. He had no advantages, except such as he gained by his own diligence + his excellent moral habits." Additional extant copies of the 1797 *Charge* belong to the Library of Congress, North Carolina Central University, and the New York Public Library.

Memoirs of the Life of Boston King, a Black Preacher. Written by Himself, during his Residence at Kingswood-School first appeared in serial numbers of *The Methodist Magazine, for the Year 1798; Being a Continuation of the Arminian Magazine, First Published by the Rev. John Wesley, A.M., Consisting Chiefly of Extracts and Original Treatises on General Redemption*, 21 (March 1798): 105–10; (April 1798): 157–61; (May 1798): 209–13; (June 1798): 261–65. The magazine was published in London "for G. Whitfield, City-Road, and sold at the Methodist Preaching-Houses in Town and Country." Our transcription is based on a microfilm of this publication produced for *Early English Newspapers* by Research Publications of Woodbridge, Connecticut. The original *Methodist Magazine* and the *Early English Newspapers* microform are available at libraries throughout the United States.

The foregoing bibliographical essay has documented freestanding editions of the texts. With the exception of the *Journal of the Rev. John Marrant* and Marrant's *Funeral Sermon*, the texts reprinted here also appear in one or more of the following anthologies: *Early Negro Writing, 1760–1837*, ed. Dorothy Porter (1971; Baltimore: Black Classics Press, 1985); *Heath Anthology of American Literature*, vol. 1, ed. Paul Lauter et al. (Lexington, Mass.: D. C. Heath, 1990); *Black Atlantic Writers of the Eighteenth Century: Living the New Exodus in England and the Americas*, ed. Adam Potkay and Sandra Burr (New York: St. Martin's Press, 1995); *Unchained Voices: An Anthology of Black Authors in the English-Speaking World of the Eighteenth Century*, ed. Vincent Carretta (Lexington: University of Kentucky Press, 1996); and *Pioneers of the Black Atlantic: Five Slave Narratives from the Enlightenment, 1772–1815*, ed. Henry Louis Gates, Jr., and William L. Andrews (Washington, D.C.: Civitas, 1998).

The editors' goal is to introduce to contemporary audiences a reliable modern edition of eighteenth-century black writings, including the previously unavailable *Journal of the Rev. John Marrant*. Bearing in mind the needs of scholarly and general readers, but also respecting the integrity of the original texts and the detractive effects of heavy annotation, we have chosen to restrict all scholarly and interpretive mediation to the introduction. Our introductory essay contains biographical, historical, and literary-critical information respecting all of the authors and texts collected in *"Face Zion Forward,"* and it includes a bibliography for further reading.

"Face Zion Forward" contains diplomatic rather than facsimile reprints of the collected eighteenth-century texts. Texts have been transcribed from microforms of the eighteenth-century originals; all transcriptions have been checked against physical copies of the base texts. All texts have been reformatted for this volume. Except for the ligature "æ," we have updated elements of eighteenth-century typography, including the eighteenth century "ſ" for "s." None of the original or authorized texts contained illustrations. Printer's devices and embellished initial capitalizations have not been reproduced in our edition, but we have preserved footnote symbols used in the originals. In the table of contents, textual note, and introduction, the titles of the collected texts and publishers' names have

been capitalized according to modern standards. Within the texts themselves, we have neither standardized nor modernized spelling, grammar, punctuation, capitalization, or italicization (except for the spelling of Philippians in Marrant's *Funeral Sermon*, which was consistently misspelled Phillipians). Where we have judged misspelling to result from a printer's error, or where the misspelling might confuse the reader, we have supplied a correction in square brackets ([ ]). Misquotations from the King James version of the Bible have not been corrected, but mistaken citations of chapter and verse have been emended with brackets. However, we have allowed Revelation of St. John the Divine to remain as "Revelations." Variant spellings of place names have not been changed, but abbreviated names have sometimes been given in full, in brackets. Misspellings of persons' names have not been changed, but for the sake of clarity an occasional bracketed note corrects a name and further identifies a person.

A

NARRATIVE

OF THE

LORD's wonderful DEALINGS

WITH

JOHN MARRANT

A BLACK,

(Now going to Preach the GOSPEL in NOVA-SCOTIA)
Born in NEW-YORK, in NORTH-AMERICA.

Taken down from his own Relation,
ARRANGED, CORRECTED, and PUBLISHED
By the Rev. Mr. *ALDRIDGE.*

THE FOURTH EDITION,
Enlarged by Mr. MARRANT, and Printed (with Permission)
for his Sole Benefit, WITH NOTES EXPLANATORY.

THY PEOPLE SHALL BE WILLING IN THE DAY OF THY
POWER, Psalm cx. 3.
DECLARE HIS WONDERS AMONG ALL PEOPLE.
Psalms xcvi. 3.

LONDON:

PRINTED FOR THE AUTHOR,
By R. HAWES, No. 40, Dorset-Street Spitalfields.

READER,

THE following Narrative is as plain and artless, as it is surprising and extraordinary. Plausible reasonings may amuse and delight, but facts, and facts like these, strike, are felt, and go home to the heart. Were the power, grace and providence of God ever more eminently displayed, than in the conversion, success, and deliverances of John Marrant? *He and his companion enter the meeting at* Charles-Town *together; but the one is taken, and the other is left. He is struck to the ground, shaken over the mouth of hell, snatched as a brand from the burning; he is pardoned and justified; he is washed in the atoning blood and made happy in his God. You soon have another view of him, drinking into his master's cup; he is tried and perplext, opposed and despised; the neighbours hoot at him as he goes along; his mother, sisters, and brother, hate and persecute him; he is friendless and forsaken of all. These uneasy circumstances call forth the corruptions of his nature, and create a momentary debate, whether the pursuit of ease and pleasure was not to be preferred to the practice of religion, which he now found so sharp and severe? The stripling is supported and strengthened. He is persuaded to forsake his family and kindred altogether. He crosses the fence, which marked the boundary between the wilderness and the cultivated country; and prefers the habitations of brutal residence, to the less hospitable dwellings of enmity to God and godliness. He wanders, but Christ is his guide and protector.——Who can view him among the* Indian *tribes without wonder? He arrives among the* Cherokees, *where gross ignorance wore its rudest forms, and savage despotism exercised its most terrifying empire. Here the child just turned fourteen, without sling or stone, engages, and with the arrow of prayer pointed with faith, wounded* Goliah, *and conquers the King.*

The untutor'd monarch feels the truth, and worships the God of the Christians; the seeds of the Gospel are disseminated among the Indians by a youthful hand, and Jesus is received and obeyed.

The subsequent incidents related in this Narrative are great and affecting; but I must not anticipate the reader's pleasure and profit.

The novelty or magnitude of the facts contained in the following pages, may dispose some readers to question the truth of them. My answer to such is,——1. I believe it is clear to great numbers, and to some competent judges; that God is with the subject of them; but if he knowingly permitted an untruth to go abroad in the name of God, whilst it is confessed the Lord is with him, would it not follow, that the Almighty gave his sanction to a falsehood?——2. I have observed him to pay a conscientious regard to his word.——3. He appeared to me to feel most sensibly, when he related those parts of his Narrative, which describe his happiest moments with God, or the most remarkable interpositions of Divine Providence for him; and I have no reason to believe it was counterfeited.

I have always preserved Mr. Marrant's ideas, tho' I could not his language; no more alterations, however, have been made, than were thought necessary.

I now commit the whole to God.——That he may make it generally useful is the prayer of thy ready servant, for Christ's sake.

W. ALDRIDGE.

London,
July 19th, 1785.

A

NARRATIVE, &c.

I, JOHN MARRANT, born June 15th, 1755, in New-York, in North-America, wish these gracious dealings of the Lord with me to be published, in hopes they may be useful to others, to encourage the fearful, to confirm the wavering, and to refresh the hearts of true believers. My father died when I was little more than four years of age, and before I was five my mother removed from New-York to St. Augustine, about seven hundred miles from that city. Here I was sent to school, and taught to read and spell; after we had resided here about eighteen months, it was found necessary to remove to Georgia, where we remained; and I was kept to school until I had attained my eleventh year. The Lord spoke to me in my early days, by these removes, if I could have understood him, and said, "Here we have no continuing city." We left Georgia, and went to Charles-Town, where it was intended I should be put apprentice to some trade. Some time after I had been in Charles-Town, as I was walking one day, I passed by a school, and heard music and dancing, which took my fancy very much, and I felt a strong inclination to learn the music. I went home, and informed my sister, that I had rather learn to play upon music than go to a trade. She told me she could do nothing in it, until she had acquainted my mother with my desire. Accordingly she wrote a letter concerning it to my mother, which when she read, the contents were disapproved of by her, and she came to Charles-Town to prevent it. She persuaded me much against it, but her persuasions were fruitless. Disobedience either to God or man, being one of the fruits of sin, grew out from me in early buds. Finding I was set upon it, and resolved to learn nothing else, she agreed to it, and went with me to speak to the man, and to settle upon the best terms with him she could. He insisted upon twenty pounds currency, which was paid, and I was engaged to stay with him eighteen months, and my mother to find me every thing during that term. The first day I went to him he put the violin into my hand, which pleased me much, and, applying close, I learned very fast, not only to play, but to dance also; so that in six months I was able to play for the whole school. In the evenings after the scholars were dismissed, I used to resort to the bottom of our garden, where it was customary for some musicians to assemble to blow the French-horn. Here my improvement was so rapid, that in a twelve-month's time I became master both of the violin and of the French-horn, and was much respected by the Gentlemen and Ladies whose children attended the school, as also by my master. This opened to me a large door of vanity and vice, for I was invited to all the balls and assemblies that were held in the town, and met with the general applause of the inhabitants. I was a stranger to want, being supplied with as much money as I had any occasion for; which my sister observing, said, "You have now no need of a trade." I was now in my thirteenth year, devoted to pleasure and drinking in iniquity like water; a slave to every vice suited to my nature and to my years. The time I had engaged to serve my master being expired, he persuaded me to stay with him, and offered me any thing or any money, not to leave him. His intreaties proving ineffectual, I quitted his service, and visited my mother in the country; with her I staid two months, living without God or hope in the world, fishing and hunting on the sabbath-day. Unstable as water, I returned to town, and wished to go to some trade. My sister's husband being informed of my inclination provided me with a master, who was a carpenter in that town, on condition that I should serve him one year and a half on trial, and afterwards be bound, if he approved of me. Accordingly I went, but every evening I was sent for to play on music, somewhere or another; and I often continued out very late, sometimes all night, so as to render me incapable of attending my master's business the next day; yet in this manner I served him a year and four months, and was much approved of by him. He wrote a letter to my mother to come and have me bound, and whilst my mother was weighing the matter in her own mind, the gracious purposes of God, respecting a perishing sinner, were now to be disclosed. One evening I was sent for in a very particular manner to go and play for some Gentlemen, which I agreed to do, and was on my way to fulfil my promise; and passing by a large meeting house I saw many lights in it, and crowds of people going in. I enquired what it meant, and was answered by my companion that a crazy man was hallooing there; this raised my curiosity to go in, that I might hear what he was hallooing about. He persuaded me not to go in, but in vain. He then said, "If you will do one thing I will go in with you." I asked him what that was? He replied, "Blow the French-horn among them." I liked the proposal well enough, but expressed my fears of being beaten for disturbing them; but upon his promising to stand by and defend me, I agreed. So we went, and with much difficulty got within the doors. I was pushing the people to make room, to get the horn off my shoulder to blow it, just as Mr. Whitefield was naming his text, and looking round, as I thought, directly upon me, and pointing with his finger, he uttered these words, "PREPARE TO MEET THY GOD, O ISRAEL." The Lord accompanied the word with such power, that I was struck to the ground, and lay both speechless and senseless near half an hour. When I was come a little too, I found two men attending me, and a woman throwing water in my face, and holding a smelling bottle to my nose; and when something more recovered, every word I heard from the minister was like a parcel of swords thrust in to me, and what added to my distress, I thought I saw the devil on every side of me. I was constrained in the bitterness of my spirit to halloo out in the midst of the congregation, which disturbing them, they took me away; but finding I could neither walk or stand, they carried me as far as the vestry, and there I remained till the service was over. When the people were dismissed Mr. Whitefield came into the vestry, and being told of my condition he came immediately, and the first word he said to me was, "JESUS CHRIST HAS GOT THEE AT LAST." He asked where I lived, intending to come and see me the next day; but recollecting he was to leave the town the next morning, he said he could not come himself, but would send another minister; he desired them to get me home, and then taking his leave of me, I saw him no more. When I reached my sister's house, being carried by two men, she was very uneasy to see me in so distressed a condition. She got me to bed, and sent for a doctor, who came immediately, and after looking at me, he went home, and sent me a bottle of mixture, and desired her to give me a spoonful every two hours; but I could not take any thing the doctor sent, nor indeed keep in bed; this distressed my sister very much, and she cried out, "The lad will surely die." She sent for two other doctors, but no medicine they prescribed could I take. No, no; it may be asked, a wounded spirit who can cure? as well as who can bear? In this distress of soul I continued for three days without any food, only a little water now and then. On the fourth day, the minister*[1] Mr. Whitefield had desired to visit me came to see me, and being directed up-stairs, when he entered the room, I thought he made my distress much worse. He wanted to take hold of my hand, but I durst not give it to him. He insisted upon taking hold of it, and I then got away from him on the side of the bed; but being very weak I fell down, and before I could recover he came to me and took me by the hand, and lifted me up, and after a few words desired to go to prayer. So he fell upon his knees, and pulled me down also; after he had spent some time in prayer he rose up, and asked me how I did now; I answered, much worse; he then said, "Come, we will have the old thing over again," and so we kneeled down a second time, and after he had prayed earnestly we got up, and he said again, "How do you do now;" I replied worse and worse, and asked him if he intended to kill me? "No, no," said he, "you are worth a thousand dead men, let us try the old thing over again," and so falling upon our knees, he continued in prayer a considerable time, and near the close of his prayer, the Lord was pleased to set my soul at perfect liberty, and being filled with joy I began to praise the Lord immediately; my sorrows were turned into peace, and joy, and love. The minister said, "How is it now?" I answered, all is well, all happy. He then took his leave of me; but called every day for several days afterwards, and the last time he said, "Hold fast that thou hast already obtained, 'till Jesus Christ come." I now read the Scriptures very much. My master sent often to know how I did, and at last came himself, and finding me well, asked me if I would not come to work again? I answered no. He asked me the reason, but receiving no answer he went away. I continued with my sister about three weeks, during which time she often asked me to play upon the violin for her, which I refused; then she said I was crazy and mad, and so reported it among the neighbours, which opened the mouths of all around against me. I then resolved to go to my mother, which was eighty-four miles from Charles-Town. I was two days on my journey home, and enjoyed much communion with God on the road, and had occasion to mark the gracious interpositions of his kind Providence as I passed along. The third day I arrived at my mother's house, and was well received. At supper they sat down to eat without asking the Lord's blessing, which caused me to burst out into tears. My mother asked me what was the matter? I answered, I wept because they sat down to supper without asking the Lord's blessing. She bid me with much surprise, to ask a blessing. I remained with her fourteen days without interruption; the Lord pitied me, being a young soldier. Soon, however, Satan began to stir up my two sisters and brother, who were then at home with my mother; they called me every name but that which was good. The more they persecuted me, the stronger I grew in grace. At length my mother turned against me also, and the neighbours joined her, and there was not a friend to assist me, or that I could speak to; this made me earnest with God. In these circumstances, being the youngest but one of our family, and young in Christian experience, I was tempted so far as to threaten my life; but reading my Bible one day, and finding that if I did destroy myself I could not come where God was, I betook myself to the fields, and some days staid out from morning to night to avoid the persecutors. I staid

A

NARRATIVE

OF THE

LORD's wonderful DEALINGS

WITH

JOHN MARRANT,

A BLACK,

(Now going to Preach the GOSPEL in Nova-Scotia)

Born in New-York, in North-America.

Taken down from his own Relation,

ARRANGED, CORRECTED, and PUBLISHED

By the Rev. Mr. *ALDRIDGE.*

THE FOURTH EDITION,

Enlarged by Mr. MARRANT, and Printed (with Permiſſion)

for his Sole Benefit, WITH NOTES EXPLANATORY.

THY PEOPLE SHALL BE WILLING IN THE DAY OF THY

POWER, Pſalm cx. 3.

DECLARE HIS WONDERS AMONG ALL PEOPLE.

Pſalm xcvi. 3.

LONDON:

PRINTED FOR THE AUTHOR,

By R. HAWES, No. 40, Dorſet-Street Spitalfields.

John Marrant authorized a 1785 version of his Narrative, *which identified him as "a black" on the title page and included accounts of his preaching to slaves in South Carolina, the cruelty of their mistress, and a young girl's deathbed visions of a shining city that might have been meant to signify Africa. Some posthumous editions of the* Narrative *deleted antislavery elements as well as any hints of Africa, transforming the work into a conversion-and-captivity narrative that*

A

NARRATIVE

of the

L I F E

OF

JOHN MARRANT,

OF NEW YORK, IN NORTH AMERICA :

Giving an

ACCOUNT OF HIS CONVERSION

When only Fourteen Years of age ;

His leaving his Mother's house from religious motives, wandering several Days in the Deserts without Food, and being at last taken by an Indian Hunter among the Cherokees, where he was condemned to die :

With

AN ACCOUNT OF THE CONVERSION OF THE KING OF THE CHEROKEES AND HIS DAUGHTER, &c. &c. &c.

The whole Authenticated
By the Reverend W. ALDRIDGE.

Halifax: Eng.
Printed at the office of J. Nicholson & Co.

1813.

was less challenging than the version Marrant authorized. The title page of the 1785 authorized edition appears courtesy of the Harry Ransom Humanities Research Center, University of Texas at Austin. The title page of an 1813 edition, from which the author's racial identification was expunged, appears courtesy of the American Antiquarian Society.

one time two days without any food, but seemed to have clearer views into the spiritual things of God.

Not long after this I was sharply tried, and reasoned the matter within myself, whether I should turn to my old courses of sin and vice, or serve and cleave to the Lord; after prayer to God, I was fully persuaded in my mind, that if I turned to my old ways I should perish eternally. Upon this I went home, and finding them all as hardened, or worse than before, and every body saying I was crazy; but a little sister I had, about nine years of age, used to cry when she saw them persecute me, and continuing so about five weeks and three days, I thought it was better for me to die than to live among such people. I rose one morning very early, to get a little quietness and retirement, I went into the woods, and staid till eight o'clock in the morning; upon my return I found them all at breakfast; I passed by them, and went up-stairs without any interruption; I went upon my knees to the Lord, and returned him thanks; then I took up a small pocket Bible and one of Dr. Watts's hymn books, and passing by them went out without one word spoken by any of us. After spending some time in the fields, I was persuaded to go from home altogether. Accordingly I went over the fence, about half a mile from our house, which divided the inhabited and cultivated parts of the country from the wilderness. I continued travelling in the desart all day without the least inclination of returning back. About evening I began to be surrounded with wolves; I took refuge from them on a tree, and remained there all night. About eight o'clock next morning I descended from the tree, and returned God thanks for the mercies of the night. I went on all this day without any thing to eat or drink.

The third day, taking my Bible out of my pocket, I read and walked for some time, and then being wearied and almost spent, I sat down, and after resting awhile I rose to go forward; but had not gone above a hundred yards when something tripped me up, and I fell down; I prayed to the Lord upon the ground that he would command the wild beasts to devour me, that I might be with him in glory. I made this request to God the third and part of the fourth day.

The fourth day in the morning, descending from my usual lodging, a tree, and having nothing all this time to eat, and but a little water to drink, I was so feeble that I tumbled half way down the tree, not being able to support myself, and lay upon my back on the ground about an hour and a half, praying and crying; after which getting a little strength, and trying to stand upright to walk, I found myself not able; then I went upon my hands and knees, and so crawled till I reached a tree that was tumbled down, in order to get across it, and there I prayed with my body leaning upon it above an hour, that the Lord would take me to himself. Such nearness to God I then enjoyed, that I willingly resigned myself into his hands. After some time I thought I was strengthened, so I got across the tree without my feet or hands touching the ground; but struggling I fell over on the other side, and then thought the Lord will now answer my prayer, and take me home: But the time was not come. After laying there a little, I rose, and looking about, saw at some distance bunches of grass, called deer-grass; I felt a strong desire to get at it; though I rose, yet it was only on my hands and knees, being so feeble, and in this manner I reached the grass. I was about three-quarters of an hour going in this form twenty yards. When I reached it, I was unable to pull it up, so I bit it off like a horse, and prayed the Lord to bless it to me, and I thought it the best meal I ever had in my life, and I think so still, it was so sweet. I returned my God hearty thanks for it, and then lay down about an hour. Feeling myself very thirsty, I prayed the Lord to provide me with some water. Finding I was something strengthened, I got up, and stood on my feet, and staggered from one tree to another, if they were near each other, otherwise the journey was too long for me. I continued moving so for some time, and at length passing between two trees, I happened to fall upon some bushes, among which were a few large hollow leaves, which had caught and contained the dews of the night, and lying low among the bushes, were not exhaled by the solar rays; this water in the leaves fell upon me as I tumbled down and was lost, I was now tempted to think the Lord had given me water from Heaven, and I had wasted it, I then prayed the Lord to forgive me. What poor unbelieving creatures we are! though we are assured the Lord will supply all our needs. I was presently directed to a puddle of water very muddy, which some wild pigs had just left; I kneeled down, and asked the Lord to bless it to me, so I drank both mud and water mixed together, and being satisfied I returned the Lord thanks, and went on my way rejoicing. This day was much chequered with wants and supplies, with dangers and deliverances. I continued travelling on for nine days, feeding upon grass, and not knowing whither I was going; but the Lord Jesus Christ was very present, and that comforted me through the whole.

The next morning, having quitted my customary lodging, and returned thanks to the Lord for my preservation through the night, reading and travelling on, I passed between two bears, about twenty yards distance from each other. Both sat and looked at me, but I felt very little fear; and after I had passed them, they both went the same way from me without growling, or the least apparent uneasiness. I went and returned God thanks for my escape, who had tamed the wild beasts of the forest, and made them friendly to me: I rose from my knees and walked on, singing hymns of praise to God, about five o'clock in the afternoon, and about fifty-five miles from home, right through the wilderness. As I was going on, and musing upon the goodness of the Lord, an Indian hunter, who stood at some distance, saw me; he hid himself behind a tree; but as I passed along he bolted out, and put his hands on my breast, which surprized me a few moments. He then asked me where I was going? I answered I did not know, but where the Lord was pleased to guide me. Having heard me praising God before I came up to him, he enquired who I was talking to? I told him I was talking to my Lord Jesus; he seemed surprized, and asked me where he was? for he did not see him there. I told him he could not be seen with bodily eyes. After a little more talk, he insisted upon taking me home; but I refused, and added, that I would die rather than return home. He then asked me if I knew how far I was from home? I answered, I did not know; you are fifty-five miles and a half, says he, from home. He farther asked me how I did to live? I said I was supported by the Lord. He asked me how I slept? I answered, the Lord provided me with a bed every night; he further enquired what preserved me from being devoured by the wild beasts? I replied, the Lord Jesus Christ kept me from them. He stood astonished, and said, you say the Lord Jesus Christ do this, and do that, and do every thing for you, he must be a very fine man, where is he? I replied, he is here present. To this he made me no answer, only said, I know you, and your mother and sister; and upon a little further conversation I found he did know them, having been used in winter to sell skins in our Town. This alarmed me, and I wept for fear he should take me home by force; but when he saw me so affected, he said he would not take me home if I would go with him. I objected against that, for fear he would rob me of my comfort and communion with God: But at last, being much pressed, I consented to go. Our employment for ten weeks and three days was killing deer, and taking off their skins by day, which we afterwards hung on the trees to dry till they were sent for; the means of defence and security against our nocturnal enemies, always took up the evenings: We collected a number of large bushes, and placed them nearly in a circular form, which uniting at the extremity, afforded us both a verdant covering, and a sufficient shelter from the night dews. What moss we could gather was strewed upon the ground, and this composed our bed. A fire was kindled in the front of our temporary lodging-room, and fed with fresh fuel all night, as we slept and watched by turns; and this was our defence from the dreadful animals, whose shining eyes and tremendous roar we often saw and heard during the night.

By constant conversation with the hunter, I acquired a fuller knowledge of the Indian tongue: This, together with the sweet communion I enjoyed with God, I have since considered as a preparation for the great trial I was soon after to pass through.

The hunting season being now at an end, we left the woods, and directed our course towards a large Indian town, belonging to the Cherokee nation; and having reached it, I said to the hunter, they will not suffer me to enter in. He replied, as I was with him, nobody would interrupt me.

There was an Indian fortification all round the town, and a guard placed at each entrance. The hunter passed one of these without molestation, but I was stopped by the guard and examined. They asked me where I came from, and what was my business there? My companion of the woods attempted to speak for me, but was not permitted; he was taken away, and I saw him no more. I was now surrounded by about fifty men, and carried to one of their principal chiefs and Judge to be examined by him. When I came before him, he asked me what was my business there? I told him I came there with a hunter, whom I met with in the woods. He replied, "Did I not know that whoever came there without giving a better account of themselves than I did, was to be put to death?" I said I did not know it. Observing that I answered him so readily in his own language, he asked me where I learnt it? To this I returned no answer, but burst out into a flood of tears, and calling upon my Lord Jesus. At this he stood astonished, and expressed a concern for me, and said I was young. He asked me who my Lord Jesus was?—To this I gave him no answer, but continued praying and weeping. Addressing himself to the officer who stood by him, he said he was sorry; but it was the law[,] and it must not be broken. I was then ordered to be taken away, and put into a place of confinement. They led me from their court into a low dark place, and thrust me into it, very dreary and dismal; they made fast the door, and set a watch. The judge sent for the executioner, and gave him his warrant for my execution in the afternoon of the next day. The executioner came, and gave me notice of it, which made me very happy, as the near prospect of death made me hope for a speedy deliverance from the body: And truly this dungeon became my chapel, for the Lord Jesus did not leave me in this great trouble, but was very present, so that I continued blessing him, and singing his praises all night without ceasing: The watch hearing the noise, informed the executioner that somebody had been in the dungeon with me all night; upon which he came in to see and to examine, with a great torch lighted in his hand, who it was I had with me; but finding nobody, he turned round, and asked me who it was? I told him it was the Lord Jesus Christ; but he made no answer, turned away, went out, and fastened the door. At the hour appointed for my execution I was taken out, and led to the destined spot, amidst a vast number of people. I praised the Lord all the way we went, and when we arrived at the place I understood the kind of death I was to suffer, yet blessed be God, none of those things moved me.

When the executioner shewed me a basket of turpentine wood, stuck full of small pieces like skewers; he told me I was to be stripped naked, and laid down on one side by the basket, and these sharp pegs were to be stuck into me, and then set on fire, and when they had burnt to my body†[2], I was to be turned on the other side, and served in the same manner, and then to be taken by four men and thrown into the flame, which was to finish the execution; I burst into tears, and asked what I had done to deserve so cruel a death? To this he gave me no answer. I cried out, Lord, if it be thy will that it should be so, thy will be done: I then asked the executioner to let me go to prayer; he asked me to whom? I answered, to the Lord my God; he seemed surprized, and asked me where he was? I told him he was present; upon which he gave me leave. I desired them all to do as I did, so I fell down upon my knees, and mentioned to the Lord his delivering of the three children in the fiery furnace, and of Daniel in the Lion's den, and had close communion with God. I prayed in English a considerable time, and about the middle of my prayer, the Lord impressed a strong desire upon my mind to turn into their language, and pray in their tongue. I did so, and with remarkable liberty, which wonderfully affected the people. One circumstance was very singular, and strikingly displays the power and grace of God. I believe the executioner was savingly converted to God. He rose from his knees, and embracing me round the middle was unable to speak for about five minutes; the first words he expressed, when he had utterance, were, "No man shall hurt thee till thou hast been to the king†."[3]

I was taken away immediately, and as we passed along, and I was reflecting upon the deliverance which the Lord had wrought out for me, and hearing the praises which the executioner was singing to the Lord, I must own I was utterly at a loss to find words to praise him. I broke out in these words, what can't the Lord Jesus do! and what power is like unto his! I will thank thee for what is past, and trust thee for what is to come. I will sing thy praise with my feeble tongue whilst life and breath shall last, and when I fail to sound thy praises here, I hope to sing them round thy throne above: And thus with unspeakable joy, I sung two verses of Dr. Watts's hymns:

"My God, the spring of all my joys[,]
"The life of my delights;
"The glory of my brightest days,
"And comfort of my nights.
"In darkest shades, if thou appear
"My dawning is begun;
"Thou art my soul's bright morning star,
"And thou my rising sun."

Passing by the judge's door, who had before examined and condemned me, he stopped us, and asked the executioner why he brought me back? The man fell upon his knees, and begged he would permit me to be carried before the king, which being granted, I went on, guarded by two hundred men with bows and arrows. After many windings I entered the king's outward chamber, and after waiting some time he came to the door, and his first question was, how came I there? I answered, I came with a hunter whom I met with in the woods, and who persuaded me to come there. He then asked me how old I was? I told him not fifteen. He asked me how I was supported before I met with this man? I answered, by the Lord Jesus Christ, which seemed to confound him. He turned round, and asked me if he lived where I came from? I answered, yes, and here also. He looked about the room, and said he did not see him; but I told him I felt him. The executioner fell upon his knees, and intreated the king in my behalf, and told him what he had felt of the same Lord. At this instant the king's eldest daughter came into the chamber, a person about nineteen years of age, and stood at my right hand. I had a Bible in my hand, which she took out of it, and having opened it, she kissed it, and seemed much delighted with it. When she had put it into my hand again, the king asked me what it was? And I told him the name of my God was recorded there; and after several questions, he bid me read it, which I did, particularly the fifty-third chapter of Isaiah, in the most solemn manner I was able; and also the twenty-sixth chapter of Matthew's Gospel; and when I pronounced the name of Jesus, the particular effect it had upon me was observed by the king. When I had finished reading, he asked me why I read those names*4 with so much reverence? I told him, because the Being to whom those names belonged made heaven and earth, and I and he; this he denied. I then pointed to the sun, and asked him who made the sun, and moon, and stars, and preserved them in their regular order; He said there was a man in their town that did it. I laboured as much as I could to convince him to the contrary. His daughter took the book out of my hand a second time; she opened it, and kissed it again; her father bid her give it to me, which she did; but said, with much sorrow, the book would not speak to her. The executioner then fell upon his knees again, and begged the king to let me go to prayer, which being granted, we all went upon our knees, and now the Lord displayed his glorious power. In the midst of the prayer some of them cried out, particularly the king's daughter, and the judge who ordered me to be executed, and several others seemed under deep conviction of sin: This made the king very angry; he called me a witch, and commanded me to be thrust into the prison, and to be executed the next morning. This was enough to make me think, as old Jacob once did, "All these things are against me;" for I was dragged away, and thrust into the dungeon again with much indignation; but God, who never forsakes his people, was with me. Though I was weak in body, yet was I strong in spirit: The executioner went to the king, and assured him, that if he put me to death, his daughter would never be well. They used the skill of all their doctors that afternoon and night; but physical prescriptions were useless. In the morning the executioner came to me, and, without opening the prison door, called to me, and hearing me answer, said, "Fear not, thy God who delivered thee yesterday, will deliver thee to-day." This comforted me very much, especially to find he could trust the Lord. Soon after I was fetched out; I thought it was to be executed; but they led me away to the king's chamber with much bodily weakness, having been without food two days. When I came into the king's presence, he said to me, with much anger, if I did not make his daughter and that man well, I should be laid down and chopped into pieces before him. I was not afraid, but the Lord tried my faith sharply. The king's daughter and the other person were brought out into the outer chamber, and we went to prayer; but the heavens were locked up to my petitions. I besought the Lord again, but received no answer: I cried again, and he was intreated. He said, "Be it to thee even as thou wilt;" the Lord appeared most lovely and glorious; the king himself was awakened, and the others set at liberty. A great change took place among the people; the king's house became God's house; the soldiers were ordered away, and the poor condemned prisoner had perfect liberty, and was treated like a prince. Now the Lord made all my enemies to become my great friends. I remained nine weeks in the king's palace, praising God day and night: I was never out but three days all the time. I had assumed the habit of the country, and was dressed much like the king, and nothing was too good for me. The king would take off his golden ornaments, his chain and bracelets, like a child, if I objected to them, and lay them aside. Here I learnt to speak their tongue in the highest stile.

I began now to feel an inclination growing upon me to go farther on, but none to return home. The king being acquainted with this, expressed his fears of my being used ill by the next Indian nation, and to prevent it, sent fifty men, and a recommendation to the king, with me. The next nation was called the Creek Indians, at sixty miles distance. Here I was received with kindness, owing to the king's influence, from whom I had parted; here I staid five weeks. I next visited the Catawaw Indians, at about fifty-five miles distance from the others; Lastly, I went among the Housaw Indians, eighty miles distant from the last mentioned; here I staid seven weeks. These nations were then at peace with each other, and I passed among them without danger, being recommended from one to the other. When they recollect, that the white people drove them from the American shores, they are full of resentment. These nations have often united, and murdered all the white people in the back settlements which they could lay hold of, men, women, and children. I had not much reason to believe any of these three nations were savingly wrought upon, and therefore I returned to the Cherokee nation, which took me up eight weeks. I continued with my old friends seven weeks and two days.

I now and then found, that my affections to my family and country were not dead; they were sometimes very sensibly felt, and at last strengthened into an invincible desire of returning home. The king was much against it; but feeling the same strong bias towards my country, after we had asked Divine direction, the king consented, and accompanied me sixty miles with one hundred and forty men. I went to prayer three times before we could part, and then he sent forty men with me a hundred miles farther; I went to prayer, and then took my leave of them, and passed on my way. I had seventy miles now to go to the back settlements of the white people. I was surrounded very soon with wolves again, which made my old lodging both necessary and welcome. However it was not long, for in two days I reached the settlements, and on the third I found a house: It was about dinner-time, and as I was coming to the door the family saw me, were frightened, and ran away. I sat down to dinner alone, and eat very heartily, and, after returning God thanks, I went to see what was become of the family. I found means to lay hold of a girl that stood peeping at me from behind a barn. She fainted away, and it was upwards of an hour before she recovered; it was nine o'clock before I could get them all to venture in, they were so terrified.

My dress was purely in the Indian stile; the skins of wild beasts composed my garments; my head was set out in the savage manner, with a long pendant down my back[,] a sash round my middle, without breeches, and a tomohawk by my side. In about two days they became sociable. Having visited three or four other families at the distance of sixteen or twenty miles, I got them altogether to prayer on the Sabbath days, to the number of seventeen persons. I staid with them six weeks, and they expressed much sorrow when I left them. I was now one hundred and twelve miles from home. On the road I sometimes met with a house, then I was hospitably entertained; and when I met with none, a tree lent me the use of its friendly shelter and protection from the prowling beasts of the woods during the night. The God of mercy and grace supported me thus for eight days, and on the ninth I reached my uncle's house.

The following particulars, relating to the manner in which I was made known to my family, are less interesting; and yet, perhaps, some readers would not forgive their omission: I shall, however, be as brief as I can. I asked my uncle for a lodging, which he refused. I enquired how far the town was off; three quarters of a mile, said he. Do you know Mrs. Marrant and family, and how the children do? was my next question. He said he did, they were all well, but one was lately lost; at this I turned my head and wept. He did not know me, and upon refusing again to lodge me, I departed. When I reached the town it was dark, and passing by a house where one of my old school-fellows lived, I knocked at the door; he came out, and asked me what I wanted? I desired a lodging, which was granted: I went in, but was not known. I asked him if he knew Mrs. Marrant, and how the family were? He said, he had just left them, they were all well; but a young lad, with whom he went to school, who, after he had quitted school, went to Charles-Town to learn some trade; but came home crazy, rambled in the woods, and was torn in pieces by the wild beasts. How do you know, said I, that he was killed by wild beasts? I, and his brother, and uncle, and others, said he, went three days into the woods in search of him, and found his carcase torn, and brought it home and buried it. This affected me very much, and I wept; observing it, he said what is the matter? I made no answer. At supper they sat down without craving a blessing, for which I reproved them; this so affected the man, that I believe it ended in a sound conversion. Here is a wild man, says he, come out of the woods, to be a witness for God, and to reprove our ingratitude and stupefaction! After supper I went to prayer, and then to bed. Rising a little before day-light, and praising the Lord, as my custom was, the family were surprised, and got up: I staid with them till nine o'clock, and then went to my mother's house in the next street. The singularity of my dress drew every body's eyes upon me, yet none knew me. I knock'd at my mother's door, my sister opened it, and was startled at my appearance. Having expressed a desire to see Mrs. Marrant, I was answered, she was not very well, and that my business with her could be done by the person at the door, who also attempted to shut me out, which I prevented. My mother being called, I went in, and sat down, a mob of people being round the door. My mother asked, "what is your business;" only to see you, said I. She said she was much obliged to me, but did not know me. I asked, how are your children? how are your two sons? She replied, her daughters were in good health, of her two sons, one was well, and with her, but the other,—unable to contain, she burst into a flood of tears, and retired. I was overcome, and wept much; but nobody knew me.†⁵ This was an affecting scene! Presently my brother came in: He enquired, who I was, and what I was? My sister did not know; but being uneasy at my presence, they were contriving to get me out of the house, which, being overheard by me, I resolved not to stir. My youngest sister, eleven years of age, came in from school, with a book under her arm. I was then sitting in the parlour, and as she passed by the parlour door, she peep'd in and seeing a strange person there, she recollected me; she goes into the kitchen, and tells the servants, her brother was come; but her report finding no credit, she came and peep'd again, that she might be certain it was me; and then passing into the next room, through the parlour where I was sitting, she made a running curtsy, and says to my eldest sister, who was there, it is my brother John! She called her a foolish girl, and threatened to beat her: Then she came again and peep'd at me, and being certain she was not mistaken, she went back, and insisted that it was me: Being then beat by my sister, she went crying up-stairs to my mother, and told her; but neither would my mother believe her. At last they said to her, if it be your brother, go and kiss him, and ask him how he does? She ran and clasped me round the neck, and, looking me in the face, said, "Are not you my brother John?" I answered yes, and wept. I was then made known to all the family, to my friends, and acquaintances, who received me, and were glad and rejoiced: Thus the dead was brought to life again; thus the lost was found. I shall now close the Narrative, with only remarking a few incidents in my life, until my connection with my Right Honourable Patroness, the Countess of HUN-TINGDON.

I remained with my relations till the commencement of the American troubles. I used to go and hear the word of God, if any Gospel ministers came into the country, though at a considerable distance, and thereby got acquainted with a few poor people, who feared God in Wills' Town, and Borough Town, Dorchester Town, and other places thereabouts; and in those places we used to meet and associate together for Christian Conversation, and at their request I frequently went to prayer with them, and at times enjoyed much of the Lord's presence among them.

About this time I went with my brother, who was a house-carpenter, to repair a plantation belonging to Mr. Jenkins, of Cumbee, about seventy miles from Charles-Town, where after I had done work in the evening, I used to spend my time in reading God's Word, singing Watts's Hymns and in Prayer, the little negro children would often come round the door with their pretty wishful looks, and finding my heart much drawn out in Love to their souls, I one evening called several of them in, and asked them if they could say the Lord's Prayer, &c. [F]inding they were very ignorant, I told them, if they would come every evening I would teach them, which they did, and learned very fast, some of them in about four weeks could say the Lord's Prayer, and good part of the Catechism, after teaching, I used to go to prayer with them before we parted; this continued without interruption for three or four months, in which time, by the children acquainting their parents with it, I soon had my society increased to about thirty persons; and the Lord was pleased often to refresh us with a sense of his love and presence amongst us; one of the negro boys made very great proficiency in that time, and could exercise in extempory prayer much to my satisfaction. We are well advised in Ecclesiast[es], chap. ii. *v.* 1. *My Son, if thou come to serve the Lord, prepare thy heart for temptation:* Nor was it long before they were made to pledge our dear Lord in the bitter cup of suffering; for now the old Lion began to roar, their mistress became acquainted with our proceedings, and was full of rage at it, and determined to put a stop to it. She had two of the children brought before her to examine, and made them say the Lord's prayer to her, she then asked who taught them? and they told her the free Carpenter. She also enquired, how many he had instructed, and at what time he taught them; and they told her, it was in the Evening after they had done work. She then stirred up her husband against us, who before had several times come in while I was instructing the children, and did not appear displeased with it: she told him it was the ready way to have all his negroes ruin'd, and made him promise to examine further into the matter, and break up our meeting; which he then very soon did, for a short space; for he, together with his overseer and negro-driver, and some of his neighbours, beset the place wherein we met, while we were at prayers; and as the poor creatures came out they caught them, and tied them together with cords, till the next morning, when all they caught, men, women, and children were strip'd naked and tied, their feet to a stake, their hands to the arm of a tree, and so severely flogg'd that the blood ran from their backs and sides to the floor, to make them promise they would leave off praying, &c. though several of them fainted away with the pain and loss of blood, and lay upon the ground as dead for a considerable time after they were untied. I did not hear that she obtained her end of any of them. She endeavoured to perswade her husband to flog me also, but he told her he did not dare to do it because I was free, and would take the law of him, and make him pay for it; which she told him, she had rather he should run the hazard of, than let me go without the benefit of a good flogging, and was afterwards very angry with him because he was afraid to gratify her. He told me afterwards that I had spoiled all his Negroes, but could not help ac-knowledging, that they did their tasks sooner than the others who were not instructed, and thereby had time after their tasks were done, to keep their own fields in better order than the others, who used to employ the Sabbath for that purpose, as is the common practice among the Negroes. He then said, I should make them so wise that he should not be able to keep them in subjection. I asked him whether he did not think they had Souls to be saved? He answered, yes. I asked him whether he thought they were in the way to save their Souls whilst they were ignorant of that God who made and preserved them. He made me no answer to that. I then told him that the blood of those poor negroes which he had spilt that morning would be required by God at his hands. He then left me. Soon after, meeting with his wife, I told her the same; but she laught at it, and was only sorry that she had not been able to get me flog'd with them. Finding I could not any longer live peaceably there, I encouraged the poor creatures to call upon God as well as they could, and returned home; where I afterwards heard that their Mistress continued to persecute them for meeting together as often as she discover'd them, and her husband for not being more severe against them; they were then obliged to meet at midnight in different corners of the woods that were about the plantation, and were sure to be flog'd if ever she caught them, they nevertheless continued their meetings though in such imminent danger, and by what I have since heard, I believe it continues to this day, by which it appears that the work was of God; therefore neither the devil nor his servants could overthrow it; and to our faithful Covenant God be all the Glory.

In about two months after I left them, it pleased God to lay his hand upon their Mistress, and she was seized with a very violent fever, which no medicine that they could procure would remove, and in a very few days after she was taken ill, she died in a very dreadful manner, in great anger with her husband, for not preventing their meetings, which she had heard they continued, notwithstanding all her endeavours to stop it. After she was dead, her husband gave them liberty to meet together as before, and used sometimes to attend with them; and I have since heard that it was made very useful to him.

About this time I was an eye-witness of the remarkable conversion of a child seven and a half years old, named Mary Scott, which I shall here mention, in hopes the Lord may make it useful and profitable to my young readers. Her parents lived in the house adjoining to my sister's. One day as I was returning from my work, and passing by the school where she was instructed, I saw the children coming out, and stop'd and looked among them for her, to take her home in my hand; but not seeing her among those that were coming out, I supposed she was gone before, and went on towards home; when passing by the church-yard which was in my way, I saw her very busy walking from one tomb to another, and went to her, and asked her what she was doing there? She told me, that in the lesson she had set her at school that morning, in the Twentieth of the Revelations, she read, "I saw the Dead, small and great, stand before God," &c. and she had been measuring the graves, with a tape she then held in her hand, to see if there were any so small as herself among them; and that she had found six that were shorter. I then said, and what of that? She answered, "I will die, Sir." I told her I knew she would, but hoped she would live till she was grown a woman; but she continued to express her desire to depart, and be with Christ, rather than to live till she was grown up. I then took her by the hand and brought her home with me. After this, she was observed to be always very solid and thoughtful, and that passage appeared always to be fresh upon her mind. I used frequently to be with her when in town, and at her request we often read and prayed together, and she appeared much affected. She never afterwards was seen out at play with other children; but spent her leisure time in reading God's word and prayer. In about four months after this, she was taken ill, and kept her room about three weeks; when first taken, she told me, she should never come down stairs alive. I frequently visited her during her illness, and made light of what she said about her dying so soon; but in the last week of her illness, she said to me in a very solemn manner, "Sir, I shall die before Saturday-night." The Physicians attended her, but she took very few if any medicines, and appeared quite calm and resigned to God's will. On Friday morning, which was the day she died, I visited her, and told her that I hoped she would not die so soon as she said, but she told me that she should certainly die before six o'clock that Evening. About five o'clock I visited her again. She was then sitting in a chair, and reading in her Bible, to all appearance pretty well recovered. After setting with her about a quarter of an hour, she got up, and desired me to go down, and send her mother up with a clean shift for her; which I did; and after a little time, when I went up again, I found her lying on the bed, with her eyes fixed up to heaven; when turning herself and seeing me, she said, "Mr. Marrant, don't you see that pretty town, and those fine people, how they shine like gold?—O how I long to be with my Lord and his redeemed Children in Glory!" and then turning to her parents and two sisters, (who were all present, having by her desire been called to her) she shook hands with them, and bade them farewell; desiring them not to lament for her when she was dead, for she was going to that fine place where God would wipe away all tears from her eyes, and she should sing Hallelujahs to God and to the Lamb for ever and ever, and where she hoped afterwards to meet them; and then turning again to me, she said— "Farewell, and God bless you[,]" and then fell asleep in the arms of Jesus. This afterwards proved the conversion of her mother.

In those troublesome times, I was pressed on board the Scorpion sloop of war, as their musician, as they were told I could play on music.—I continued in his majesty's service six years and eleven months; and with shame confess, that a lamentable stupor crept over all my spiritual vivacity, life and vigour; I got cold and dead. What need, reader, have we to be continually mindful of our Lord's exhortation, *"What I say unto you, I say unto all, Watch."* My gracious God, my dear Father in his dear Son, roused me every now and then by dangers and deliverances.—I was at the siege of Charles-Town, and passed through many dangers. When the town was taken, my old royal benefactor and convert, the king of the Cherokee Indians, riding into the town with general Clinton, saw me, and knew me: He alighted off his horse,†⁶ and came to me; said he was glad to see me; that his daughter was very happy, and sometimes longed to get out of the body.

Some time after this I was cruising about in the American seas, and cannot help mentioning a singular deliverance I had from the most imminent danger, and the use the Lord made it of to me. We were overtaken by a violent storm; I was washed overboard, and thrown on again; dashed into the sea a second time, and tossed upon deck again. I now fastened a rope round my middle, as a security against being thrown into the sea again; but, alas! forgot to fasten it to any part of the ship; being carried away the third time by the fury of the waves, when in the sea, I found the rope both useless and an incumbrance. I was in the sea the third time about eight minutes, and several sharks came round me; one of an enormous size, that could easily have taken me into his mouth at once, passed and rubbed against my side. I then cried more earnestly to the Lord than I had done for some time; and he who heard Jonah's prayer, did not shut out mine, for I was thrown aboard again; these were the means the Lord used to revive me, and I began to set out afresh.

I was in the engagement with the Dutch off the Dogger bank, on board the Princess-Amelia, of eighty-four guns.*7 We had a great number killed and wounded; the deck was running with blood; six men were killed and three wounded, stationed at the same gun with me; my head and face were covered with the blood and brains of the slain; I was wounded, but did not fall, till a quarter of an hour before the engagement ended, and was happy in my soul during the whole of it. After being in the hospital three months and sixteen days, I was sent to the West-Indies on board a ship of war, and, after cruising in those seas, we returned home as a convoy. Being taken ill of my old wounds, I was put into the hospital at Plymouth, and had not been there long, when the physician gave it as his opinion, that I should not be capable of serving the king again; I was therefore discharged, and came to London, where I lived with a respectable and pious merchant, near three years, who was unwilling to part with me. During this time, I saw my call to the ministry fuller and clearer; had a feeling concern for the salvation of my countrymen: I carried them constantly in the arms of prayer and faith to the throne of grace, and had continual sorrow in my heart for my brethren, for my kinsmen, according to the flesh.——I wrote a letter to my brother, who returned me an answer, in which he prayed some ministers would come and preach to them, and desired me to shew it to the minister whom I attended. I used to exercise my gifts on a Monday evening in prayer and exhortation, in Spa-fields chapel, and was approved of, and sent down to Bath; where I was ordained, in Lady Huntingdon's Chapel. Her Ladyship having seen the letter from my brother in Nova Scotia, thought Providence called me there: To which place I am now bound, and expect to sail in a few days.

I have now only to intreat the earnest prayers of all my kind Christian friends, that I may be carried safe there; kept humble, made faithful, and successful; that strangers may hear of and run to Christ; that Indian tribes may stretch out their hands to God; that the black nations may be made white in the blood of the Lamb; that vast multitudes of hard tongues, and of a strange speech, may learn the language of Canaan, and sing the song of Moses, and of the Lamb; and anticipating the glorious prospect, may we all with fervent hearts, and willing tongues, sing Hallelujah; the kingdoms of the world are become the kingdoms of our God, and of his Christ. Amen, and Amen.

Nor can I take my leave of my very dear London Friends without intreating GOD to bless them with every blessing of the upper and nether Springs:—May the good will of Him that dwelt in the bush ever preserve and lead them! is the fervent prayer of their affectionate and grateful Servant in the Gospel,

J. MARRANT.

London, N° 69,
MILE-END ROAD,
Aug. 18. 1785.

PSALM CVII. Dr. WATTS.
1 GIVE Thanks to God; He reigns above;
Kind are his Thoughts, his Name is Love;
His Mercy Ages past have known,
And Ages long to come shall own.
2 Let the Redeemed of the LORD
The Wonders of his Grace record;
Isr'el, the Nation whom he chose,
And rescu'd from their mighty Foes.
3 When GOD's Almighty Arm had broke
Their Fetters and th'Egyptian Yoke,
They trac'd the Desert, wand'ring round
A wild and solitary Ground!
4 There they could find no leading Road,
Nor City for a fix'd Abode;
Nor Food, nor Fountain to assuage
Their burning Thirst, or Hunger's Rage.
5 In their Distress to GOD they cry'd;

John Marrant 74

GOD was their Saviour and their Guide;
He led their March, far wand'ring round,
'Twas the right Path to Canaan's Ground.
6 Thus when our first Release we gain
From Sin's old Yoke, and Satan's Chain,
We have this desert World to pass,
A dang'rous and a tiresome Place.
7 He feeds and clothes us all the Way,
He guides our Footsteps lest we stray;
He guards us with a pow'rful Hand,
And brings us to the heav'nly Land.
8 O let the Saints with Joy record
The Truth and Goodness of the LORD!
How great his Works! how kind his Ways!
Let ev'ry Tongue pronounce his Praise.

FINIS

A
SERMON
PREACHED ON THE 24TH DAY OF JUNE 1789,
BEING THE FESTIVAL
OF
ST. JOHN THE BAPTIST,
AT THE REQUEST
OF THE
RIGHT WORSHIPFUL THE GRAND MASTER
PRINCE HALL,
AND
THE REST OF THE BRETHREN
OF THE
AFRICAN LODGE
OF THE
HONORABLE SOCIETY
OF
FREE AND ACCEPTED MASONS
IN BOSTON.

BY THE REVEREND BROTHER MARRANT,
CHAPLAIN.

JOB xxxii. 17 ver. I said, I will answer also my part, I
also will shew mine opinion.——

BOSTON:
PRINTED AND SOLD AT THE BIBLE AND HEART

A SERMON.

ROMANS xii. 10.

*Be kindly affectioned one to another, with brotherly
love, in honour preferring one another.*

IN this chapter, from whence my text is taken, we find the Apostle Paul
labouring with the Romans to press on them the great duties of Brotherly
Love.

By an entire submission and conformity to the will of God, whereby
are given to us exceeding great and precious promises, that by these we
might be made partakers of the divine nature, having escaped the corruption that is in the world through lust—That being all members of
the body of Christ with the Church, we ought to apply the gifts we have
received to the advantage of our brethren, those of us especially who are
called to any office in the church, by discharging it with zeal and integrity
and benevolence, which is the most important duty, and comprehends
all the rest, and particularly the following—which the apostle here sets
down—which are to love one another sincerely, to be ready to all good
offices—to sympathize in the good or evil that befals our brethren, to
comfort and assist those that are in affliction, and to live together in a
spirit of humility, peace and unity. Benevolence does yet further oblige
christians to love and bless those who hate them and injure them, to
endeavour to have peace with all men, to abstain from revenge, and to
render them good for evil; these are the most essential duties of the
religion we profess; and we deserve the name of christians no further
than we sincerely practise them to the glory of God and the good of
our own souls and bodies, and the good of all mankind.

But first, my Brethren, let us learn to pray to God through our Lord
Jesus Christ for understanding, that we may know ourselves; for without
this we can never be fit for the society of man, we must learn to guide
ourselves before we can guide others, and when we have done this we
shall understand the apostle, Romans xii. 16. "Be not wise in your own
conceits," for when we get wise in ourselves we are then too wise for

God, and consequently not fit for the society of man—I mean the christian part of mankind—Let all my brethren Masons consider what they are called to—May God grant you an humble heart to fear God and love his commandments; then and only then you will in sincerity love your brethren: And you will be enabled, as in the words of my text, to be kindly affectioned one to another, with brotherly love in honour preferring one another. Therefore, with the apostle Paul, I beseech you therefore brethren, by the mercies of God, that ye present your bodies a living sacrifice, holy, acceptable unto God, which is your reasonable service—let love be without dissimulation, abhor that which is evil, cleave to that which is good. These and many other duties are required of us as christians, every one of which are like so many links of a chain, which when joined together make one complete member of Christ; this we profess to believe as Christians and as Masons.—I shall stop here with the introduction, which brings me to the points I shall endeavour to prove.—

First, the anciency of Masonry, that being done, will endeavour to prove all other titles we have a just right as Masons to claim—namely, honourable, free and accepted: To do this I must have recourse to the creation of this our world.—After the Grand Architect of the Universe had framed the heavens for beauty and delight for the beings he was then about to make, he then called the earth to appear out of darkness, saying, let there be light, and it was so; he also set the sun, moon and stars in the firmament of heaven, for the delight of his creatures—he then created the fishes of the sea, the fowls of the air, then the beasts of the earth after their various kinds, and God blessed them.

Thus all things were in their order prepared for the most excellent accomplished piece of the visible creation, Man.—The forming [of] this most excellent creature Man, was the close of the creation, so it was peculiar to him to have a solemn consultation and decree about his making, and God said, let us make Man.—Seneca says, that man is not a work huddled over in haste, and done without fore-thinking and great consideration, for man is the greatest and most stupendous work of God.—Man hath not only a body in common with all inferior animals, but into his body was infused a soul of a far more noble nature and make—a rational principle to act according to the designs of his creation; that is, to contemplate the works of God, to admire his perfections, to worship him, to live as becomes one who received his excellent being from him, to converse with his fellow creatures that are of his own order, to maintain mutual love and society, and to serve God in consort. Man is a wonderful creature, and not undeservedly said to be a little world, a world within himself, and containing whatever is found in the Creator.—In him is the spiritual and immaterial nature of God, the reasonableness of Angels, the sensative power of brutes, the vegetative life of plants, and the virtue of all the elements he holds converse with in both worlds.—Thus man is crowned with glory and honour, he is the most remarkable workmanship of God. And is man such a noble creature and made to converse with his fellow men that are of his own order, to maintain mutual love and society, and to serve God in consort with each other?—then what can these God-provoking wretches think, who despise their fellow men, as tho' they were not of the same species with themselves, and would if in their power deprive them of the blessings and comforts of this life, which God in his bountiful goodness, hath freely given to all his creatures to improve and enjoy? Surely such monsters never came out of the hand of God in such a forlorn condition.—Which brings me to consider the fall of man; and the Lord God took the man and put him into the garden of Eden, to dress it and to keep it, and freely to eat of every tree of the garden; here was his delightful employ and bountiful wages, and but one tree out of all that vast number he was forbidden to eat of. Concerning this garden, there have been different opinions about it by the learned, where it was, but the most of them agree that it was about the center of the earth, and that the four rivers parted or divided the four quarters of the world. The first was Pison, that was it which compasseth the land of Havilah; this river Pison is called by some Phasis, or Phasi Tigris, it runs (they say) by that Havilah whither the Amalekites fled, see I Sam. xv. 7. and divides it from the country of Susianna, and at last falls into the Persian Gulf, saith Galtruchius and others; but from the opinions of christian writers, who hold, that Havilah is India, and Pison the river Ganges. This was first asserted by Josephus, and from him Eustubius, Jerom, and most of the fathers received it, and not without good reason; for Moses here adds, as a mark to know the place by, that there is gold, and the gold of that land is good; now it is confessed by all, that India is the most noted for gold, and of the best sort. It is added again, a note whereby to discover that place, that there is bdellium and the onyx stone—and India is famous for precious stones and pearls.—The name of the second river is Gihon, the same is it which compasseth the whole land of Ethiopia (or Cush as it is in the original) there is reason to believe that this Gihon is the river of Nile, as the forenamed Josephus and most of the ancient writers of the church hold, and by the help of the river Nile, Paradise did as it were border upon Egypt, which is the principal part of the African Ethiopia, which the ancient writers hold is meant there: The name of the third river is Hiddekel, that is it which goeth toward the east of Assyria, ver. 14. That it was a river belonging to Babylon is clear from Dan. x. 4; this is concluded to be the river Tygris, which divides Mesopotamia from Assyria, and goeth along with Euphrates, this being the great middle channel that ran through Edom or Babylon, and may be thought to take its name from its fructifying quality. These are the four grand land marks which the all-wise and gracious God was pleased to draw as the bounds and habitation of all nations which he was about to settle in this world; if so, what nation or people dare, without highly displeasing and provoking that God to pour down his judgments upon them.—I say, dare to despise or tyrannize over their lives or liberties, or incroach on their lands, or to inslave their bodies? God hath and ever will visit such a nation or people as this.—Envy and pride are the leading lines to all the miseries that mankind have suffered from the beginning of the world to this present day. What was it but these that turned the devil out of heaven into a hell of misery, but envy and pride?—Was it not the same spirit that moved him to tempt our first parents to sin against so holy and just a God, who had but just (if I may use the expression) turned his back from crowning Adam with honour and glory?—But envy at his prosperity hath taken the crown of glory from his head, and hath made us his posterity miserable.—What was it but this that made Cain murder his brother, whence is it but from these that our modern Cains call us Africans the sons of Cain? (We admit it if you please) and we will find from him and his sons Masonry began, after the fall of his father. Altho' Adam, when placed in the garden, God would not suffer him to be idle and unemployed in that happy state of innocence, but set him to dress and to keep that choice piece of earth; here he was to employ his mind as well as exercise his body; here he was to contemplate and study God's works; here he was to enjoy God, himself and the whole world, to submit himself wholly to his divine conduct, to conform all his actions to the will of his Maker; but by his sudden fall he lost that good will that he owed to his God, and for some time lost the study of God's works; but no doubt he afterwards taught his sons the art of Masonry; for how else could Cain after so much trouble and perplexity have time to study the art of building a city, as he did on the east of Eden, Gen. iv. 17. and without doubt he teached his sons the art, ver. 20, 21.—

But to return, bad as Cain was, yet God took not from him his faculty of studying architecture, arts and sciences—his sons also were endued with the same spirit, and in some convenient place no doubt they met and communed with each other for instruction. It seems that the allwise God put this into the hearts of Cain's family thus to employ themselves, to divert their minds from musing on their father's murder and the woful curse God had pronounced on him, as we don't find any more of Cain's complaints after this.

Similar to this we have in the 6 Gen. 12 & 13, that God saw that all men had corrupted their way, and that their hearts were only evil continually; and 14, 15, 16 verses, the great Architect of the universe gives Noah a compleat plan of the ark and sets him to work, and his sons as assistants, like deputy and two grand wardens. One thing is well known, our enemies themselves being judges, that in whatsoever nation or kingdom in the whole world where Masonry abounds most, there hath been and still are the most peaceable subjects, cheerfully conforming to the laws of that country in which they reside, always willing to submit to their magistrates and rulers, and where Masonry most abounds, arts and sciences, whether mechanical or liberal, all of them have a mighty tendency to the delight and benefit of mankind; therefore we need not question but the allwise God by putting this into our hearts intended, as another end of our creation, that we should not only live happily ourselves, but be likewise mutually assisting to each other. Again, it is not only good and beneficial in a time of peace, in a nation or kingdom, but in a time of war, for that brotherly love that cements us together by the bonds of friendship, no wars or tumults can separate; for in the heat of war if a brother sees another in distress he will relieve him some way or other, and kindly receive him as a brother, prefering him before all others, according to the Apostle's exhortation in my text, as also a similar instance you have I Kings, [x]x. from 31st to 38th verse, where you find Benhadad in great distress, having lost a numerous army in two battles, after his great boasting, and he himself forced to hide himself in a chamber, and sends a message to Ahab king of Israel to request only his life as a captive; but behold the brotherly love of a Mason! no sooner was the message delivered, but he cries out in a rapture—is he alive— he is my brother! Every Mason knows that they were both of the craft, and also the messengers. Thus far may suffice for the anciency of this grand art; as for the honour of it—it is a society which God himself has been pleased to honour ever since he breathed into Adam the breath of life, and hath from generation to generation inspired men with wisdom, and planned out and given directions how they should build, and with what materials. And first, Noah in building the ark wherein he was saved, while God in his justice was pleased to destroy the unbelieving world of mankind. The first thing Noah did upon his landing was to build an altar to offer sacrifice to that great God which had delivered him out of so great a deluge; God accepted the sacrifice and blessed him, and as they journeyed from the east towards the west, they found a plain in the land of Shinar and dwelt there, and his sons.

Nimrod the son of Cush, the son of Ham, first founded the Babylonian monarchy, and kept possession of the plains, and founded the first great empire at Babylon, and became grand master of all Masons, he built many splendid cities in Shinar, and under him flourished those learned Mathematicians, whose successors were styled in the book of Daniel, Magi, or wise men, for their superior knowledge. The migration from Shinar commenced fifty three years after they began to build the tower, and one hundred and fifty four years after the flood, and they went off at various times and travelled east, west, north and south, with their mighty skill, and found the use of it in settling their colonies; and from Shinar the arts were carried to distant parts of the earth, notwithstanding the confusion of languages, which gave rise to Masons['] faculty and universal practice of conversing without speaking, and of knowing each other by signs and tokens; they settled the dispersion in case any of them should meet in distant parts of the world who had been before in Shinar. Thus the earth was again planted and replenished with Masons the second son of Ham carried into Egypt; there he built the city of Heliopolis—Thebes with an hundred gates—they built also the statue of Sphynx, whose head was 120 feet round, being reckoned the first or earliest of the seven wonders of arts. Shem the second son of Noah remained at Ur of the Chaldees in Shinar, with his father and his great grandson Heber, where they lived in private and died in peace: But Shem's offspring travelled into the south and east of Asia, and their offspring propagated the science and the art as far as China and Japan.

While Noah, Shem and Heber diverted themselves at Ur in mathematical studies, teaching Peleg the father of Rehu, of Sereg, Nachor, and Terah, father of Abram, a learned race of mathematicians and geometricians; thus Abram, born two years after the death of Noah, had learned well the science and the art before the God of glory called him to travel from Ur of the Chaldees, but a famine soon forced him down to Egypt; the descendants of Abram sojourned in Egypt, as shepherds still lived in tents, practised very little of the art of architecture till about eighty years before their Exodus, when by the overruling hand of providence they were trained up to the building with stone and brick, in order to make them expert Masons before they possessed the promised land; after Abram left Charran 430 years, Moses marched out of Egypt at the head of 600,000 Hebrews, males, for whose sakes God divided the red sea to let them pass through Arabia to Canaan. God was pleased to inspire their grand master Moses, and Joshua his deputy, with wisdom of heart; so the next year they raised the curious tabernacle or tent; God having called Moses up into the mount and gave him an exact pattern of it, and charges him to make it exactly to that pattern, and withal gave him the two tables of stone; these he broke at the foot of the mount; God gave him orders to hew two more himself, after the likeness of the former. God did not only inspire Moses with wisdom to undertake the oversight of the great work, but he also inspired Bezaleel with knowledge to do all manner of cunning workmanship for it.——Having entered upon the jewish dispensation, I must beg leave still to take a little notice of the Gentile nations, for we have but these two nations now to speak upon, namely, the Gentiles and the Jews, till I come to the Christian æra.

The Canaanites, Phenicians and Sidonians, were very expert in the sacred architecture of stone, who being a people of a happy genius and frame of mind, made many great discoveries and improvements of the sciences, as well as in point of learning. The glass of Sidon, the purple of Tyre, and the exceeding fine linnen they wove, were the product of their own country and their own invention; and for their extraordinary skill in working of metals, in hewing of timber and stone; in a word, for their perfect knowledge of what was solid in architecture, it need but be remembered that they had in erecting and decorating of the temple at Jerusalem, than which nothing can more redound to their honour, or give a clearer idea of what this one building must have been.——Their fame was such for their just taste, design, and ingenious inventions, that whatever was elegant, great or pleasing, was distinguished by way of excellence with the epithet of Sidonian.——The famous temple of Jupiter Hammon, in Libian Africa, was erected, that stood till demolished by the first Christians in those parts; but I must pass over many other cities and temples built by the Gentiles.

God having inspired Solomon with wisdom and understanding, he as grand master and undertaker, under God the great architect, sends to Hiram king of Tyre, and after acquainting him of his purpose of building a house unto the name of the Lord his God, he sends to him for some of his people to go with some of his, to Mount Lebanon, to cut down and hew cedar trees, as his servants understood it better than his own, and moreover he requested him to send him a man that was cunning, to work in gold and in silver, and in brass, iron, purple, crimson and in blue, and that had skill to engrave with the cunning men, and he sent him Hiram, his name-sake; this Hiram, God was pleased to inspire with wisdom and understanding to undertake, and strength to go through the most curious piece of workmanship that was ever done on earth.—Thus Solomon as grand master, and Hiram as his deputy, carried on and finished that great work of the temple of the living God, the inside work of which, in many instances as well as the tabernacle, resembles men's bodies; but this is better explained in a well filled lodge; but this much I may venture to say, that our blessed Saviour compared his sacred body to a temple, when he said, John ii. 19. Destroy this temple and I will raise it up again in three days; and the Apostle, I Peter, i. 14 says, that shortly he should put off this tabernacle. I could show also that one grand end and design of Masonry is to build up the temple that Adam destroyed in Paradise—but I forbear. Thus hath God honoured the Craft, or Masons, by inspiring men with wisdom to carry on his stupendous works.

It is worthy our notice to consider the number of Masons employed in the work of the Temple: Exclusive of the two Grand Masters, there were 300 princes, or rulers, 3300 overseers of the work, 80000 stone squarers, setters, layers or builders, being able and ingenious Crafts, and 30000 appointed to work in Lebanon, 10000 of which every month, under Adoniram, who was the Grand Warden; all the free Masons employed in the work of the Temple was 119,600, besides 70,000 men who carried burdens, who were not numbered among Masons; these were partitioned into certain Lodges, although they were of different nations and different colours, yet were they in perfect harmony among themselves, and strongly cemented in brotherly love and friendship, till the glorious Temple of Jehovah was finished, and the cape-stone was celebrated with great joy— Having finished all that Solomon had to do, they departed unto their several homes, and carried with them the high taste of architecture to the different parts of the world, and built many other temples and cities in the Gentile nations, under the direction of many wise and learned and royal Grand Masters, as Nebuchadnezar over Babylon—Cyrus over the Medes and Persians—Alexander over the Macedonians—Julius Cæsar over Rome, and a great number more I might mention of crowned heads of the Gentile nations who were of the Craft, but this may suffice.—I must just mention Herod the Great, before I come to the state of Masonry from the birth of our Saviour Jesus Christ.—This Herod was the greatest builder of his day, the patron and Grand Master of many Lodges; he being in the full enjoyment of peace and plenty, formed a design of new building the Temple of Jerusalem. The Temple built by the Jews after the captivity was greatly decayed, being 500 years standing, he proposed to the people that he would not take it down till he had all the materials ready for the new, and accordingly he did so, then he took down the old one and built a new one.—Josephus describes this Temple as a most admirable and magnificent fabric of marble, and the finest building upon earth.—Tiberius having attained the imperial throne, became an encourager of the fraternity.

Which brings me to consider their freedom, and that will appear not only from their being free when accepted, but they have a free intercourse with all Lodges over the whole terrestial globe; wherever arts flourish, a man hath a free right (having a recommendation) to visit his brethren, and they are bound to accept him; these are the laudable bonds that unite Free Masons together in one indissoluble fraternity—thus in every nation he finds a friend, and in every climate he may find a house—this it is to be kindly affectioned one to another, with brotherly love, in honour preferring one another.

Which brings me to answer some objections which are raised against the Masons, and the first is the irregular lives of the professors of it.—It must be admitted there are some persons who, careless of their own reputation, will consequently disregard the most instructive lessons.— Some, I am sorry to say, are sometimes to be found among us; many by yielding to vice and intemperance, frequently not only disgrace themselves, but reflect dishonour on Masonry in general; but let it be known that these apostates are unworthy of their trust, and that whatever name or designation they assume, they are in reality no Masons: But if the wicked lives of men were admitted as an argument against the religion which they profess, Christianity itself, with all its divine beauties, would be exposed to censure; but they say there can be no good in Masonry because we keep it a secret, and at the same time these very men themselves will not admit an apprentice into their craft whatever, without enjoining secresy on him, before they receive him as an apprentice; and yet blame us for not revealing our's—Solomon says, Prov. xi. 12, 13. He that is void of wisdom despiseth his neighbour, but a man of understanding holdeth his peace; a tale-bearer revealeth secrets, but he that is of a faithful spirit concealeth the matter. Thus I think I have answered these objections. I shall conclude the whole by addressing the Brethren of the African Lodge.

Dear and beloved brethren, I don't know how I can address you better than in the words of Nehemiah (who had just received liberty from the king Artaxerxes, letters and a commission, or charter, to return to Jerusalem) that thro' the good hand of our God upon us we are here this day to celebrate the festival of St. John—as members of that honorable society of free and accepted Masons—as by charter we have a right to do —remember your obligations you are under to the great God, and to the whole family of mankind in the world—do all that in you lies to relieve the needy, support the weak, mourn with your fellow men in distress, do good to all men as far as God shall give you ability, for they are all your brethren, and stand in need of your help more or less—for he that loves every body need fear nobody: But you must remember you are under a double obligation to the brethren of the craft of all nations on the face of the earth, for there is no party spirit in Masonry; let them make parties who will, and despise those they would make, if they could, a species below them, and as not made of the same clay with themselves; but if you study the holy book of God, you will there find that you stand on the level not only with them, but with the greatest kings on the earth, as Men and as Masons, and these truly great men are not ashamed of the meanest of their brethren. Ancient history will produce some of the Africans who were truly good, wise, and learned men, and as eloquent as any other nation whatever,*1 though at present many of them in slavery, which is not a just cause of our being despised; for if we search history, we shall not find a nation on earth but has at some period or other of their existence been in slavery, from the Jews down to the English Nation, under many Emperors, Kings and Princes; for we find in the life of Gregory, about the year 580, a man famous for his charity, that on a time when many merchants were met to sell their commodities at Rome, it happened that he passing by saw many young boys with white bodies, fair faces, beautiful countenances and lovely hair, set forth for sale; he went to the merchant their owner and asked him from what country he brought them; he answered from Britain, where the inhabitants were generally so beautiful. Gregory (sighing) said, alas! for grief, that such fair faces should be under the power of the prince of darkness, and that such bodies should have their souls void of the grace of God.

I shall endeavour to draw a few inferences on this discourse by way of application.—

My dear Brethren, let us pray to God for a benevolent heart, that we may be enabled to pass through the various stages of this life with reputation, and that great and infinite Jehovah, who overrules the grand fabric of nature, will enable us to look backward with pleasure, and forward with confidence—and in the hour of death, and in the day of judgment, the well grounded hope of meeting with that mercy from our Maker which we have ever been ready to shew to others, will refresh us with the most solid comfort, and fill us with the most unspeakable joy.

And should not this learn us that new and glorious commandment of our Lord Jesus Christ to his disciples, when he urges it to them in these words—Love the Lord thy God with all thy heart, and thy neighbour as thyself.—Our Lord repeats and recommends this as the most indispensable duty and necessary qualification of his disciples, saying, hereby shall all men know that ye are my disciples, if ye have love one to another.—And we are expressly told by the Apostle, that charity, or universal love and friendship, is the end of the commandment.

Shall this noble and unparalleled example fail of its due influence upon us—shall it not animate our hearts with a like disposition of benevolence and mercy, shall it not raise our emulation and provoke our ambition— to go and do likewise.

Let us then beware of such a selfishness as pursues pleasure at the expence of our neighbour's happiness, and renders us indifferent to his peace and welfare; and such a self-love is the parent of disorder and the source of all those evils that divide the world and destroy the peace of mankind; whereas christian charity—universal love and friendship—benevolent affections and social feelings, unite and knit men together, render them happy in themselves and useful to one another, and recommend them to the esteem of a gracious God, through our Lord Jesus Christ.

The few inferences that have been made on this head must be to you, my worthy brethren, of great comfort, that every one may see the propriety of a discourse on brotherly love before a society of free Masons— who knows their engagements as men and as christians, have superadded the bonds of this ancient and honourable society—a society founded upon such friendly and comprehensive principles, that men of all nations and languages, or sects of religion, are and may be admitted and received as members, being recommended as persons of a virtuous character.

Religion and virtue, and the continuance and standing of this excellent society in the world—its proof of the wisdom of its plan—and the force of its principles and conduct has, on many occasions, been not a little remarkable—as well among persons of this, as among those of different countries, who go down to the sea and occupy their business in the great waters, they know how readily people of this institution can open a passage to the heart of a brother; and in the midst of war, like a universal language, is understood by men of all countries—and no wonder.—If the foundation has been thus laid in wisdom by the great God, then let us go on with united hearts and hands to build and improve upon this noble foundation—let love and sincere friendship in necessity instruct our ignorance, conceal our infirmities, reprove our errors, reclaim us from our faults—let us rejoice with them that rejoice, and weep with those that weep—share with each other in our joys, and sympathize in our troubles.

And let the character of our enemies be to resent affronts—but our's to generously remit and forgive the greatest; their's to blacken the reputation and blast the credit of their brethren—but our's to be tender of their good name, and to cast a vail over all their failings; their's to blow the coals of contention and sow the seeds of strife among men—but our's to compose their differences and heal up their breaches.

In a word, let us join with the words of the Apostle John in the 19th chapter of Revelations, and after these things I heard a great voice of much people in heaven, saying, Alleluia, salvation and glory, and honour, and power, unto the Lord our God; for true and righteous are his judgments—and the four and twenty elders, and the four beasts, fell down and worshipped God that sat on the throne, saying, Amen; Alleluia; and a voice came out of the throne, saying, praise our God, all ye his servants, and ye that fear him, both small and great.

To conclude the whole, let it be remembered, that all that is outward, whether opinions, rites or ceremonies, cannot be of importance in regard to eternal salvation, any further than they have a tendency to produce inward righteousness and goodness—pure, holy, spiritual and benevolent affections can only fit us for the kingdom of heaven; and therefore the cultivation of such must needs be the essence of Christ's religion.—God of his infinite mercy grant that we may make this true use of it. Unhappily, too many Christians, so called, take their religion not from the declarations of Christ and his apostles, but from the writings of those they esteem learned.—But, I am to say, it is from the New-Testament only, not from any books whatsoever, however piously wrote, that we ought to seek what is the essence of Christ's religion; and it is from this fountain I have endeavoured to give my hearers the idea of Christianity in its spiritual dress, free from any human mixtures—if we have done this wisely we may expect to enjoy our God in the world that is above—in which happy place, my dear brethren, we shall all, I hope, meet at that great day, when our great Grand Master shall sit at the head of the great and glorious Lodge in heaven—where we shall all meet to part no more for ever and ever—Amen.

A

JOURNAL

OF

The Rev. JOHN MARRANT,

From AUGUST the 18th, 1785,

TO

The 16th of MARCH, 1790.

LONDON:

PRINTED FOR THE AUTHOR:

Sold by J. TAYLOR and Co. at the Royal Exchange; and
Mr. MARRANT, No. 2, Black Horse Court, in
Aldersgate-street.

Price 2s. 6d.

THE
PREFACE

THE following Extracts will shew my Readers the impropriety of that report which prevailed so much after I left this country, among the greater sort of people, of that sum of money that they were informed I had from that Honourable connection which I was then in. To give a strict and honest account of the collection I had received at Bristol, some have taken upon them to say, that I did receive thirty odd pounds; this I contradict in the sight of God, before whom I must soon stand and give an account of the same. I received but twenty-four pounds seven shillings, and the greater part of that was from the Tabernacle people. I expended that in getting the necessaries for which it was collected, such as books, clothes, &c. and when in London had lodging to pay, which took up more than that sum by far; besides, the necessaries for the passage, such as bedding, tea, sugar, &c. and this is all that I received from that connection with the passage, which was ten guineas. My Readers may enquire what makes me so strict in putting the sums. In order to remove the prejudice of the mind of the Public in general, the above sum mentioned is all that I received from that connection from that time to the present.

The day I left London, the sum of money I had amounted to six pounds three shillings, five shillings of which I paid for the coach down to Gravesend. I arrived there one hour after the ship sailed, which obliged me to pay two guineas to get on board, and that very morning at one o'clock, paid two guineas more for a person that was sent down to me to bring me a twenty pounds Bank note, whose name I forbear to mention. And the little money I saved when I lived in the merchant's employment, this I laid out every farthing in building a Chapel, in Birch Town, which I hope is standing now. This is the true account I solemnly now give my Readers in the sight of God. And after I had been in that country, finding that the Gospel of our Lord Jesus Christ prospered among the poor people, I felt such a desire for travelling from village to village, I soon ran out the remainder of my money in paying ferryings, as that country has so many large rivers and lakes to cross; so that I was soon reduced so low that I was obliged to pawn my jacket off my body, and that I did four times, in order to get over to the different places, and repeatedly sending home every opportunity to the connection for some support, so that I might have been able to continue with the people, but never had any of any kind, which forced me to come to England to know the reason. With all the expence of coming, to pay myself, and when arrived, was not permitted to speak for myself, and so remained to the present, without any assistance, or even a Christian word out of them. And I am certain of this one thing, that there is not a Preacher belonging to the Connection could have suffered more than I have for the Connection, and the glory of God, and for the good of precious souls. No man knows my sufferings but God and myself; however, all that they have done to me I freely forgive them, from a *benevolent heart*, and I hope God will give them that benevolent disposition as to forgive me all the offences I have done against them. We must all appear at that day, where I shall be permitted to speak for myself, where might will not overcome right. I have now only to intreat the earnest prayers of all my kind Christian friends, that I may be carried safe through this troublesome world, and successfully in the Gospel of Christ, and kept humbly before God; and that the Gospel may carry its divine force in this land, and wherever God pleases to send it, and by whom, if of a strange language, that they may understand the language of Canaan. That the learned might learn to sing the Song of Moses and the Lamb, and to anticipate the glory of our Emanuel. May we all with fervent heart, and willing tongue, sing Hallelujah; the kingdoms of this world are become the kingdom of our God, and of his Christ. Amen, and Amen.

May every blessing attend every individual of my Readers in whose hands these lines may fall. May the spirit of our Lord Jesus Christ rest upon you all; that it may enable any that are in a state of suffering to hold out, and strengthen the weak in faith, so that when the storms of this world are over, we all may meet round his throne, to praise him to all eternity. To him be all praises and glory ascribed, now, and for evermore.

JOHN MARRANT.

London, June 29, 1790.

A LIST OF THE NAMES
OF THE
SUBSCRIBERS

The Rev. Mr. Cartwright, Lant-street
The Rev. Mr. Williams Ebeneza
Mr. Andrews
Mr. John Timmings, Steward-street, Spital Fields, 5 Copies
Mr. James Daniel, Shoreditch, 5 Copies
Mr. Briggs, Shoreditch, 5 Copies
Mr. Robert Thompson
Mr. John Cartham
Mr. Thomas Griffiths, 3 Copies
Mr. Enovai
Mr. Thomas Mortimer
Mr. William Thorne
Mr. Harmis
Mr. Needham, 7 Copies
Mr. Rainbow
Mr. Reynolds
Mr. Sterrange
Mr. Peter Street
Mr. Anthony Cavalier, Rosemary-lane
Mr. William Bickley
Mr. William Higgs
Mr. Philip Jones
Mr. William Whitebrook
Mr. Peter Dawson

Mr. John Burghall

Mr. John Jones

Mr. John Brown

Mr. Victixker

Mr. Mark Anthony

Mr. Barnick

Mr. Timothy Brown

Mr. Thomas Cole

Mr. George King

Mr. Thomas Butler

Mr. J. Pegge

Mr. Samuel Rolls

Mr. William

Mr. Cornelius Mounsey

Mr. Wrathall, Smithfield

Mr. May, 12 Copies

Mr. Lukesmore.

THE
JOURNAL, &c.

ON the 15th day of May, 1785, I was ordained, and put into the ministry of the word of God the Father, through our Lord Jesus Christ. In that day, I was full of the Spirit of God, and felt a willingness to tell the world the love of God in Christ; and preached many sermons in Bath and Bristol, which God was pleased to accompany with his divine power, to the conviction of souls which afterwards proved their everlasting conversion; and many precious souls in London experienced great blessings from my labours; which gave me great consolation at my return, that God was pleased to work, by so weak an instrument, to his glory, and the good of precious souls: one of whom, I am informed, is gone down to the college, to be a mouth for Christ. Here we see that God does not work as man imagines, who takes the base things of this world, and things that are despised has God chosen; yea, things that are not to bring to nought things that are, that no flesh should glory in his presence. I COR. i. 26, 27, 28, 29, verses.

On the 18th day of August, 1785, I left London for America, in the connections of the Right Honorable the Countess of Huntingdon, without any money to go into a strange country; but being filled with zeal and the love of God, and her Ladyship's promises of assistance when there.

We sailed from Gravesend on the 19th, to perform our voyage. Having arrived there an hour after the ship sailed, I was necessi[t]ated to pay two guineas to get on board; by the help of God I did get on board. The wind being fair, we kept on till the tide came against us; we then brought to, and waited for the next tide; so about six o'clock, she got on the way again, and kept on all night. At twelve o'clock at night, she was hailed by a boat, who enquired what ship that was? and was answered the Peggy, bound for Hallifax. They then asked, if Mr. Marrant was on board? and was answered, yes; so she came along side, and I was called up. A man came on board, and presented to me a pocket book, which, when I opened, I found a twenty pound bank note. Here I saw that the Lord opened the heart of a friend to sympathize with my affliction, who is now alive, but his name I forbear to mention.

We came to the Downs on the 20th, and layed there till the 23d, then we sailed, and were obliged to put into Portsmouth, where we layed four hours, and then sailed for our voyage. We came to the Needles about four o'clock in the afternoon, with a sweet and pleasant breeze, and the smiles of a gracious God, till we came as far as Cape Clare, in Ireland; the wind came about west and west north west for three weeks. The passengers, in general, swearing and playing at cards all day, and impatient with a gracious God, I spoke to them about their wicked ways; that God's frowns were upon us by reason of their wickedness on board the ship, but it proved fruitless.

In the fourth week, it pleased God to send a violent storm, wherein we shifted a heavy sea, which almost filled the cabin; then did they cry out for God to have mercy upon them, and called for the minister to pray for them. I went immediately into the cabin, and asked them what was the matter? Their answer was, "Pray for us, that we perish not.["] I told them, that they must pray for themselves; but as soon as the water was gone out of the cabin, I bid them all get up, and we went down to prayers. God was pleased to hear the prayer of an unworthy creature, so that the arrows of conviction went to the heart of one of the ladies. Indeed, when I came upon deck the sea seemed to be all on fire; running mountains high. Here I saw more of the power of Almighty God; this night the bowsprit of our ship was sprung; none of the passengers went to sleep any more, but crying for prayer all night; this was a sweet work to me, and I believe to two souls on board the ship, who saw the power and glory of God.

The next morning, about eight o'clock, it was as calm as though there never had been any storm; the captain, positively declared, he never saw such a thing in his life: then I had an opportunity of speaking to him concerning the love, and irresistable power of God; and while I was embracing the opportunity of speaking for Christ, and telling him all things were possible to them that believe, the mate went forward, and hallooed to the captain that the bowsprit was sprung. This gave me a greater opportunity to speak to the glory of God, and shewing him, by scripture proof, how good and kind God was, even in his providential ways, that he is not willing that sinners should be lost; he therefore warned them of their danger, and if we reject these repeated warnings, we must expect his judgments to fall upon us. The men went to work to secure the bowsprit, and every body about the ship tried to assist what they could.

About four o'clock they got it secure; after this we went to prayers in the cabin, and all attended that could be spared from off the deck. Here I experienced the kind goodness of a gracious God, in answering prayer, so that we had a fair wind for three days: during this time, the captain and I contrived to make a law against swearing, and playing at cards; so it was agreed to, by all the passengers, and even all the sailors, that every person was to pay one penny for every oath, and that immediately. After this we had no swearing on board; but, instead of swearing, reading, praying, singing of hymns, and preaching, every opportunity when the weather would permit; even the sailors, when their watch was below, was heard to be singing of hymns, and coming to me to teach them.

Here I had work enough to do to watch all night, and part of the day, and every body was upon the catch; so that there was a great alteration in the ship for the better. It was noticed, by all in the ship, that we never had a storm after this, but always high winds, but fair; although our passage being long, but a very good one. Here we see God fulfilling his own glorious promise, in saying, that where two or three agree to call upon his name, there he will be in the midst of them, and that to bless them; and not only so, but to take care of them in all storms and troubles of this world; God will deliver us, and bring us to his heavenly kingdom. Here I saw the land where we were bound to, and all well, not a soul lost; and this day I hoped to be in harbour, and into harbour we came at four o'clock in the afternoon, being the eleventh week, and one day; all the people were in chearful spirits.

After the ship anchored, we all went to prayers, to return thanks to God. Some of the people went on shore, being informed this harbour is called Bevan Harbour, and four and twenty leagues to the eastward of Hallifax, where the ship was bound.

The next morning, being Saturday, after prayers were over, our captain asked me and some of the passengers, whether we would go on shore to walk; and the wind being a-head, we thought it best to take the ladies on shore, to give them a walk. After we got on shore, we went into the woods, and on our knees, returned God thanks for landing us once more on shore. The captain and I, and two other passengers went into the woods after rabbits, and by following them who were shooting, we missed our way, and were out all night in the woods, till Sunday afternoon, four o'clock, without victuals, except two partridges they killed, that we dressed on Saturday night, keeping a fire all night; and on the Lord's day morning, the sun being risen, we walked on until we came to a high mountain; and, after prayers, the captain climbed up into a tree, in order to see whether he could discern the sea; having a sight of the ocean, he cried out "We are near the shore;" so we were all encouraged, and soon came to the sea; but we were about twelve miles westward from the ship. Prayer was made for direction from God which way we should go. The captain and the other went to the westward, and I and another to the eastward; we were to make signal by a gun, if any of us should spy the ship.

An hour after we parted, my companion and I got up on a high mountain, and fired a gun, and were answered from the ship, still eastward from us. We fired a signal gun to our companions, and they followed us to the ship. It was twelve o'clock, before we came to the boat, which had been rowing about all night with provisions for us; so we waited two hours till the captain and the other came to us.

It was past four o'clock on the Lord's day afternoon, before we got on board. After we had got some refreshment we performed divine service. I continued on board till Tuesday the 24th of November, and then four of us hired a fishing boat, to take us to Hallifax, and gave them twenty dollars, thinking to be before the ship, the wind being in the west. The same evening, we came to a place called Littleziddo, when I performed divine service among a congregation of Irish Romans; after divine service I had conversation with them, they seemed to express a great desire for me to stay with them, so I preached again in the morning, and left them in the hands of God.

On the 25th, we arrived at Ship Harbour; I preached to a number of Scotch and Irish together, and afterwards visited several of their small huts, and found the greater part of them very desirous to hear the gospel; and expressing their desire, as many of them had not heard the gospel for many years; so after praying in the morning, we sailed from thence.

On the 26th, in the evening, we arrived at Shag Harbour. Here we stayed four days, weather bound; and very few souls to preach to.

The 1st day of December we sailed from thence, and arrived at Threefathomed Harbour, and attempted to perform divine service, but was prevented, by the violence of the Irish Romans.

On the 2d, we sailed for Hallifax, and arrived in the evening at nine o'clock; where we found the ship had arrived before us, and there was no small stir concerning us. Being strangers, we were obliged to lodge in Golden Ball Tavern, where I found it was impossible to join together in prayer; however two of us did join together, while the others forgot their God. After supper, I went to bed, leaving the other four behind, making themselves merry: by this I learned, that many will pretend to serve God while in danger, but soon forget his mercies. In the morning I came out to go to the ship, and met with the captain, who expressed great satisfaction in seeing me; and hearing all was well, he soon took me to the ladies, where we all joined in prayer together. I then went down to the ship, and found the sailors expressing themselves full of joy; I then returned to the tavern, and found my companions had done breakfast, and the bill was brought in to the amount of six pounds sterling; so I paid the bill, and took myself from thence. On the 4th night, I preached in Hallifax to a large congregation.

The 5th day, we had all our things from on board the ship, and we met in the evening, in order to settle our accounts with the captain and passengers; after which we had prayers, and parted in peace.

The sixth day, being the Lord's day, I preached twice to a crowded congregation, and God was pleased to manifest his divine power both to black and white, which proved the conversion of several present.

On Monday, the 7th, I went over to Dartmouth, to see the place.

Tuesday, the eighth, I preached again in Hallifax to a large concourse of people. Here I was encouraged, because many were crying, "What shall I do to be saved." The Reverend Mr. Furmage took me from place to place, so I had opportunities of conversing with many precious souls, who were groaning for redemption through the blood of Christ.

The 11th, I preached a farewell sermon to a large concourse of people. I preached from the thirteenth chapter of the second epistle of Paul to the Corinthians, the eleventh and following verses. The Lord was truly present with us, so that there was groaning, and sighing, heard throughout the congregation. After I had dismissed the congregation, I conversed with a great number of them, finding their desire that I should stay a little longer with them, I replied, that the pacquet could not stop, but I promised them that I would come through Hallifax once a year; so we had prayers, and commended them to God, who was able to build them up, and give them an inheritance among all them that are sanctified.

The next morning I was accompanied down to the pacquet by Mr. William Furmage, and some of his people. The wind being fair, we sailed on the 12th morning for Shelborne Port Rosway; but we had a violent storm on the passage, which kept us four days, and arrived in Shelburn Harbour on the 15th.

On the 16th, I landed on shore, but did not see any body I knew, neither did I think to stay in the place, seeing it was a new uncultivated place. The people seemed all to be wild; I was obliged to conclude with Abraham, and said, "Sure the fear of God is not in this place." About three o'clock in the afternoon, I went into a coffee house to get something to refresh me; there I met with a gentleman, whom I had some knowledge of, and he of me. I asked him several questions about the people; he informed me of several of them of whom I knew, and persuaded me to get my things from on board the pacquet. Accordingly I did, and lodged at the coffee house that night, without seeing any body else that I knew, and still retained a strong desire to return with the pacquet; but, about midnight I arose up and went to prayer, and I had it impressed on my mind, that God had some people in this place, and so concluded in my mind to stay one week; but on the 17th, in the morning, after addressing the throne of grace once more, I came down stairs, and ordered my breakfast. In the mean time, a gentleman came in, whom I had a perfect knowledge of; and that because we went both to school together. We breakfasted together at one table; but he did not know me, until after breakfast, when I took him into a private room and made myself known to him; he then burst into a flood of tears, and I wept also. He went with me to many others that I perfectly knew, and was gladly received by them.

On the 18th, in the morning, I went over to Birch Town, with two others in company; but was not known by any body there; but one man, who was not at home, but came in about six o'clock in the evening, and was very glad to see me; so we talked about old times, which made us to shed many tears, and I continued all night with him.

On the 19th, in the morning, we returned to Shelbourn Town, in order to get my things over to Birch Town, and returned the same evening back again, when I had many to visit me; and was informed by them, that Mr. Marchenton, in Hallifax, had wrote a letter to them, informing them that I was not an Arminian, and did not come from Mr. Westley, and preached, there was no repentance this side the grave; and thus inflamed the minds of the people. Some cried one thing and some another; but God over-ruled all things for his glory, and I was permitted to preach in the Arminian meeting (because there was no other in the place) to a very large congregation.

On the 20th, being the Lord's day, I preached from the third chapter of the Acts of the Apostles, twenty-second and twenty-third verses; and here God displayed his divine power, in convincing them of the truth of the gospel. Ten of them were pricked to the heart, and cried out, "Men and brethren what shall we do to be saved." In the afternoon, I [was] preaching again to a larger congregation than the morning, of white and black, and Indians, when groans and sighings were heard through the congregation, and many were not able to contain; but cried out to God to have mercy upon them, and would not depart from the place.

In the evening, I preached again from the 5th chapter of the gospel by St. John, at the twenty-eighth and twenty-ninth verse, when God's spirit was very powerfully felt both by the preacher and hearer, and for five minutes I was so full I was not able to speak. Here I saw the display of God's good spirit; several sinners were carried out pricked to the heart. Here Mr. Marchenton's letter proved fruitless; the people determi[n]ed to hear for themselves; all this week I was engaged very much in visiting those poor wounded souls; six of whom God was pleased to manifest himself to.

On the 25th, being Christmas day, I did not administer the sacrament, being not well acquainted with the people. In the afternoon, I baptised ten of them, and married four couple[s]. In the evening, I preached from the sixtieth chapter of Isaiah, and the Lord was pleased to rise and shine in the hearts of those that were wounded; so that they could glorify God through our Lord Jesus Christ. Seven more, also, God was pleased to awaken, under the same discourse. For three days I preached three times a day, and the people were running from all quarters, very desirous to hear the word of God. Preaching the gospel became my meat and my drink; and the mighty work of God spread as far as Barrington, Cape Negro, Shelborn, and Jordan River. I had letters from those places to come over to them, but could not go till after new year's day.

On new year's day, I preached to a large congregation, from the first epistle of Paul to the Corinthians, first chapter, twenty-ninth, thirtieth, and thirty-first verses; when God was pleased to manifest himself again, and got himself great glory in the [conversion] of many precious souls; after which I administered the sacrament to them; where I had great rejoicing with them whom God had been pleased to add as seals to the ministry of his unworthy servant; thirteen in number, who testified the love of God in Jesus Christ, by his unworthy servant; and I may add, many more groaning for redemption in the blood of Christ. I stayed with them until the 7th of January, and then set off for Green's Harbour.

I passed over Jordan River on the 8th day, in a violent storm of snow. About three o'clock, we came up to a ferry house, and enquired the way to Green's Harbour[.] About five o'clock we came to the Indian's wigwam; and after a little discourse, I went to prayers with them; after prayers, I went on my journey, with three of them to accompany me to the house where I stayed all night.

The next morning, a small company of people came together; I preached from the twenty-eighth of Matthew, nineteenth verse; after which I had some discourse with them, and finding that none of them had been baptised, and expressing themselves very desirous, I preached again in the evening from the sixteenth of Mark, sixteenth verse; and the Lord was pleased to manifest himself, and send the words to their hearts: four of them were very much distressed. I gave notice that I would preach in the morning of the 9th, at five o'clock, but the greater part of the people would not go home, so I got no sleep this night; but conversed with them till five o'clock, and found that the master of the house, with his wife and seven children had not been baptised.

On the 10th, at five o'clock, I preached from the first of John, latter part of the nineteenth verse; when there was much of God's presence with us. After breakfast, we went over to Ragged Island, with about thirty persons. In the evening, I preached at Ragged Island from the eleventh chapter of Matthew's Gospel, twenty ninth and thirtieth verses; and afterwards conversed with many of them. Nobody seemed to have any sleep in their eyes, but wanted to hear of the Lord continually.

On the 11th in the morning, about nine o'clock, I preach[e]d again to a large congregation: here was manifested the mighty power of God, in giving me strength to go through the important work, and sealing his own word of divine truth to the hearts of the hearers. I then left them in the hands of God, with an intent to go to Sable River, with three of the people of Ragged Island; but when we came to a place called Little Harbour, the people stopped me, and desired preaching.

On the 12th, I preached from the twenty-third chapter of St. Luke's Gospel, the latter part of the fortieth verse. Here the Lord was pleased to add one son to the Ministry; and tears and groanings were seen and heard throughout the congregation. After conversing with them, and commending them into the hands of God, I attempted to go on my journey, but was prevented by the weather; and the people earnestly desired me to stay with them, to let them hear more of Christ.

On the 13th, in the evening, I preached from the first chapter of Genesis, second verse; and at this time the Spirit of God did move upon the waters; and I conversed with them part of the night. I preached again in the morning on the 14th, at six o'clock, from the sixth chapter of St. Matthew, the thirty-third and thirty-fourth verses; although there was a violent storm of snow, yet I had [a] greater congregation in the morning than in the evening. Here the Lord brake the bread of eternal life amongst poor hungry souls.

After dinner, commending them into the hands of God, I passed on my journey, and arrived at Savel River in the evening. Finding a congregation waiting, I preached from the sixth chapter of St. Mark, the twelfth verse. Here the Lord was pleased to shew them the absolute necessity of repentance; indeed they were led to cry out, "What shall we do to be saved."

On the 15th, at six o'clock in the morning, I preached from the second chapter of the Acts of the Apostles, the thirty-eighth verse, to a large congregation. Here the Lord was pleased to display his divine power, in giving them true repentance. I tarried with them till the 17th, and preached twice every day; and found that my labours were not in vain in the Lord.

On the 18th, after preaching, I had a desire to go over to Jones's Harbour, where, I was informed, the inhabitants were all free-thinkers, and was persuaded not to go over to them, but their persuasions proved fruitless. At ten o'clock, all that could conveniently go, went with me, both men, women and children. We arrived at Jones's Harbour about twelve o'clock; I entered into the first house we came to, determined to have divine service, with God's permission. God was pleased to open the old man's heart, insomuch that he sent all round to the neighbours, and informed them, that there was preaching at his house; and they all came with willingness. I preached from the first chapter of the Acts of the Apostles, the seventh verse. Here God was pleased to manifest himself by his divine power, even to those free-thinkers, and several were set at liberty, and could rejoice in the love of God through Jesus Christ; God deepened his works in the hearts of others. After preaching, I had some conversation with the free-thinkers, asking them what they thought of Jesus Christ, through the gospel? I found three of them were convinced. I insisted that they could not think any good thing of themselves, but some said they never had any bad thoughts, and I insisted upon it they never had any good ones; upon this we parted, and I left them in the hands of God, and we returned again to [Sable] River. In the evening, I preached again from the second chapter of James, the twenty-sixth verse, shewing the nature of true faith. In the heart, the Lord was pleased to open their understanding, so that some of them were constrained to cry out, saying, "Not unto us, not unto us, but unto thy name be all the glory."

In the morning of the 19th, I preached from the thirteenth chapter to the Hebrews, first verse. After preaching, I had some little conversation with them. I left them in the hands of God, promising them that I would return again, if God spared me; I then pursued my journey home again, quite a different way; on which account, I had not an opportunity of seeing those to whom I had preached. Five of them accompanied me through the wood to the seashore, and then we parted in prayer; they returned home again, and I pursued my journey.

I reached at Green's Harbour about nine o'clock at night; being very tired, and having lost two hours in the day, I did not preach, but called the family together; we went to prayers, and committed ourselves to the Lord for refreshment.

On the 20th, being Saturday, I told the man to prepare his children to be baptised on the sabbath day; and I took a little walk as far as the Indian wig-wam, to see how they did. After discoursing with them, they expressed a great desire to hear me preach. I gathered them together, and preached from St. Paul's epistle to the Romans, first chapter, thirty-second verse. Here I found the Lord was pleased to strengthen my weak-ness; it was enough to melt the heart of any man, to hear how these poor creatures expressed their desires to know the true and living God. After a little discourse with them, from their different places, I told them that I should preach on the Lord's day. They asked me, if they came up in the evening, whether I would go to prayers with them? I answered, yes; and in the evening, on the 21st, they came up more than thirty of them. The family gathered together, and filled the room; the Lord en-abled me to speak from the second of Romans, the seventh verse, and the power of God was present to wound, and to heal. After preaching was over, the Indians would not go away till twelve o'clock. I informed them that on the 22d, there would be preaching in the morning early, that they had better go home and get a little sleep. Three of the women answered, they did not want any sleep. However they went home, but I believe they did not sleep, for in the morning they were there before five o'clock. I preached from the sixth chapter of Romans, and the third verse; and here I found that God did not fail to manifest himself, in such a manner, that we all got a good sabbath's breakfast.

Some of the poor creatures went home, weeping; the master of the house, his wife and three children, reflected much upon the nature of the ordinance they were about to submit to. At half after ten o'clock, a large body of people came from Ragged Island, and round about, so that the place could not contain them, and many of them were obliged to stay out of doors; and my reader will be pleased to take notice, that the snow was four feet deep, and in some places five feet deep. I preached from the twenty-eighth chapter of St. Mat[t]hew's gospel, the nineteenth and twentieth verses. My soul was filled with the glorious power and love of God; I could perceive solemnity in the faces of all the people within the audience of my voice; so that the convincing power of God was manifested; instead of nine, the number of the family, there were added to it twelve, which made twenty-one; and in the time of baptising, I desired all the grown people to kneel down upon their knees; fourteen kneeled, then did I lift up my voice aloud to the Lord for the baptising Spirit to fall upon us; and here I would have my readers to take notice, that, for about five minutes, I was not able to speak, being overpowered with the love of God; when, rising from my knees, I looked upon the people, and saw tears in their eyes, and the congregation at large, filled with solemnity. I took the bason in my hand, and attempted to baptise them; when I had baptized five, the rest were fallen to the ground; however I baptised them on the floor, while they were crying out, and saying, "Lord Jesus have mercy upon us." I immediately called for the children to be brought up, two of which I took in my arms, the other five I commanded to kneel down, and I baptised them all with tears running down their cheeks; then I lift up my voice to God to bless the means. There was such crying in the congregation, that my voice could hardly be heard; and one particular circumstance I would have my reader to note; a girl of twelve years of age was continually calling for God to have mercy upon her. I went to her, and asked her, what she cried out so much for after the rest. Her answer was, that she was afraid she should not be able to fulfil the charge that was then given her. I asked her if she was not afraid her soul would be lost to all eternity? Looking me earnestly in the face, she burst out in tears. I left her, finding that she was not able to express her feelings. The congregation was then dismissed, but would not go home. I went into private, and returned God thanks for the mercies received, imploring his presence, that he would not leave them comfortless.

In the evening, I preached from St. John, xiv. 1, 2; when God was pleased to comfort the mourners. I intended to set off in the morning for home; but this night was a blessed night, it was spent in reading, praying and singing. In the morning, half after four, I preached from the same chapter, verse the 27th.

On the 23d, the girl I have already mentioned, rose up in the time of preaching, crying out, and declaring to the congregation—that her sorrow and sighing had fled away, and she had received that peace from God, which the tongue could not express. Then we sung, for joy, one of Dr. Watts's hymns, "My God, the spring of all my joy[s]." In singing the hymn, the mother was able to testify of the love of God; and, after conversing with them, I commended them in the hands of God.

About nine o'clock, we came to the Indian wig-wam, and found several wounded souls; I stayed with them all this day, and from place to place, we had prayer, if God would be pleased to display his divine power, and deliver their precious souls from the distresses they were then in. I prayed the best part of the night, saying, "O Lord, is thine arm shortened, that it cannot save? O Lord, for Jesus Christ sake, have mercy upon these poor creatures:" but the heavens seemed as brass to my prayers, and they continued in distress all night.

In the morning, on the 24th, we had prayers, and I left them, deeply wounded for their sins, and we came to Jordan River about eleven o'clock, and crossed over the upper part of the river upon ice, and reached Shelbourne Town about seven o'clock in the evening, and stayed there all night.

On the 25th, very early in the morning, we set out for Birch Town, and arrived at eight o'clock.

At nine o'clock, I had a letter from Barrington, wherein the people expressed a great desire for me to come to them. I very readily answered them by a letter that I would come to them as soon as I could. I abode in Birch Town eight days, attending the classes, and confirming the people; in the evening, we had a great love feast, and we continued all night praying to and praising of God, and God was in the midst of us: six souls were pricked to the heart. I left them on the 3d of February, and on the 7th day after I had left the town, I was informed that these souls were set at liberty. In the evening we arrived at Shelbourn, and stayed all night.

On the 4th, we crossed Jordan River very easy, because the ice had reached as far as Green Harbour. The next morning we had a great number of Indians and white people. I preached from II Cor. ch. xiii. verse 5. God was pleased to manifest himself to those precious wounded souls, and we had great joy indeed. At two o'clock we set off for Ragged Island; we had a great multitude singing praises to God through the woods.

In the evening I preached at Ragged Island, from Psalm lxxiii. verse 1. when we had a love feast, and Christ was the master of the feast. The people here seemed to want no sleep; however I left them praising of God, and I went to bed and got a little sleep. I awoke about three o'clock, and hearing them praising the Lord, I rose up and joined them, and so continued till morning.

On the 5th, I preached from Isaiah xl. verse 31; then leaving them in the hands of God; some of them accompanied me across the river on the ice; and then we parted with prayer. I felt much of the presence of the Lord. Here the Lord was preparing me for tryals; the people persuaded me not to enter into this man's house, because his wife was an abandoned woman, one that had been on board a man of war all the last war; however, when I came up to the house, it was impressed upon my mind to go in and see them. I knocked at the door, and had much such a reception as my Lord had among the Jews; she called me a pickpocket; I told her I thought she had nothing to lose; she then took the tongs, and gave me several blows on my arm with much violence, and wounded me much on my head; she also cut my hand, and I was constrained to hold her, with the blood running down on the side of my face and from my hand, which fell upon her and enraged her worse than before; however, being stronger than she was, I held her fast; my little boy was frightened, and cryed, and ran away. After a while, her rage seemed rather to abate, and I was enabled to speak to her in the name of the Lord. I let her go, to see what was become of the boy, not thinking she would rage again in the former manner; but as I was going out of the door, she got the broom, and struck me on the head. I went to seek the child, and afterwards went into a house, where cows are kept in the winter; I kneeled down, and laid my complaint before my God, and lifting my hand up which was then bleeding, and the blood trickling all over my face, begging the Lord to search my heart, whether I had lost these drops of blood for the gospel of Christ, and the good of souls; that he would be pleased to show me a token for good, so that I might not deceive myself. The Lord was pleased to pour down his blessing upon my soul, in answer to my poor petition; then was I strengthened and encouraged to go back, and said, If it is his will that I should spill more blood, in his cause, I was willing, for I know that he will not let the words return void. I intreated him to go with me, that he would seal the word of divine truth to his glory, and the good of her soul; so I came up to the door again, and she retalliated with more violence than at first. I was met with the poker and tongs, but the Lord, who over-rules all things, prevented her from hurting me. I caught hold of her two shoulders, and held her for some considerable time, but she raged like a lion; and the Lord furnished me with words, particularly out of St. Matthew's gospel, chapter xxvii; and she struggled hard as long as she could, till she was allmost out of breath; she then set herself down, and I [was] continually speaking to her concerning the sufferings of Christ, and his resurrection power, and she seemed to be somewhat calm; I continued speaking of the glory of God, and the happiness of the saints in heaven, who had suffered for his names sake; and of the dreadful torment of hell, and of the long continuance of the same.

She sat for about five or six minutes and never said a word; then I asked her, if I should go to prayers? she answered, in a very rough manner, I might if I pleased. I went on my knees, and she set down on the side of a bed. Whilst I was in prayer, I felt much of God's spirit, and about the middle of the prayer, she fell from off the bed, as though she was shot, and screamed out with a loud voice, and stretched herself off, as though she was going out of the world. I rose from off my knees, and put a smelling bottle to her nose, and washed her face with cold water. All this while the old man, about eighty-two years of age, sat in the corner, crying, and both were despised in the neighbourhood[.]

I attempted the second time to go to prayer, but found I was shut up; I came out and went to another house, about a quarter of a mile off, and left her on the floor. When I arrived at this house, they received me kindly; seeing my clothes were daubed with blood, they were rather surprised; they asked me the meaning of all this—I told them I had received all this at the next house. They were surprised that I was suffered to go in. I told them I did go in, and received these wounds, and left her on the floor. The young man was surprised, and said, "I hope you have not been fighting." I told them, no, she fought with me, but I did not with her.

He set off, and finding her lying on the floor, he took her up and laid her on the bed, and searched her to see if there were any wounds upon her; asked her several questions, but she answered none. Then turning to his father, the old man related the story to him. She cried out, with a lamentable voice, "Lord have mercy upon me!" which surprised him. He ran out immediately, and came home for his wife, and told her that her mother-in-law was very ill, and she must go over to her.

They both set off, and one of the boys; and after being absent about half an hour, I looked and saw them dragging something upon a sledge. I continued walking about till they came up to the door, and found they had the old woman upon a bed, covered up. They brought her into the house, and seemed to be very much scared; but she continued as though she was dead. I looked on her, and smiled. They asked me what I had done to her. I told them—nothing, but went to prayers with her, and spoke to her in the name of the Lord. They asked me, if they had not better send for the doctor to her. I answered—no, I told them that she was only sin sick, and no doctor in this life could cure her; but there was a good physician in Gilead, and in his good time he would apply his balm of Gilead to her soul. Then they stared at me, and I asked them to let me go to prayers over her; so we kneeled down, and I poured out my spirit before God in behalf of her. The poor creature was slain worse, and cried out—she was sinking into hell.

I bid them get her out of the way to sleep; so after we had joined in family duty, we all went to bed; but she had no sleep, but cried out all night, for Christ to have mercy upon her; but she would sometimes say, that she was too vile a sinner to be saved.

On the 6th, when we rose in the morning, I went to speak to her, but her soul was filled with great anguish. At ten o'clock, a great multitude came together, I preached to them from St. Luke, xiii. verse 5. They all seemed to be frightened, and in the evening I preached again from St. John, iii. verse 5. Here was much of the out-pouring of God's spirit. The people did not seem inclined to go home to their houses; but afterwards, when I informed them that I would preach again in the morning, God willing, of the 7th, they dispersed; and I had some conversation with this poor woman again; but finding she was not able to contain herself, by reason of her distress, I left her in the hands of God, and went to rest.

In the morning, when the people gathered together, I preached from St. John, i. 1 and 2 verses. Then I dismissed the people, telling them, that I would preach again on the next day, that I might have an opportunity of speaking with her, but she seemed to grow worse and worse, and God seemed to shew her the evil of her ways, by filling her soul with strong conviction.

On the 8th, I preached from St. John, i. 29. Here the Lord was pleased to manifest his divine love, and many sinners felt the power of the everlasting gospel; yet this poor woman was still in agonies, worse and worse; she looked as pale as death, having eaten nothing, but at times took a little water, and one cup of tea. I preached again in the evening from Isaiah, lx. 1 and 2; when God was pleased to arise and shine in her heart. She got up, and praised God in a remarkable manner, which surprised all the people in the room; and, after I had dismissed the people, I had some conversation with her, and her joy was so great, that she could not express herself, but looking upon my hand which she had cut, she burst out in tears and fell upon her knees, and begged me to pardon her for the blood she had spilled. I told her that Christ had pardoned her, and I had nothing against her. She then got up and clasped me round my neck, then sat down again, and was not able sometimes to speak for five or six minutes, being so filled with the peace of God. This brought to my mind, St. Luke, xv. 7; and my soul was ready to leap out of the body for joy. Here we see the Lord turned a lion into a lamb, and as her sins were great, so were her joys. The people were so amazed, that some of them did not go home all night. I went to bed to get some rest; but she did not sleep all night, but was heard praising of God, and telling the people the wonders that God had done for her soul.

On the 9th, in the morning, I preached from II Peter, iii. 8; and the glory of God was in the midst of us; and after preaching, I set off for [Sable] River, and arrived in the evening, two men accompanying me.

On the 10th, I preached once to a large body of people, then went from house to house visiting. On the 11th, I preached once up the river.

On the 12th, I preached at Jones's Harbour, once more amongst the free-thinkers; but finding them hardened in sin, I conversed with them after preaching, and left them in the hands of God. In the evening, I arrived at [Sable] River again.

On the 13th, I preached at eleven o'clock, and after preaching, set off for Little Harbour, with a great company, and arrived there in the evening; being tired, I did not preach.

On the 14th, I preached from St. Luke, xxiii. 42, 43; when we felt the great out-pouring of God's divine spirit in this place, and also at [Sable] River. I stayed a whole month, intending to go to Liverpool, but finding the wind was contrary, on the 10th of March we set out for Birch Town, and arrived in the evening at Captain Church's, where we stayed all night.

On the 11th, at twelve o'clock, we arrived at Green's Harbour again; after dinner, we went down as far as the Indian wigwam: finding them all preparing to remove, I stayed two hours with them, and returned back to Green's Harbour, and in the evening preached to them. Here we stayed all night, and in the morning, after prayer, I set off for Jordan River, and arrived at twelve o'clock; after dinner, set off for Shelbourn Town, where we arrived in the evening. Finding all well, I preached to a large company, and commended them into the hands of God.

On the 13th, I set off to Birch Town, where we arrived at ten o'clock in the morning. I staid till the 16th, having received a letter from Jordan River, wherein they expressed their warm desire to hear the word of God; so I thought it best to take it before the throne of grace, to know whether it was the Lord's will.

On the 18th, while I was contemplating upon this, somebody knocked at my door, and gave me a letter that came from Ragged Island, from Mr. John Lock, with a recommendation to his son, who then lived at Jordan River.

On the 19th, in the morning, I set off, at ten o'clock, with two little boys; we went through Shelbourn about twelve o'clock, but made no stay there, and arrived at Jordan about five o'clock in the afternoon. The first house I entered in was Mr. Lock's mother-in-law; they asked me to sit down by the fire to warm myself. I did so, and the little boys also. She had four daughters in the house[,] women grown. I sat down, and was in deep contemplation, and they walked about, viewing of me. A little while afterwards, I held up my head, and looking the old lady in the face, asked her if she knew Christ? She never answered me a word, but began to cry. I asked one of the young women if she knew how far Mr. Lock lived? She came to the door, and shewed me the house. I thanked her, and wished her a good night, leaving the mother weeping.

I went to Mr. Lock's house, and delivered the letter to him, but he could not read it; so I took it and read it to him. He then asked me to take off my knapsack. I abode there all night, and discoursing with him, I found that he was ignorant of God and himself. I asked him what he thought would become of his wife and three children, if they should die in that state. He answered nothing, but cried; so after supper I went to prayers with them, and he continued sobbing the whole night. In the morning, about ten o'clock, they gathered a large body of people together.

On the 20th, I preached from St. Luke, xxiv. 47; and the Lord's presence was in the midst of this people, all seemed to be astonished, having lived there above twenty years, and never heard the word of God; so after preaching, I discoursed with them, shewing them the absolute necessity of an interest in Christ. The Lord was pleased to follow the weak attempt with his divine power; seven of them cried out under this sermon, being pricked to the heart. In the evening, I preached again from the Acts of the Apostles, iii. 19; and there was a wonderful display of the power of God among this people; they went away, hanging down their heads like bullrushes. After preaching, I conversed with Mr. Lock and his wife till bed time; finding that they were not baptised, nor any of their family, they expressed a great desire to be baptised.

On the 21st, I preached to a larger congregation than I did at first, from St. John, v. 28, 29; and on the 22d, I preached from St. Matthew, xxviii. 19, 20; and, after preaching, such as desired to be baptised were brought up. There were eight in number, the grown people kneeled down upon their knees, and while I was baptising them outwardly, God was pleased to set Mr. Lock at perfect liberty; and great awe was upon the minds of the rest; three of them were pricked to the heart. There was a great stir among the people of Jordan River at this time, so that the fame of Christ reached as far as Shelbourn and Green Harbour. I stayed with them till the 27th, going from house to house, conversing with them, and preaching to them all opportunities.

On the 28th, in the morning, I preached from St. John, xiv. 27; and then set off for Green Harbour; I thought best to leave one of the boys at Jordan River till I returned; being a calm morning, we crossed from Jordan Point, with an intent to reach Blue Island; but the wind began to blow very hard, and the boy was frightened because of the seas break-ing in the boat; however, through the help of God, we got as far as Jenkins' Point, with the boat half full of water, which obliged us to go on shore; and we had to turn the boat upside down to get the water out. It being a desolate place, we went to return God thanks for our safe landing. All the while we were crossing from Jordan Point, the people were looking after us and mourning, thinking we should be lost. After staying at Jenkins' Point, we set off again with the tide with us; but the wind against us, which made the seas very rough; and after we had gone a mile, we had hard work to get her on shore, being half full of water; but by the help of God, we got on shore on an island just entering on Green Harbour. Here we were obliged to stop till near four o'clock; we kindled a fire to dry ourselves. Seeing nobody coming to our assistance, and night coming on, being very cold, I went to prayer, that God would enable us to carry my plan into full execution; and afterwards we set off again and reached at Sun Town, our desired haven, where we were received kindly.

The next morning, being the 29th, I preached to a large congregation, and after preaching, we set off for Ragged Island; where we arrived in the evening, and were gladly received. I preached from Jeremiah viii. 20, 21, 22; and the Lord was pleased to display his divine power to many, and brought them under deep convictions. Here I stayed till the 4th of April, confirming them in the faith of the Lord Jesus Christ. About this time, I had several messages from Little Harbour, and [Sable] River, which obliged me to leave them on the 5th morning, and we passed over the Ragged Island, to Little Harbour shore, in boats. We had six to accompany us to Little Harbour, being six miles distant.

We passed over a lake two miles in length, and arrived at Little Harbour one hour before sun set; where the people were all waiting. I preached from St. Luke xiii. 24; and we had the presence of the Lord amongst us. After preaching, I conversed with them, and found several of them were convinced before, and now justified by the faith of Jesus Christ.

On the 6th, I passed on for [Sable] River, and arrived in the evening. I did not preach, but went to prayers with them.

On the 7th, I preached from St. John iii. 14, to a large multitude. After preaching, I baptised six persons, and then went up the river three miles.

On the 8th, I preached in the morning from St. John iii. 22; and stayed all this day, going from house to house. On the 10th, I passed over to the other side of the river, to inter the bodies of two persons departed this life, but no reason to believe that they died in peace, having neglected God's great salvation, and died without any evidence. Here I took occasion to address the spectators in the words of the Apostle Paul, from Ephesians v. 16; when there were tears in every face[.] Here I stayed all night, conversing with them from house to house.

On the 11th, I preached in the morning, from St. Matthew, v. 3, and a wonderful display of God's mercy was shewn amongst this people; then I passed over the River. In the evening, I preached from St[.] Matthew, v. 16, to a large congregation. Here I staid all night.

On the 12th, I preached from St. Matthew, vi. 10, 11, 12, 13. About ten o'clock, we set off through the woods, and reached Green Harbour in the evening. We stayed all night, intending to set off for Shelbourn on the 13th; but, before we set off, I received a message to visit an old woman about eighty-seven years of age, who was then on a bed of sickness, and without the knowledge of God. When I asked how matters stood between her soul and God; she said, she never had done any body any harm, and always went to prayers, night and morning. I asked her, if she had ever felt the power of God's love in her heart? but she seemed to be very ignorant. I asked her farther, if she knew her own heart? she said, they that did not know their own hearts must be fools. I asked her by what she knew her own heart? she said, she was born with a good heart. I told her, if she had not a better heart than what she was born with, it was a wicked heart, and full of enmity against God; that if she died with this heart unchanged, where God is she cannot come. She asked me, where she should go then. I answered her, among devils and wicked spirits, where all people go that die without a change of heart. At this she was silent. I asked her if I should go to prayers with her. She answered, yes; so I went to prayers with her. When prayers was concluded, finding myself rather bound, I went down upon my knees again, then I did feel a little assistance and comfort from God's spirit; and after prayer, I asked her how she felt herself; but she never answered me a word, but looked very earnest at me, and tears ran down her cheeks; so we parted, and I went to Mr. Hewit's, intending to set off in the morning.

On the 14th, after prayers, we got our knapsacks on our backs, and took our leave of Mr. and Mrs. Hewit for Jordan River, and when we got down to the boat, after putting our things on board, ready to set off, a little girl came running down, and I stopped to know what was the matter. She said, her grandmother desired that I would come to see her; so I left the boy with the boat, and I went up to her, and after discoursing with her a little, she acknowledged she had a wicked and deceitful heart. I asked her, how she came to know that? She said, she felt it. So I went to prayers with her again; and here I was obliged to stay all day, reading, praying, and conversing.

I returned in the evening to Mr. Hewit, and slept there. He persuaded me to go by the ferry, on the 15th, saying, that we should have a snow storm on that day, and very probably be blown off. I told him, I had no money to go over the ferry, and I promised to bring the boat back.

Being a fine morning, the wind fair, we set off, and after we had been an hour from the shore, we had a snow storm, and finding that I could not turn back, I kept on; for some time we could not see one another, the snow fell so thick; the boy began to cry, but I encouraged him, as well as I could, and took hold of both the oars myself, and made him take a little bowl, and throw the snow out of the boat, while I was rowing; and, by the help of God, we just got over before the wind shifted about W. N. W. and brake the ice in the Cove; so we could not land for some time; we got entangled with the ice, but, by the help of the Almighty, I got her out of the ice, and run her right a-shore. Six men came down to our assistance, and got her on the shore, and dragged her into the wood, out of the way of the ice. We went up to the house, and got some refreshment; and I do really believe, if we had stayed out another hour, the boy would have died, for his blood began to be chilled, and it was some time before we could get him to feel himself.

I preached in the evening at Jordan River, from Isaiah iii. 10, 11. We had much of the presence of the Lord: while I was describing the former clause of my text, I was overpowered with the love of God. The people wept and groaned throughout the congregation. Here I continued till the 17th, confirming them in the faith of Christ.

On the 18th, in the morning, I preached from II Corinthians xiii. 11, 12; when there was much crying and mourning. I then set off for Shelbourn; six of them accompanied me part of the way, and desired to know why I would not stay with them a little longer. I told them I had a call to go as far as Barrington, and could not be with them again this spring; so we had prayers and parted.

I passed through Shelbourn about three o'clock, but made no stay, and reached Birch Town in the evening, where I found they were all gathered in the chapel. I preached from St. John vii. 37, 38; and we had a great out-pouring of God's spirit. The people all rejoiced to see me once more, for they had heard I was drowned, going across from Jordan Point to Blue Island; so when I came out of the pulpit, they would not let my feet touch the ground, for the Arminian had been amongst them, endeavouring to draw them away, and had drawn some of the weak ones away, telling them that they would never see me any more: but here God disappointed the devil of his hope, by restoring me to them in such a wonderful manner, which he did in the fullness of his gospel thus, in this time of mourning. The hour of rejoicing was near at hand, so that they did not depart from my house all the night.

On the 19th, in the morning, the chapel was filled, all praising of God in prayer, and singing. I came in, and preached from Psalm lxxiii. 24, 25, when we had a fresh shower of God's grace, and great rejoicing in the morning; so after meeting was over, such as had been drawn aside through error, came, trembling, and expressed great sorrow because they had been deceived, and had joined the Arminians; but they returned back again, so I continued to attend classes, and set the people right; and many were added to the church every week.

Here I stayed with them till the 12th of May, on the same evening we had a love feast, when we had much of the presence of God, and three souls were struck down on the floor, apparently dead, for some time; they were taken up and carried out, and we continued till three o'clock next morning, when we all returned to our houses to get a little rest.

About six o'clock, I arose and went to see how the people did, and found them in the same condition, or rather worse. I left them in the hands of God, and told the elder to take care of them, and prayed with them; I then sent an order to the captain of my boat to get her ready, as I wanted to go to Barrington. About eleven o'clock, he came and informed me that she was ready.

At half after eleven o'clock we set off for Barrington, by sea, but could not reach any farther than Lance Point, where we went on shore and staid all night, and I preached from St. Luke xiv. 17, to a small company of people.

On the 14th, in the morning, I preached from St. Mark vi. 12, and then we sailed from thence for Barrington; going into the Harbour, we run on shore, upon the sand bank; but after a little while, with the help of the Lord, we got off again without any hurt; so we went up to Barrington Town, to visit the man to whom I had a very strong recommendation by letter.

I went to his house, and he seemed somewhat shy, for the Arminians had been there, and had told them falsehoods, desiring them not to let me go into the chapel to preach, and by that there was a great division, for one half was for me to go to preach, and the other half was not; so the contention was so sharp, that they parted assunder, those upon Rose Island, were part Dissenters, part Baptists, and part Presbyterians[;] so I staid upon Rose Island, and preached for them ten days, and the Arminians could not stay away.

On the 15th, we had a love feast, when we had much of the outpouring of God's spirit, and many souls rejoicing. Here I staid till the 25th, going from house to house; by this time the greatest part of the Arminians were convinced of the false reports, and declared, when Mr. Garrison [Freeborn Garrettson] came, they would have their names taken out of the book; and I was informed afterwards, that there was a great division among them.

We sailed on the 25th, and reached as far as Glance Point, and preached there that evening from St. Matthew vi. the two last verses; where we had a great body of people from Cape Negro. They expressed a great desire for me to go to Cape Negro with them. I told them I could not go, as I was obliged to return to Birch Town at present.

I preached in the morning of the 26th from St. Paul's second epistle to the Corinthians iv. 10; when there was a great out-pouring of God's spirit, so that many were crying in the congregation, "What shall we do to be saved.["] After a little conversation with them we sailed for Birch Town, where we arrived at midnight.

On the 27th, in the morning, several people came into my house, after prayer meeting, with three petitions in their hands, which, when I opened and read, I found them expressing a great desire for me to go to Hallifax, to the governor, to request tools, spades, hoes, pickaxes, hammers, saws and files, such as they should want, and blankets. I told them it was not in my power to comply with their request, that they should go to their colonel. They answered me, that he was gone out of town, and had left them. However, after eight days, having collected the people together, I found it was the request of the whole. I enquired into those things they had, and found they really stood in want of more.

I took their petition on the 14th, and sailed for Hallifax, and arrived on the 15th; and on the 16th, I presented the petition to the governor, which was complied with.

On the 24th, I sent them to Birch Town, by a man, and desired him not to let any of them be given out before I arrived.

On the 26th, I left Hallifax, for the Eastward Preston Town, and arrived there the same evening, and preached to a large concourse of people. I staid here till the 29th, preaching and visiting, finding much comfort among the people rejoicing in God.

On the 30th, I set off for Cold Harbour, where I arrived at two o'clock, and preached from St. Matthew xi. two last verses, to a small company of people.

Next morning; the 31st, I preached from St. John iii. 5, to a greater congregation than in the evening; and, after conversing with them, finding but few of them protestants, I took my leave of them. About ten o'clock in the day, I arrived at Dartmouth. At five o'clock in the afternoon, we got over to Hallifax. In the evening, finding the pacquet arrived from Shelbourn, I received letters expressing that I must return immediately.

On June the 1st, I preached to a large congregation in Hallifax, and on the 2d I sailed for Shelbourn.

I arrived on the 4th, and was saluted upon the wharf; I was much distressed, when I found the man that I had delivered the things to, had taken them all out and given them to the Arminians. I made the best way over to Birch Town, in order to rectify this mistake. When I arrived there, I found the Town in an uproar; the old blind man, who preaches for the Arminians, had broken his agreement, and had sold the place for three guineas to the Arminian preachers. I went to him to know the certainty of it. He told me, that I should not preach there any more. I answered him, that the place was built for the people at large, not more for one connection than another; and, with God's leave, this night I was determined to preach in it.

In the evening, a multitude of people gathered together, and found the doors shut against them; but when some of the elders came, they went and demanded the key, and were denied, but they took it away. The doors were opened, and the people went in and prepared for preaching. The old man, in order that I should not preach, came and sat in the desk, and began to give out an hymn, but nobody would sing with him until I came in, and he not knowing that I was in, I gave out the same hymn over his head, when the house rang with the praises of God. After singing, he went immediately to prayers. Some of the people touched him, and asked him whether he knew what he was about; and while they were talking together, I went to prayer, and when he heard me, he crept out, and I saw him no more that night. We here see, by this, that the devil can never stand against the truth, but will always fly. I preached from St. Luke xiii. 21; when the Lord was pleased to bless the souls of the people; so that we found that the devil was disappointed of his hope, and hell of her expectation.

On the 5th, after prayer meeting in the morning was over, I desired to have all the people together, and this man brought before them all. After examination, he was found guilty of all the reports, and desired them to go and gather all the things that he had given out; and two of the elders went with them. Finding, from house to house, that they all had one saying, That he did not give them away, but bought them of him, and would not deliver them without they had the money back. I afterwards went and conversed with them, telling them the consequences, that it was the king's property, and it would go hard with them if we went to law; they then freely gave them up.

On the 6th day, they brought them all to my door, expressing their sorrow for being so foolish as to listen to what he had said, and declared they would be paid back again their money.

I continued the remainder of this month, confirming the people, and setting all right again.

On July the 1st, I sailed for Jordan River, to be with them on the sabbath day, and to return again on Monday; but when I came there, the devil had also been among them, for the Arminian preacher had been among them, and insinuated into their mind that I was not right. When they asked, why? they said he did not come from Mr. Westley, therefore could not be right. When they could not alledge any thing else, they drove them away, and told them that they must not come there any more. Here the devil was disappointed also; and here I was two days, preaching and confirming them.

On the 4th Morning, I preached from I John iv. 1. and then set off for Birch Town again. I arrived in the evening, and found the people all turned upside down again, for the Arminian had been amongst the people again; the people expressing how glad they were I came that day; I asked them, why that day more than another? they answered, because Mr. Garrison was to be there on the 5th evening, to read Mr. Wesley's society book, and to take all their names down that would join them, and that was to be done before I returned; so they were all invited to hear. I told them not to make a noise that I was come, and I would be there too. So in the evening a vast concourse of people gathered together; after the candles were lighted, I went in, but was not discovered by the preacher, nor them that accompanied him. I got pretty close to the pulpit, that nothing should slip; he began with an hymn, and then engaged in prayer, and told the people he should not preach, but read Mr. Wesley's society book, and expound from that, and shew them how the order of their society was, and it was the best order that could be adopted, and expressed himself thus to the people—that he was very sorry that they had a man come from England, and was not of Mr. Wesley's society, and had sown the seeds of discord; he even went so far as to call me a devil; but one of the elders rose up, and told him if he came to preach the Gospel of Christ, for to preach it; if not, to come down out of the pulpit; for, says he, you had no business to rail against a person that you never discoursed with, nor have seen; but this one thing we know, we never heard the Gospel of Christ till he did come, and we know that God hears not the prayer of a sinner. I can testify, and several others who are now in the congregation, that God made him the instrument of our souls conversion, for the devil never converted a soul in his life, nor never can he; I wish Mr. Marrant was here to answer for himself; to this he made no answer, only said, please to let me go on till I have done, and then you will know. So there was silence, and he went on until he came to a place that Mr. Wesley speaks that ministers must not speak against ministers behind their backs, nor brethren against brethren. He did not expound this part; the elder then arose again, and desired him to go back and explain that part he answered, and said that Mr. Wesley only meant his own preachers. The elder told him, he knew the meaning as well as he did, and he found that very passage gave him the lie to the face. So another of the elders arose and told him, that this was a bar that he could not get over; after this, silence was made, and he went on till he concluded, and all this while I was standing close to him, but said nothing.

My Reader must understand I never saw this person before, nor he me; but before he concluded, he told the people that he and his brothers came over on purpose to take all their names down that would join him, hoping that all would, after hearing the book explained, and those that would not, begged they would depart. The people all fixing their eyes upon me, I stared about five minutes to see if any person or persons left the place, and finding that they would not go without me, I thought I would give them leave to go on with their plan, and see how far the devil could go. So I moved towards the door, and the whole house moved and went out, all but fourteen. I got behind the door to see what would follow, hearing him expressing himself very much distressed because of the people being so ignorant as to leave the way which he thought was right; so one of them came to the door, in order to shut it, but I would not let him, and when they found that I was in the house, they all returned again into the house. So I went from behind the door unto the pulpit, and requested him to come down. At this he seemed to look somewhat amazed, and said he did no harm. I answered him, that he did no good there, and therefore bid him come down again, and told him, that if he did not come down by fair means, that I would force him out of it; and when he found that I was resolute, he came down, and I bid him to walk out[.] And after the door was made fast.

On the 6th day in the morning, the people were gathered again, and after I had engaged in prayer with them, told them that they should come to my house; and whilst they were gathering themselves at my door, Mr. Garrison and his company went into meeting, and he preached, and all the people returned and went to hear what he had to say; he preached from the xiiith chapter of St. Paul's 2d epistle to the Cor. 11th and following ver. and then he did preach the Gospel, and gave great satisfaction in recommending that love which he destroyed the evening before, and wept much in the time of service, and expressed himself much hurt for what had happened the past evening, and begged that the congregation would forgive him for wounding their precious souls.

When he came down out of the pulpit, I went up to him, and caught hold of his hand, and he wept, and I sympathized with him, and wept also. We joined in love, and went to prayer in the congregation, and here we had a manifestation of God's love, for all the people were much affected. I then dismissed the people, and took Mr. Garrison by the hand, in order to take him home with me to breakfast, but he could not spare the time, for he had to preach at Shelbourn that evening, so he begged to be excused, and that he would do himself the pleasure of breakfasting with me when he came over again; so we walked both together up the road, and thus he began to make a confession of the impropriety of his own conduct, for believing what was told him, without examining into the matter and knowing the certainty of it, and declaring that he had wounded his own soul by so doing; and after we had a little farther conversation, we went aside into the wood, and kneeled down to prayer, and then parted in peace and love. He went on his way to Shelbourn, and I returned to Birch Town, finding all the people waiting for me, and it being late in the day, I dismissed them, and told them that I would meet them in the evening, God willing. So in the evening there was gathered a great multitude, and I preached from I John iv. 1 where we felt much of the out-pouring of God's spirit, for there was groaning and crying through the whole congregation, the devil was disappointed of his hope, and hell of her expectation.

On the 7th day I preached from St. Matthew v. 3d and following verse. After preaching and dismissing the people, I determined to stay at home for the summer, having a large number of children to take care of in a school, the number soon increased to an hundred and four; finding that I was not able to take care of them and preach four times a week, and having letters from the neighbouring villages, I was obliged to decline the instruction of the children, and got a man to take care of them, so that I might be enabled to go down to the villages once a month. This I did all the summer, (by the help of God) till the 23d of November, and found great pleasure in travelling, and that my labour was not in vain among them.

The 24th I arrived from Green Harbour, being my last visit for this fall, and had a great storm, which took us after we left Green Harbour this morning at ten o'clock, wind being at N. E. blew very violent, we were not able to carry sail, but went under bare pol[e]s, and sometimes she went under water, insomuch that she was filled up to the thwarts three times in our short passage, which obliged us to run in at Berry's Cove, Jordan River; when we did come in, the shore was covered with people, expecting every moment to be our last, although we had one very shocking stroke, whereby our foremast was sprung, and she sprung a leak, but the people ran down to our assistance, and the God who saved Paul, saved us and brought us safe on shore, not one being hurt. We soon got the boat high up on the shore, and then went up to the house to return God thanks for his divine mercy, in delivering us from the deluge of the seas; we had much of the presence of the Almighty, for I had much reason to believe that God answered our prayer.

John Marrant 128

After prayer was over we got dinner, and about three o'clock the wind got about to the north, and blew moderately; finding it was fair wind, I got the people together, and the boat in order, and asking their advice, we all with one consent thought it was best to pursue our way to Birch Town while it was fair; but we went up to the house to ask God's permission, and to put our souls and bodies under his care, and then we sat off a quarter before four o'clock, leaving the people on shore, and begging that we should not go, but by the help of the Almighty, we arrived about five o'clock in the evening, in Birch Town, all well. We went into the house of God with those that were gathered, and returned thanks to him for his divine mercy in delivering us from the dangers of the sea. Here I remained till Christmas, meeting the classes, and preparing the people and the church for the solemn worshiping of God on that day. On Christmas eve we sat up in the chapel all night, we had much of the out-pouring of God's spirit upon us; I preached about half past ten o'clock in the morning, from Luke ii. 13. after which we administered the sacrament, and had a most glorious time, for whilst we broke the bread outwardly, God was pleased to break the bread of eternal life to our souls. There were seventy-four of us went to the table that day, and we had new life from God, several were pricked to the heart, and said men and brethren what shall we do to be saved. In the afternoon I did not preach, being up all the night I went to get a little rest to be ready for the evening; but whilst I was lying on the bed musing, I heard them singing in the chapel, which caused me to get up, and found that they had a prayer meeting, and much people came up from the villages round about, and continued till six o'clock. I preached from Luke ii. 14. here I stood astonished to hear the shout[s] of the people, and the groans of poor sinners, God's word went as a two-edged sword, and poor sinners were slain. I concluded the discourse, and came out, leaving several of them lying on the floor stretched out as though they were dead. I went immediately to bed, in order to get me some rest, and awoke about two o'clock, finding the people were still in the meeting, and continued till four o'clock before they left the meeting.

On the 27th of December I was informed in the morning by one of the elders, that God had begun a good work in the chapel among the precious souls, that two of them were set at perfect liberty. At half after ten I preached from Psalm lxxiii. ver. 1. and in the evening from the same Psalm, the 24th and 25th verses, where there was much out-pouring of God's spirit. Here I went from house to house, meeting the classes, confirming the people, and preparing myself for the journey. We kept a watch night, watched the old year out, and the new year in; we had a happy time, for God was in the midst of us, for there was one soul born with the new year, and I believe two at Mr. Wesley's meeting. We kept a covenant night on the 1st of January, and so did they; we administered the sacrament again this night, but they had nobody to give it to them, for a great many of them came and begged to be partakers with us, and were admitted. Here I staid till the 9th of January, and had a love-feast on that night with Mr. Wesley's people, and had a very happy time with them, after which I commended them to God in love.

In the morning at five, being the 10th, I preached in my own chapel, to a very crowded congregation of both chapels, from St. John xivth chap. and 27th verse; after which I departed for Jordan River, but when I came as far as Shelburn, the water prevented me from going any farther that evening, and I preached there to a large congregation, and on the 11th we set off for Jordan River. We arrived there at ten o'clock, and were there till eleven before we could get over the ferry, and then were obliged to pawn a jacket. However, by the help of God, we got over, and a snow storm overtook us in the wood, which was so violent, and fell so thick, that we lost our way; just before the sun sat, we came up with an Indian, and he put us in the way: so we got to Green's Harbour about seven o'clock. Being very tired, travelling that day through the snow, which was three and four feet deep, which rendered me incapable of preaching on the 12th.

On the 13th, a large body of people gathered together; I was enabled to set up, and preached from the two first verses of the lxxviii Psalm, when the Lord was pleased to bless his word with a divine power to the hearts of the people. Here I was not able to preach any more until the 23d, when the Lord was pleased to strengthen me so that I was enabled to preach on the 24th, from the xxxviith chapter of Job, and 7th verse. And on the 25th, through much weakness I reached as far as Ragged I[s]land, and was not able to preach for two days; but on the 28th I preached to a large body of people from the second epistle of Peter, chap. ii. and 9th verse, where we had much of the presence of God. Here I staid four days, and was not able to preach, but kept my bed part of the time.

On the 3d of February I was enabled to preach from the xiiith chapter of Hebrews, verse the 7th, to a large concourse of people, and the people had much rejoicing. In the evening I was permitted to preach again from Hebrews the xiiith chapter, and 14th verse, where I had remarkable liberty in speaking, though weak, and felt a great desire and eagerness to leave this body, and then was not able to preach any more, until the 14th, and was much persuaded by the people to return home, or not to travel.

On the 15th I preached in the evening, from the xiith chapter of St. Paul's second epistle to the Cor. the latter clause of the 10th verse. On the 16th we went over from Ragged I[s]land, to young Mr. Matthews; there I abode till the 19th. Not being able to preach, on the 20th I set off for Little Harbour about nine o'clock. We arrived there about two, being not able to walk very fast, and accompanied with a few of the people from Ragged I[s]land. Finding myself incapable of preaching[,] I was persuaded by the people not to travel, nor preach any more, until I was better; so I kept my bed from the 20th of February to the 27th. I had a great many people coming in to see me from every quarter, which kept me talking to them, which made me much weaker than I should otherwise have been, and by this time the news had got far and near that I was dead.

On the 28th, I was able to walk across the floor, and found a willingness to speak unto the people, but was prevented, and sickness continued increasing till the 6th of March; and here I said with Job, although he slay me, yet I will trust him; and with David, I can say that sickness was good unto me, for it was sanctified to my soul. Although the people did all that they could, and gave the best attendance that laid in their power, yet that was very poor nourishment for a sick person in the state

I was then in; for I must inform my readers, that in my greatest illness my chief diet was fish and potatoes, and sometimes a little tea sweetened with treacle, and this was the best they could afford, and the bed whereon I laid was stuffed with straw, with two blankets, without sheets; and this was reckoned a very great advantage in these parts of the globe; for in some places I was obliged to lay on stools, without any blanket, when the snow was five and six feet on the earth, and sometimes in a cave on the earth itself.

On the 8th of March I was permitted to preach from Hosea, xiiith chap. and 9th ver. where we had a great out-pouring of God's spirit, and was strengthened much. On the 9th they would not let me preach, for fear of my hurting myself, but I went from house to house praying with them, and confirming them in the faith. In the evening I had a violent fever again, and continued so till midnight. On the 10th I was able to go about again. In the afternoon a great many people came in to see me, and I found a great desire to speak to them from the vith chapter of St. Matthew, 33d verse, and conversed with them till evening, and finding a strong desire of something fresh to eat, I spoke to an Indian in his own language, and after they were all gone away, I was put to bed again. All this night I had no fever, and in the morning felt very well, and had a desire to preach in the morning, but was prevented. I begged very hard for them to let me go as far as Sable River, but was not permitted; in the evening the Indian came back with some mouse-meat [possibly moose], I had some stew made, but was prevented from eating so much as I would for fear of its hurting me.

On the 12th I found myself a great deal better; after 10 o'clock I asked them to let me go as far as Sable River again, and was permitted so to do, and was accompanied by six of the people, where we arrived at three o'clock, but was not able to preach until the 15th. I preached to a large body that came down the River, from the xth chapter of St. John and 11th verse; here I was empowered to speak very wonderfully, and was filled with the love of God. Groans and tears were heard and seen through the whole congregation, and after preaching I conversed with the greater part of them. Finding they had some children to be baptized,

I bid them to bring them on the 16th, and when they came my illness prevented me; they were brought again on the 20th, which was the sabbath day, when they brought fourteen of them. After preaching from the xxviiith chapter of St. Matthew, verses 19 and 20, the children were brought up, and I baptized them in the name of the Father, Son, and Holy Ghost; then gave out that I should preach again in the afternoon, but when the people gathered together, I found that I was not able, so they met in prayer.

I staid here till the 25th, but did not preach, but going from house to house conversing and confirming them, was called on the 26th day to commit the body of an old man, about eighty years of age, to the earth, after which I returned over the River again.

On the 27th I staid at Sable River all day, in order to get my boots mended.

On the 28th we sat off through the wood for Green's Harbour, four men accompanying me, with my two little boys. We arrived at Green's Harbour in the evening, all well, but very tired.

On the 29th I was not able to travel, felt my spirits very low and dull, having a very poor night's rest, having only a stool for my bed, and I found that I had caught a fresh cold.

On the 30th I set off in order to reach Birch Town; at twelve o'clock we came to Jordan River, the River being frozen, we had a ready passage over, and were able to get as far as Shelbourn Town that night, which surprised the people, who had heard in time past that I was dead.

I remained at Shelbourn till the 31st; about ten o'Clock, we sat out for Birch Town, and when we had got about half way, we came up with two women in the road, one was lying down and just expiring, and the other stood over her weeping; they had both been over to Shelbourn, to beg something to eat, and were then returning back to Birch Town, and had got a little Indian meal, but had not strength to reach home with it. When I came up to her, I found that she was irrecoverable; and had I not arrived as I did, the other would have been soon dead also, for her body was partly chilled with the cold, the snow being four feet on the earth, and was then snowing; so I sent one of my little boys to town to inform the people that I was on the road, and that some of them must come to my assistance; in the mean time, I took some rum out of my knapsack, and gave her a little of it to drink, and rubbed her face with some, and moved her about as well as I was able, and sometimes we both fell down together, I being so weak after my late illness; but, by the help of the Almighty God, I got her a mile nearer the town, where I met the two men, and they took the charge of the living woman, and got her to town as fast as they could; and when we arrived in town, we got all the necessaries we could for her recovery; and dispatched two men off to bring the dead body of the other woman.

I continued visiting this woman, while I was able, and committed the body of the other to the earth; and in about six days after I was taken very ill myself, and was not able to go about, and did spit blood for eight days continually.

On April the 17th, I was somewhat better, and was able to walk across the floor.

On the 18th, I had a second doctor from the next town, he informed me that I was in a very dangerous condition, and desired me not to preach nor walk a mile, and ordered me to get some honey, and to drink honey in every thing that I used; but the honey was fifteen pence sterling a pound, and I was not able to purchase one pound, but the Lord was so kind as to open the heart of the doctor, that he sent me two pounds, and said that I must pay him when I could.

I continued here without preaching till April the 24th; and on the 25th, I preached in the chapel from Genesis i. 1, 2. I then began to bleed in the pulpit and was taken out of the pulpit, and staid in doors till the 6th of May, and had many distressing objects before me, who were continually coming begging, and were really objects of pity, and were perishing for want of their natural food for the body.

On the 7th of May, I set off for Jordan Point in a boat, where I staid till the 10th, preaching and meeting the society, where I had an opportunity of hearing their complaints and distresses, by reason of a long winter, and for want of provision and clothes.

On the 11th in the morning, I preached from the ixth chapter of Isaiah,

6th verse, and then set off for Green Harbour, in a skiff; but the wind began to rise from the N. E. which forced us to put ashore on Jenkins Point, and had the boat to overset to get the water out of her. After we had prayer, and committed ourselves to the care of God, we set off again with intent for Green Harbour; but was prevented by the violence of the wind, which forced us to make for the nearest shore; and, by the help of God we got on shore on the Ragged Island Beach; we hauled the skiff up, and turned her upside-down, so we made our way through to the woods for to go to the Ragged Island. When we came we had a small river to cross, we crossed over the ice, and had like to have been lost, for the ice broke, but the Lord helped us, and we got over safe and was gladly received by the people, but did not preach this evening, being very tired.

On the 12th I preached from the viiith chapter of St. Mark, 36th and 37th verses.

On the 13th, after preaching in the morning, I felt a desire to proceed on my journey, so we were let go from thence for Sable River. We arrived there in the evening, very much tired.

On the 14th I preached to a large congregation, from the xiith chapter of St. John, 37th verse, where we had a great out-pouring of God's spirit, and after conversing with them till evening, I commended them to God.

On the 15th we set off for Little Harbour, and arrived there at two o'clock in the day, and found a vessel bound to Liverpool, which forced me to preach this evening, from the iid chapter of St. Luke, 51st verse, after which I had a little conversation with them till nine o'clock, then committing them to God.

On the 16th we sailed for Liverpool, with recommendation to one of the brethren, who had a good report among the church. We arrived in the evening there, got on shore, and was received at his house kindly; but after a little conversation, finding that he was a New-light, (so called) I found his love began to change. However, I was permitted to stay all night.

On the 17th I preached in the New-light meeting house, from chap. i. of St. Paul's epistle to the Romans, verse 16; but they gnashed upon me with their teeth, and was exceeding mad with me. I conversed with one of the elders afterwards, when I asked him what it was that he was offended at; his answer was, that it was all true gospel, but one thing he could by no means allow that it was the power of God unto salvation to every one that believed; and for this reason I was not permitted to preach any more there. I went home to his house, in order to stay all the night, but he was for putting me out, and that because I was not a New-light, but his wife prevented him; so we staid there till the 19th, and in the morning he ordered us out without any breakfast. We came out, and went down the wharf, in order to take shipping for Hallifax; but as we were going aboard, we met a gentlemen who heard me preach in the New-light meeting. I passed by him, and went on board the vessel, and in a little while he sent his son down to call me up to his house, and when I came, he said to me; Sir, I perceive Mr. Parker has turned you out this morning. I answered he had, and that without supper or breakfast. He answered, I think it was not the spirit of a Christian; and said, that he only turned you out of one door, in order that you might come in at a better; whenever you are travelling through this country, when you come to Liverpool, take my house for your home; so said his wife, and I had every thing that I could wish for, and I preached four times in the large chapel, to a large congregation.

On the 25th I sailed for Hallifax, but he would not permit me to take my boy with me, for fear I should not come back to Liverpool; so I left the boy, and he furnished me with such things as were necessary for my passage.

On the 26th I arrived at Hallifax; I did not preach that day.

On the 27th I left Hallifax for Preston Town. I arrived there in the evening, and I preached to a large concourse of people, and preached again on the 28th in the morning, then set off for Cold Harbour, and arrived in the evening. Preached on the 29th to a small body of people, greater part of them Roman Irish.

I left them on the 30th day, and arrived in the evening at Preston Town again. Here I remained till the 4th of June, meeting the classes and society. Finding the place of worship to be too small, I gathered the people together to know their mind concerning the building [of] another; they all unanimously agreed with one voice: but one obstacle was in the way, and that was they had no nails, nor were they able to buy any, nor a piece of ground to put the house on, and they requested me to go over to the governor and to lay their complaints and distresses before him.

On the 5th I sat off for Hallifax, in order to accomplish this business.

On the 6th I presented their complaints before his Excellency, and met with his approbation. Set off at two o'clock in the afternoon again for Preston Town, with their petition signed by his Excellency.

On the 7th I had them all together again, and the ground laid out, and they all with one consent went to work, some cutting down, some hewing, and some sawing, and the women bringing it out from the woods. In the evening I preached from the xivth chapter of St. John, 1st and 2d verses, where the out-pouring of God's spirit was much felt, and great joy was among the people; after preaching, I had some conversation with them. In the morning of the 8th, I preached from the vth chapter of St. Matthew, and the 18th verse, and then commended them into the hands of God.

I set off for Hallifax, arrived there in the evening, preached for Mr. Furmage, to a large concourse of people; after which I requested him to visit Preston Town, and to keep the people in order.

On the 9th I sailed from Hallifax to Liverpool again; arrived the same evening, and was received by Mr. Benjamin Collins, where I staid till the 14th, preaching and conversing with the people.

On the 15th I sailed from Liverpool for Port Murtoun, where we arrived in the evening, but through much difficulty. Here I did not preach, being one day later than I thought to have been, having sent a letter from Liverpool to inform the people at Sable River, that I would be there on the sabbath-day, which obliged me to leave them without preaching, and leave one part of my luggage, and we sat off on Saturday morning the 16th, to accomplish my promise to the people at Sable River. I got over [Big] Port Jolly, we had a very thick swamp to go through; in the midst of the swamp there was a brook, I stepped over, my little boy heedless fell in, and with a little difficulty I got him out again, and by the help of Almighty God we got out of this place, and he went down to a little pond to wash the mud from off him, without acquainting me any thing of it; so I went on for a mile and an half, not knowing but he was following me; but looking round I missed him, sat myself down on the rock to wait till he came up. After waiting half an hour, and not seeing him, I turned back to seek for him, but found him not; I hallowed, but hearing no answer, it gave me great concern, which caused me to wander part of the afternoon in pursuit of him. In doing so, I lost myself, and did not find that I was lost till five o'clock, when I was surprised to find myself in the situation I was then in, but a great deal more concerned for the boy. My troubles rose so great, that it caused drowsiness to fall on me, and being tired, I laid me down in among a parcel of high grass, in order to take some rest; but after I had been lying down for near half an hour, I felt something push me, but being heavy with sleep laid myself down again without taking any notice, but in the space of a quarter of an hour I was again pushed in the same manner, with more power, which caused me to rise up on my feet, and I looked to see whether it was not the boy that pushed me, for I verily thought that he had found me sleeping, and seemed rather glad at the thoughts of finding him. But walking a little distance, looking about, and could not discover any thing of him, my former sorrow returned again. I took my bible out of my pocket, and read part of the Psalms, after which I went to prayer, and found much of the presence of the Lord. I sat myself down musing upon the goodness of God, I grew drowsy and laid me down again to sleep; but after half an hour, as near as I can perceive, I was touched again in the former manner, but more powerfully, which was accompanied with a voice which I thought said arise, why sleepeth thou in a dangerous place? I arose with surprise, and searched all about for a quarter of a mile round, and fancying that there was some human person laid by, but had hid himself; but after a little while it came into my mind that it was the Lord, then I wept, and was full of trouble, because of my slothfulness in going to sleep in a wilderness, where I was certain I had lost my way. Here I discovered more of the frailty of human nature; O what poor creatures we all are, even the best of Christians, and we cannot be kept unless we are kept by God through our Lord Jesus Christ. I wandered in this manner till evening, and having not a mouthful of victuals from Friday dinner till now, which was Saturday evening, I went to prayer, and committed myself into the hands of God, and laid me down by the side of a rock, and laid for half an hour, then I got up and went and broke some boughs, and I laid upon them all the night; but no man can conceive the distress I went through in the course of the night.

On the 17th, which was the Lord's day, I got up with much difficulty, and walked all the day, sometimes praying, sometimes reading, and sometimes crying, continuing so till half past five o'clock in the afternoon; but my mind was very much troubled concerning the boy, fearing that he had perished in the wilderness, or fallen into the paws of some wild beasts: but about six o'clock coming through a very thick swamp upon the side of a river, where I perceived an house on the other side. Not being able to hallow, I took my handkerchief out of my pocket, and made a signal on a pole, and after some time they perceived the signal, and there came three persons in a boat, two women and a little girl. So they helped me into the boat, and got me over into the house, and gave me such things as they had. So I had a little refreshment, and was strengthened in body, but was not able to converse with them; they informed me that all Sable River was gathered together down at Mr. Pride's, waiting for me; to this I gave no answer, being much afflicted in my mind concerning the boy. They also informed me that my boy arrived at Sable River on the 16th, at five o'clock in the afternoon, and when he was asked where was his master, he said he came along before him. I sat still, and hearing all that they had to say, but upon hearing the boy was arrived safe, it gave me a great deal of joy and satisfaction, so I asked them to join in prayer, and the Lord was present with us, and that to bless us; so I continued with them until the 18th.

About ten o'clock we went down the River in a boat, and were gladly received. I preached that evening from the xvth chapter of St. Luke, and 24th verse, where we had great joy, and much of the out-pouring of the spirit of God, after which I conversed with them the best part of the evening.

On the 19th, at five o'clock in the morning, I preached from the Prophet Joel, ii. 15, 16, to a very crouded audience, where the Lord was present to wound and to heal. After breakfast I sat off for Little Harbour, and arrived there at half past eleven o'clock in the morning; and, at one o'clock, preached from chapter ii. of Joel verse 31, to a crouded audience, conversed with them and dined, which took my time up till four o'clock; I then set off for the Ragged Island Point, and lodged at Mr. Mat[t]hews's house that night.

On the 20th, we made a fire on the shore, for a signal, which, when it was discovered, a boat was sent over from the Ragged Island. We got over in the evening, and here I staid till the 23d, conversing and confirming the people in the faith, and preaching.

On the 24th, we set off for Jordan River, we had a good deal of rain on this day, and with much difficulty we reached Jordan River at one o'clock, I and my boy were bare-footed, and covered with rags. We came to the Ferry, but had no money to get over; we passed by the Ferry, and went as far as Judge Hogsdon, but he was not at home. We went as far as the upper Ferry, which is four miles distance, and when there we could not get over without a shilling, which I had not; so I was obliged to give them a handkerchief and four pennyworth of halfpence, which made the shilling. We pushed off as hard as we could for Shelbourn Town, and arrived there in the evening, very much tired, by reason of a hard journey, which prevented me from preaching that night.

On the 25th we set off for Birch Town, and arrived there at ten o'clock in the forenoon, where the town was much alarmed, and a numerous congregation gathered in the evening; I preached from the ixth chapter of Jeremiah, 1st and 2d verses. O what an out-pouring of God's spirit was felt this evening, both in doors and out of doors, and I was filled with the spirit of God; there was crying and groaning through the whole congregation. Here I continued meeting the classes and the society till the 4th of July.

On the 5th we had a love-feast, where the Lord was pleased to convince several of sin, and set at liberty four persons who were groaning for Redemption in the Blood of Christ; they could rejoice and praise his holy name, and there was great joy in the whole congregation. Here the Lord was preparing me for a sick bed.

I continued here not very well until the 16th, when I was taken with a violent fever after morning service was over, and was attended also with spitting of blood. This spitting of blood lasted for seven days. On the eighth day I attempted to perform divine service, it being the Lord's day, and seeing a crouded multitude coming from the neighbouring villages round about. I was persuaded by the elders not to go; but having a strong desire, they permitted me. I went in and read the church prayers all through, and the lessons for the day; that being done, I got up in the pulpit, and preached from Genesis i. 1st and 2d verses, where we had much of the out-pouring of God's spirit. About the middle of the discourse I found myself pretty warm, had much liberty, so exerted myself, forgetting my former illness. But before I concluded, I was nearly strangled with blood. The blood came running out at my nose and mouth, so that the people were all frightened. They took me out of the pulpit and carried me into my house, which was next door to the chapel, where I laid for two hours in that condition. Some said one thing, and some another[.] [I]n the midst of the hurry I asked them for some water, and they gave me a pint. A little after the blood stopped; I got up and came out of the room, and was grieved to see so many precious souls that came so far that morning to hear the word of God, and was deprived of hearing of it.

About five o'clock in the afternoon, God was pleased to send one to my relief, so I got him to preach in the evening, and meet the society; he staid all night with me, and went away in the morning. So we see that God will always provide for himself.

I beg leave to pause here, and give my reader a small account of those false brethren, who say they are Christians, and love to rejoice at the fall of their brethren, and when down, do all in their power to keep them down, and going from house to house, speaking disrespectfully of their brethren, and bringing a reproach upon the religion and the gospel of

Christ, stabbing their brethren with their wicked deceitful words, and scattering the flock of God. Yea, they go so far as to invent wicked malicious lies to cause part of the church to be called before the judgment-seat of this world; and I through such was compelled to come before Shelbourn court with them, and was charged there with things that I knew nothing of, and had then witnesses to prove that I was an hundred and twenty miles off, and did prove it to be so, and was dismissed from the court that time, and my enemies fell into their own netts; they were put in gaol, and kept there till they could find security, and we went home in peace. But soon after this the devil began again, and they brought another accusation against me for marrying a woman, and they declared in court she was another man's wife; so I was brought to court a second time, and part of the congregation for witnesses. I was called up before the judge in the open court, and the first question that was put to me was, "How came you to marry a woman that was another man's wife.["] I asked the justice for the woman's name, and when I knew it from him, I told him that she was not another man's wife; and if she was, she was lawfully published, and the man should have stopped the marriage if it was his wife, for it was four weeks after it was published before they were married. The justice pointing with his finger, shewed me the man. I said that he was not worthy of such a woman for his wife; and all this while the man who lately married the woman standing by, but said nothing; but I proved to the court that she was not the man's wife, and that the woman told me that he was only her servant man, that she had to drive up her cows; turning round, I desired the man to prove otherwise if he could, and when he found that he could not, he was asked if he did not hear the publication, he answered yes; then the court discharged me.

Here the devil was disappointed again of his aim, and hell of her expectation; I came right through the body of my enemies, some gnashing their teeth, and I laughing them to scorn. After this my enemies were silent as to bringing me before courts, they could do nothing but backbite and give me an ill name, which upon examination they could not prove; so I did not think it was worth my while to mind them any more.

About six weeks after they came and acknowledged their wicked ways and their envious hearts against me without a cause, and wished to join my society; but I could not in conscience receive them till farther proof, and when I examined them closely, found that every one of them were class-leaders of the Methodist society. So we see here the greatest enemies of Christ's church frequently make a great profession, and have a name or an office in the church, when at the same time [they] are destitute of the vital power of true godliness; they live by a name themselves, and they want a great many names to be set down in their society books to make a fair shew, but they care nothing about real religion; from such religion as this, good Lord deliver us.

Here I continued all the summer, and visiting the neighbouring village, until the 10th of November, and met with many trials from false brethren; so that I might say with Paul, in peril at sea, in peril in the wood, in peril in the city; but through all these things I was made more than conqueror, through our Lord Jesus Christ, who always comforts them that wait upon him for their support.

On the 11th of November I took my journey with an intent to reach Liverpool; we came to Jordan River, and we continued there till the 13th. We passed over Jordan River to Green Harbour. We abode there till the 15th, and because I would not lose time, I hasted if it was possible to be back by Christmas.

On the 16th we set off for Green Harbour, in the morning, and we called at Ragged Island, but passed through the woods, in order to accomplish my purpose, and when we got about half way, we lost the marked trees, which were our guide, so we wandered in the wood for two hours, then I went to prayer to God to guide me into the right way, and found much of the presence of the Lord while in prayer. When we got up, one said one thing, and another said another thing, for there were five of us with the boys; I said to the boys, follow me. The snow was about a foot and a half on the earth; I went this way for about a mile, and then came right into the road that was newly cut, and I hallowed for the other two men; so they followed me, and we passed on, and got to Sable River half after three o'clock, and were gladly received, and had such things set before us as they could afford, and we refreshed ourselves. The neighbours were alarmed that I was at Sable River, and there came more than thirty together, and I preached from the vth chapter of St. Paul's epistle to the Ephesians, and 16th verse, and the presence of the Lord was with us. The next morning the 17th, at ten o'clock, I preached again to a large concourse, from the ivth chapter of St. Paul's second epistle to the Corinthians, and 10th verse; after which I set off to go down to Mr. Pride's, which was three miles distant, and I arrived there about one o'clock, and preached again from St. Paul's epistle to the Hebrews, the iid chapter and 3d verse, to a crouded audience, and God was pleased to manifest himself, for there was groaning and crying through the whole congregation.

On the 18th, at five o'clock in the morning, I preached again to a large congregation, from the iiid chapter of St. John, and 14th verse, and had a little conversation with them, and then set off to go up the River to see some sick people, which employed me all this day at Sable River.

On the 19th I set off for Jones's Harbour, and arrived there about ten o'clock in the morning, but did not tarry. We set off from there at eleven, and arrived at Big Port Jolly about three in the afternoon. We staid here all night, and in the morning of the 20th, after prayer, we set off for Little Port Jolly. We arrived here at twelve o'clock. This place consisted of only eleven houses, a parcel of very poor people, for their children and themselves had scarcely clothes enough to cover their bodies, but seemed to be very willing to hear the word of God. My congregation consisted of forty-seven, great and small, all the number of souls in this place. Here I staid till the 25th, and did not stay in vain, though this was the first visit I made in this place, yet it pleased God to call five souls, and justify their souls by faith through the blood of Christ. Ten others were pricked to the heart, and were groaning for redemption in the blood of Christ.

On the 26th day I proposed to go on to Port Martoun, but they informed me that the small-pox was there, but I did not believe them, and was not afraid of the small-pox for myself, but my little boy never had it. However, I set off about ten o'clock to accomplish my purpose, and met a man half way, who informed me that the small-pox was there in reality, and said that the people of Liverpool would suffer nobody to come into town from the westward, so I thought it was prudent to return back. We came back to Little Port Jolly again that evening, and abode there till the 28th, then set off on my way back. We got to Big Port Jolly, at half after eleven o'clock, and the people were desirous that I should stay with them a few days. I concluded to send the boys with some people that were going to Sable River, to inform the people that I would be with them on the Lord's day, by the permission of God. I abode here till the 30th, then set off very early in the morning to accomplish my design, and about one o'clock in the day I was lost, by reason of the snow falling so very thick, and no road, only marked trees; and at times I could not see twenty yards before me, by reason of the violence of the snow-storm. In this case I wandered all the day, sometimes reading, sometimes praying, and sometimes crying, till evening, when I came up to a very large rock, and finding it was bitter cold, and must have perished if I had laid out in the open air, for the air was very keen and sharp, I went down on my knees to God, to direct me what I should do; and whilst I was praying, my little dog went under the rock and brought a bit of bone in his mouth. So when I rose up I thought I would go in, taking the tommihawk in my hand, and I went in; the place was very warm, I felt about for a considerable time, but found no opposition. I sat me down, and took my knapsack off, in order to get a tinder-box, and I struck a light, and took my pencil and began to write the transaction of the day, and how kind God was to provide me with a place of abode. In the space of an hour, I heard something walk on the snow, my little dog ran away to the mouth of the cave. I arose up and went and met a bear at the mouth of the rock, but was prevented from coming in by seeing me. He drew back, and growled very fiercely, and continued for an hour; whilst he was raging, I was praying to God to encourage me, and strengthen me to stand against him. But, I must confess to my Readers, at the first sight of the beast I trembled and became very faint, and had he attempted then to attack me, I should have fell an easy prey in his paws; but the God who saved David and Paul from the mouths of the lions and the bears, prevented him from coming in upon me in that state, and my God strengthened me and encouraged me, and turned him away that I saw him no more till half after two in the morning. At that time no man can tell what distress I felt in my mind, but God alone. At half after two I had another visit from him, but met him in the name of the Lord, and with much boldness, trusting upon the promises of the Lord. He strengthened me wonderfully; he staid three quarters of an hour this time, and then the Lord turned him away again, and I saw him no more until half after eight in the morning of the 1st of December.

After I had left the cave, committing myself into the hands of God, I set off in order to find my way to Sable River. I came by a very large rock, a little way from the rock I saw the bear again, but he never growled at me. After I had passed him about thirty yards, he went in my track back to his former lodging. I went my ways along wandering till about twelve o'clock on the Lord's day, and I began to feel myself so weak that I was not able to travel, having eat nothing from the 30th of November to the 2d of December, I sat myself down; I had a small box of wafers in my pocket, I eat them, and put some snow into my mouth for water. After which I got up and went my way; but not long after my knapsack grew too heavy for me. I sat me down, in order to lighten it by taking my bible and gown out, and left the knapsack with all the rest of the things. But not long after I set off, I had occasion to lighten myself again, by leaving the gown, and by this time I heard some people blowing a horn in the wood, but I could not answer by reason of weakness, which obliged me to lay down with my bible under my head, and commend my spirit to God who gave it. But God did not think proper to receive it at that time, and the people continued hallowing, and my little dog began to howl, so the people heard it, and made towards me; soon after the dog left me, and went to the people. So they knew the dog, and followed him. Two women came to me, one was rather frightened, and started back, the other came up and laid her hand upon me, perceiving life was still in me; she said to the other, he is alive, so they raised me up, and two men came and took me away, but I was insensible of the whole till the 3d of December, when I began to recover and found myself in a strange place; and asking how I came there, they told me they found me in the wood. I asked them what place they called this, they informed me it was the upper end of the River Sable. I asked them if they took up nothing where they found me. They answered, nothing but the bible. I begged them to go back and follow my track, they would find the rest of my things, which they did, and they found my words true. I was now five miles from the preaching-house.

Here I staid till the 6th of December, conversing with them, and I found the boy had informed them that I was set off in order to be with them on the Lord's day. After waiting till past ten, and having no information of me, they concluded that I was lost. There were more than ten men sent out to blow the horn in different parts of the wood, in order that I might hear. So by this way I perceived I was found by the commandment of God. Here we see the ama[z]ing and boundless love of God, in delivering his people from the jaws of death. O where shall we find language sufficient to celebrate his praises? [W]hilst our pilgrimage is here below, may we not join with Paul, and say, "O the depths of the wisdom and knowledge of God." I assure thee, Reader, I am at a loss for words; but this I know, experience goes beyond expression. All I can say upon this is, that whilst I am in this mortal body, by his mighty power I will praise him with my stammering tongue; and when I am swallowed up in death, and faith is lost in sight, then shall I praise him in a nobler strain around his throne in glory, where I hope to meet all who are made perfect through suffering, to suffer no more, where suffering will be turned into joys and praises. Then what are all my sufferings here, if I be made [meet] at last for eternal glory. Many more things could be said on this head, but I forbear, fearing it will tire my Readers.

On the 7th day I had a desire to go down the River, and towards evening I went; but not being able to preach, I continued till the 8th, conversing with them, and praying with them.

On the 9th, in the morning, I received a letter from Birch Town, wherein I was informed that I must go to Hallifax to receive some relief arrived from her Ladyship. I made the best of my way for Shelbourn, that very evening I arrived at Green Harbour.

On the 10th I arrived in Shelbourn; at eleven o'clock I went to Esquire White, to get farther information. He assured me that there was some money come by the letter he had received from Mr. James Earl, but did not know how much it was; he persuaded me to go and see after it. So I arrived at home that very evening.

On the 11th I prepared myself for the journey, finding the weather very mild, I thought it was prudent to go in my own boat for quickness.

I set off on the 13th of December, and got down as far as Gunnell Cove, the wind being calm and a very thick fog, we thought it prudent to go on shore till midnight. We did so, and we had prayer on shore in the house of an old disciple. After twelve o'clock we sailed from thence to perform our voyage. After we had got two miles out at sea, it became very calm; so we thought proper to lower our sails and come to an anchor. We laid there till the 14th; at eleven o'clock in the morning we had a breeze of wind about south-west. We weighed anchor, and hoisted our sails. About half after one o'clock we ran into Sable River to land a little child we had, and staid there till nine o'clock at night, then sailed from thence with a fair wind, and a moon-light night. The next evening the 15th, we arrived on the eastward of Margate Bay.

On the 16th we made an attempt to get into Hallifax, but the wind coming a-head, prevented us. We ran into Sambury Harbour. We laid there till the 17th, and had a good deal of snow. We sailed for Hallifax, and by the help of God, arrived at Hallifax at nine o'clock in the evening. We had a violent snow storm this night, which filled our boat with snow, and rendered us unable to return with her this winter, which obliged us to haul her up, and one of the hands returned in a schooner to Shelbourn, but I remained at Hallifax, waiting for Mr. James Earl, until the 27th day of January, but I did not see him, which concluded my travels in Nova Scotia.

I sailed for Boston, and left one hand to take care of the boat. I had five days passage from Hallifax to Boston. Here I was in a strange country, knowing nobody; but having a few letters of recommendation, the first house I went to deliver these letters was Mr. Watts's; finding him not at home, his wife behaved with all the kindness she could. She sent a man with me to shew me the way to the Rev. Dr. Stillman, where he kindly received me, and shewed me all that respect that becometh a Minister of the Gospel of Christ. Here I got some refreshment, and he gave me two notes to some friend which he could recommend, and was so kind to send the boy to shew me their houses; the first was Mr. Samuel Beans, who kindly received me, and his wife shewed all that respect that became her station. So he took me from thence to Mr. [Prince] Hall, one of the most respectable characters in Boston, where I was kindly received by him and his wife; also between these two houses I divided my time, and had many Christian friends to visit me, both in town and country. I preached my first sermon in Boston, at a society room of Dr. Stillman's people. Then on the Lord's day in the evening, which was on the 3d day of February, I preached to a large concourse of people, at the west end of the town, from the iiid chapter of the Acts of the Apostles, 22d verse, and had much of the presence of the Lord. There was no small stir among the people in Boston that week, I obtained a large place, and preached every Friday afternoon to a large concourse of people; and on the Sabbath evenings at the west end of the town, to a very crouded audience. I continued preaching twice and thrice a week, and all the people heard for themselves. But one thing I must take notice of, is a very singular deliverance which God shewed towards me in Boston. I was preaching at the west end of the town, on the 27th day of February, 1789, after preaching to a large concourse of people, there were more than forty that had made an agreement to put an end to my evening preaching, and in order to accomplish it, they came prepared that evening with swords and clubs, and other instruments, to put an end to my life. So they set watches at the two gates, in order that I should not escape their hands, and all this time I was innocent of any danger of that kind near at hand, until a gentleman came in who saw what they were about to do. He informed me of their scheme, and bid me follow him. So I took my gown and wrapped it round me, so that it hid my band, and I followed him. And passing through the croud, I arrived at the gate; there were four of these men put at the gate to watch, and the Lord seemed to blind their eyes, for I passed betwixt them, and escaped out of their hands like a bird out of the snare of the fowler. So when we arrived at the Commons, the gentleman bid me make the best of my way to his house, which was at the Bank, and he would go back and see if he knew any of them, and so I escaped for my life, and four other persons with me; and when I came to the Bank, I thought I would venture to my lodging, all this while my enemies were waiting with full expectation of accomplishing their design. But when the last man came out who locked the door, they ran upon him, and I was informed that he was obliged to run for his life; still they thought to catch me before I got down to my lodgings, and they dispersed themselves and ran in hopes of taking me before I got in; but here they were disappointed again, for when I came to the corner of School-lane, I saw them running across, and after they passed me, I passed thro' the croud in the street, and went the back way, and got into my lodging, and when they found that they had lost their aim, they throwed three or four stones through the window. But the master of the house soon came home, and dispersed them; and the next morning there was no little stir, for the constables had their orders from the Justice, with one of the men who knew them; they went to one of their houses, and he was taken, and then he discovered the rest; and when the Justice examined them, and found that they were guilty of the crime, he asked them what they did all this for? They answered, because in the evening when we left our work, we used to go and see our girls, and when we came to their houses, we always found they were gone to meeting, and we were determined to put an end to the meeting; so the Justice asked them how they would do it, they answered, by killing him; then the Justice reproved them, and shewed them the impropriety of such conduct, by breaking the laws of their country, and what sore punishment they would be brought to if they were severely dealt with; so they began to weep, and they were bound over for their better behaviour in future, and paid all costs and damages, and then were dismissed. I was never disturbed by them any more.

Here I continued keeping school and preaching, and visiting from house to house, till the 24th of June, where I was called upon to preach a sermon for the Free-masons. I complied with their request, and preached to a great number of people that day. The sermon, by the request of the brethren of the lodge, was printed for the benefit of the Free-masons lodge.

On the 26th of June I was called upon to go into the country, and when the horse was sent down for me, I went as far as Bridgwater Town, East Town, and Sherham. Here I staid eleven days, preaching the gospel twice every day, and the people coming from every quarter with their mouths open to hear the word of God, and much of the out-pouring of God's spirit was among them, and many was pricked to the heart, and it proved their conversion.

On the 12th day I sat off for Boston again, by receiving a letter. I arrived in Boston about six o'clock in the evening, and was gladly received, and could never get an opportunity to leave that people to go any distance in the country. Here I continued to keep school and to preach, and had continually a crouded audience, and many precious souls were convinced under the word of God, both white and black. I had many very good friends, and many enemies; so after writing repeatedly home to England, to her Ladyship, and receiving no relief nor answer by letter, I thought it best to come to England, to know what her Ladyship intended to do; and accordingly I prepared for the voyage, but it was a lamentable sight to see the people the last night I preached in Boston, weeping and mourning; but I said the will of the Lord must be done. So they gave me such things as were necessary for the passage, and accompanied me down to the ship, with very heavy hearts.

On the 5th day of February, 1790, we sailed for England, with Captain Loud, a very religious young man, and the wind blowing at W. N. W. and continued for four days very cold, and our decks were covered with ice, and then came about north, and continued there three days, and then came about S. W. for two days, and then came about S. E. and blew a gale for two days and a half, and then came about S. W. and blew, and this is the 14th day; and on the 15th the wind blew about S. all the day, and in the morning of the 16th blew a very hard gale N. E. all day, and all the 17th, which caused us to lay too that night, and on the 18th the Lord was pleased to favour us with a fair wind and a pleasant day, and that continued all the 19th, with the blessings of God the Father, through our Lord Jesus Christ, the wind blowing at west.

On the 20th we had the wind E. S. E. until four in the afternoon, then came about N. W.

On the 25th day the wind being at S. W. and continued till the 28th day of February, and continued all the 1st of March.

On the 3d day, the wind blowing at west, all well, and expecting to see the land every moment.

On the 4th day, the wind blowing S. E. and blew fresh, all well, and in good spirits.

On the 27th day of our being out, we arrived at the North of Ireland; so we were twenty-seven days from land to land, all well, through our Lord Jesus Christ.

On the 5th day of March, the wind blowing S. and the land bore S. of us. At four in the afternoon we came up to Black Rock. She bore S. of us, and the wind S. W.

On the 6th day of March we came in sight of the island of Tory, bearing south-east, and we steering for it, wind S. W. all well, by the blessing of God, and hoping on the Lord's day to preach the gospel to the people on board.

On Sunday the 7th of March, we entered the harbour of Londonderry, in Ireland, and took a pilot on board, the wind blowing S. E. all well, thanks be to God the Father, through our Lord Jesus Christ; and this is the thirtieth day since we left Boston, and all well. We were then in sight of Copeland lights, and the land bearing S. of us, and all well, thanks be to God. O what a kind God we have to do with, and kind to us when we deserve to be banished from his presence for our ingratitude. We had prayers every morning, and preaching when the weather would permit, and a very civil ship's crew; a number of fine sober men, and a Captain a very worthy man, and I hope the blessing of God will be with him, and prosper him; in the things of this world may he have an hundred fold, and in the world to come, life everlasting.

Now, to God the Father, God the Son, and God the Holy Ghost, be all praises and glory for evermore. Amen and Amen.

I have been giving my Readers a large account of God's dealings with me in Nova Scotia, likewise of many precious souls, the greater part of them are now living witnesses of these things, whose souls must rejoice when they read this and experience the same, and will have reason to bless and adore the infinite wisdom of God, to a never ending eternity; each of them can testify and bear witness to the truth of this book.

I thought proper also to give a few names of those whom the Lord has been pleased to take to himself, who are now, I hope, singing his praises in glory, whose death-bed I had the opportunity of attending. The first was Mr. Jonathan Lock, who had a short pilgrimage here, after his conversion. He was set at liberty on the 14th day of February, 1786, and left this world the 26th of March, thro' the small-pox, and in his greatest extremity of pains of body, he was always heard to say, that he longed to depart this life. And when the blood was running out at his mouth and his nostrils, he was asked by one if he felt any pain; he answered no, and Death, said he, has lost its sting, and the grave its victory. He was asked again by one what he thought of his wife and dear children; he answered, the God who gave them to me, will provide for them; and then bid them to call up his mother-in-law[,] and all his sisters, and he gave them an admonition against dancing and swearing, and following foolish diversion, and begging them to serve the Lord Jesus Christ in this world, and to forsake all the ways of sin, that they might meet in glory, to part no more. And then bidding them farewell, he said unto them, tell Mr. Marrant not to forget his promises that he made to me, that is to preach a funeral sermon for me, from these words: "For me to live is Christ, and to die gain;" and to have it printed and given to my father, mother, and sisters; and that the Lord will please to be with him in all his journies through this world: And then turning himself said, Lord Jesus Christ into thy hands I commend my spirit, and fell asleep in Christ. So according to his request I preached a sermon, which is added to this Journal.

The second name I would give my Readers the account of, is a little girl about twelve years of age, who died in full triumph of faith, and left a sweet testimony behind, which may be of great use to all young people, and to shame old Christians. This girl was one whom I had in school, and had frequent opportunity of conversing with her concerning her soul; but it seemed to prove fruitless, until four days before her death, when God was pleased to manifest himself to her in a most extraordinary manner, on the 4th of May, 1787, whereon she sent for me, and related to me the great display of God's glory that was shewn to her on the evening past, and sent for all her school-mates, and gave them a very solemn charge, which made them all to weep, and then turned round to her mother, and said, "O my mother, I am afraid I shall never see you any more, for you are not serving God," said she, "and you cannot[,] mother[,] deceive God, but you will deceive your own precious soul. Mother[,] leave off backbiting God's people, and perse-cuting the church of God; mother[,] God is angry with you every mo-ment of the day." She continued for the last three days of her life speaking in this manner to every one that came in to see her, so that she caused tears to trickle down the cheeks of every one that came in. The last two hours before she died, she said unto me, "master, I must go, for the angel of the Lord is come for me;" and she desired me to preach a sermon for her, from the xivth chapter of the Revelations, the 1st to the 4th verses. She then desired me to call for the elder of the church, and all the children; so the room was filled with small and great. We prayed and sung according to her desire. After which, she called her mother again, and began in the former manner to her, which made the whole room to be astonished. Then bid all her school-mates farewell, and turned herself round on the bed, and said fare ye well every body, God Almighty bless you all, and bring you to heaven. And then said, Lord Jesus receive my soul, and fell asleep in Christ, and left every body in floods of tears, God over-ruled her death for good; so she proved a saving conviction of her mother, and three of her school-mates. Thus died Kitty Bligh.

The next name I would give is Mrs. Murray, who died the 24th of July, 1787, in the full triumph of faith. She longed to go before the hour came. I found great satisfaction in visiting her all her illness. In my last visit her request was that I should preach a funeral sermon for her, from the viith chapter of the Revelations, 15, 16, and 17 verses, and desired that we should go singing before her to the grave. I did according to her desire.

The next name I beg leave to mention is, Diana Elliott, who died the 27th day of September, 1787, in the full triumph of faith; who left this world singing the praises of God. Here I might mention a great many more names, who died in faith since I have been in Nova Scotia; but I forbear, for fear of tiring my Readers. May the eternal God who rules the inhabitants of this world, give a blessing to those triumphant believers I have already mentioned in this account, and to such as may read this book, and an encouragement to weak believers. May God grant the Author and the Reader may meet them around the throne, where parting shall be no more.

Now, to him be all praise and glory, for evermore. Amen and Amen.

I think it is proper also to give my Readers a list of the names of those principal gentlemen in Nova Scotia, who knew and were eye-witnesses of my sufferings in that country, for want of temporary necessaries, and who I applied to, and was assisted by them; their names I mention by their leave and permission, to give my Readers a greater satisfaction of the truth of this book. The first name whom I applied to, and was supplied by is,

Stephen Skinner, Esq. of Shelbourn Town.

Benaja Collins, Esq. of Liverpool, at whose house I lodged three weeks.

Gideon White, Esq. whom I applied to as a Magistrate.

Isaac Wilkins, Esq. the Chief Judge of Shelbourn Court, with whom I had the honour of being passenger with in returning from my numerous journies.

James Clark, Esq. of Hallifax, Sheriff.

The Rev. Dr. Walter, of the Church of England, in Shelbourn Town, who well knew my sufferings, and has sympathized with me in my afflictions many times.

The Rev. Dr. Stillman, of Boston, one of the most respectable characters that is in that country, and whose house was the second I entered into.

And Mr. Prentice, and Mr. Skinner, who supplied my last wants in Boston.

Mr. Prince Hall, at whose house I lodged, one of the most respectable characters in Boston Town.

Mr. John Edmonds, who came passenger with me, and is now in London, who well knew my distress and sufferings in Nova Scotia for the want of the necessaries of this life. These names my Readers may satisfy themselves with, for the reality of what I have advanced. And if this book should fall into the hands of any of my enemies, let them be satisfied also with the reality of it. But I am sorry to say, that there are some of these that the Bible, with all its divine beauties, is not sufficient to satisfy, for they will even find fault with the holy scriptures of God, and like the Pharisees of old, cast a contempt upon the religion of our Lord Jesus Christ; and if Christ was to be on earth now, they would, with the Rabbies of Jerusalem, condemn him, and crucify him. For they are men lovers of their ownselves, covetous boasters, proud and unholy without natural affection; truth breakers, and awful despisers of those that are good, having a form of godliness, but denying the power thereof. These are ever learning, but never able to come to the knowledge of the truth; let such as these tremble whilst they read these lines, and no longer reject the spirit of God against their own souls.

Now, may God bless them in reading of these words, so that God may be glorified in their conversion. To him be glory for ever and ever. Amen.

THE END.

Copy of a Letter from the Right Honourable the Countess of Huntingdon, to the Rev. Mr. John Marrant, Minister of the Gospel in the secreting connection, dated South Wales, Oct. 25, 1786.
"I Have received with great pleasure your two letters; my ill state of suffering bad health prevents my writing so exactly as I would desire to do, and begging our Lord's tender mercy to make me the means of strength-

ening your hands in his work, and comforting your heart, that you may abide faithful unto death. Many must be the tribulations of the diligent in the Lord's service; but faith, *true Gospel faith*, will cause us to ride out every storm, and sing our great and glorious deliverer's praises for eternity. I have wrote to enquire after that Mr. Brown you mention, and shall order tickets as you desire, and only writ for your further wants, tickets to send what you want. I think a faithful account of the spread of the Gospel in England and Wales, would cause you and your society to rejoice in the Lord abundantly. Remember me in Christian love to all who love the Lord Jesus; and believe me your truly faithful friend, for his sake,

S. HUNTINGDON.

"Direct for me at Spa Fields, London."

Copy of a Letter from Mr. Jonathan Allstyne, to the Rev. Mr. Marrant, dated Boston, May 23, 1787.

"REV. SIR,

"I Have just left our friend the Rev. Mr. William Farmadge, whose strong recommendations in your behalf, assures me that you are a worthy soldier and servant of the great *Emanuel*, and that your exemplary life and pious workings for the spiritual welfare of the flock you now lead towards *Zion*, becomes the shepherd of *Isrol*. I am sorry that I did not meet you in your circular visits, as it would have prevented me from troubling you with this invitation of meeting me at Liverpool, about the latter end of July. I long to converse with you, and to settle means for our correspondence. Should you have occasion for money to travel with, pray apply to some friend, and I will furnish you (when we meet) with the opportunity to repay them. Should you be in want of any temporary provision, pray let me know by your answer, and I will send you a supply. And as I hear that you have a chapel, and that your people are drove to some extremes, you may very probably need some assistance towards its present establishment. Should that be the case, and you will bring along with you an estimate signed by two or three of the most respected of your followers, I will on account of your brethren at home, enable you to carry your plans in full execution, as I am persuaded that you will obey this brotherly invitation. Pray bring along with you a list of your congregation, with the names of those you entrust with the classes. My reason I shall make known when we meet. Let me further exhort you my beloved, that as you struggled with the difficulties of this temporal tabernacle, to manfully maintain the banner as becomes the true soldier and servant; so that we may jointly *hail* and receive the prize of immortal bliss, to our eternal and everlasting joy. Grace be to you, and all them of whatever denomination that love our Lord, our common father, in sincerity. Amen, Amen, prays your fellow labourer, brother and servant,

JONATHAN ALLSTYNE.

"P.S. Direct to me at Dr. Pembrook's, State-Street, Boston."

Copy of a Letter from the Rev. Mr. Marrant, to Lady Huntingdon, dated North America, Nov. 24, 1788.

"I Hope these few lines will find your Ladyship in good health, and all them that love the Lord Jesus Christ. I am now getting a little better, thanks be to God the Father, through our Lord Jesus Christ, for sparing me to see this day. One of the greatest favours we can receive from virtuous human beings, is to find an opportunity of opening our hearts to them; in doing so we communicate to them an account of our afflictions; our friends naturally sympathize with us, and we are glad of their advice, that advice gives us the same refreshing pleasure as a shower of rain does the weary traveller in the desart of Arabia. It is with a view of obtaining such comfort that I write to your Ladyship. These lines informs your Ladyship my reason in doing so. The bill your Ladyship will find inclosed is drawn by me in favour of Mrs. Margaret Neal. The sum of ten pounds sterling, for value received; it is for things I had in the time of my illness, and the Lord blessed the means that was made use of for my body, so that I am able to go about. I can say that it was good for me that I was afflicted, for here I learn the will of God. I hope to go to Liverpool in a few days, to see the people of God, whom I long to see, that the Lord Jesus Christ will be pleased to enable me to go this journey to the glory of God, and to sing of his name in this world, so that I might die in the works of the Gospel. If your Ladyship will be so kind to accept this bill, it will be the means of set[t]ing your unworthy servant on his way to the glorious works in the Gospel of our Lord Jesus Christ. May this meet with your Ladyship's approbation and love. So no more from me at present,

I remain your humble Servant, in Christ,

JOHN MARRANT."

⁎ The first, second, and third [letters], were of the same tenor.

Copy of a Letter from Mrs. Blucke, to the Rev. Mr. Marrant, dated New-York, Oct. 12, 1789.

"REV. SIR,

"I Am favoured by your very kind and affectionate letter, dated the 17th of last month, and in return receive my hearty thanks for your kind attention in writing to me; and indeed, my dear friend in *Christ*, your letter has refreshed, and is comfortable to me, and I may say as the wise man saith, ointment and perfume rejoice the heart; so doth the sweetness of a man's friend by hearty council, and they that seek the Lord, understand all things. And may the spark of divine love (which you always cherish) extend in all the hearts of your hearers, and that you may have that comfort of seeing the success of the Gospel fully accomplished among your people. I would be glad to hear the Gospel tidings you would give of them, as it would give me joy and welcome news of the renewal of the holy spirit in their hearts and precious souls, and that God, out of his infinite mercy, may pour down into their hearts and souls, that enlightened grace which Cornelius and family renewed by the hands of Peter, which I shall not fail to make my earnest prayers to God for them. And now, my dear respected friend for temporal concerns, believe me I answered every letter I received from you that came from Nova Scotia. The first letter I sent you, I enclosed it to Mr. Blucke, wherein he informed me that he delivered it into your own hands. Indeed, I was doubtful of it; however, the very last I wrote you and sent you, I here inclose a copy of it now for your satisfaction, and you will see that I did not shew that neglect for you that you thought I did. I sent it under cover to York Lawrence, then living with Mr. Stephen Skinner, as I was almost certain York Lawrence would deliver it to yourself, as I charged him in my letter not to deliver it into any body's hands but your own. I would be glad to know if you received it; believe me, my mind and heart is filled with concern and trouble on account of that poor unhappy girl Isabella, in the manner she lives. I would wish to God it was in your power to contrive to get her to Boston, and any expence you would be at of getting her away, I would gladly pay; indeed it would be an act of charity and mercy of restoring her from the unhappy life she lives in. I have wrote to Mr. Blucke, and that repeatedly, but no satisfaction I can receive from him, or nothing I can depend on. I request you will write to me every opportunity, and let me know how your children and yourself does, and how you like the place where you are, and to let me know if it would be possible you could do any thing of getting Isabella away; and likewise I request you will let me know what news about Mr. Blucke and the place, as I cannot find out what he is doing. I would take it as a favour if you would enquire after Peter Gray and wife, and please to take notice of him, and let him know his mother is well, (she is my sister) and all his friends and relations are well. Please to acquaint me how he makes out; my dear friend I believe I almost tire you with this long letter, but excuse me for the present, as my next letter shall be shorter; and believe me to be, with every affectionate regard, wishing yourself and family every spiritual and temporal blessing, is the sincere prayer of,

YOUR'S,

MARGARET BLUCKE.

"N. B. Please to let me know what Street you live in, and Number, as I shall direct my letter to you; so please to direct your letters to me, No. 40, Smith's Street, New-York. Those directions are necessary, as the letters will sooner come to hand.

YOUR'S,   M.B.

"My good SIR,

"You see I am entirely at a loss how Mr. Blucke goes on, and you will be pleased to give me as full an account as you can about him."

A

FUNERAL SERMON

PREACHED

By the Desire of the deceased, JOHN LOCK;
the TEXT chosen by himself,

FROM THE

EPISTLE of ST. PAUL to the PHILIPPIANS,

CHAP. i. VER. 21.

And was PREACHED according to PROMISE,
Before his Father and Mother, Brothers and Sisters, and
all the Inhabitants round the neighbouring Village,

BY

The Rev. JOHN MARRANT

LONDON:

PRINTED FOR THE AUTHOR:

Sold by J. TAYLOR and Co. at the Royal Exchange; and
Mr. MARRANT, No. 2, Black Horse Court,
in Aldersgate-street

A

SERMON,*1 &c.

PHILIPPIANS i. 21.

For me to live, is Christ; and to die, is gain.

IN this Chapter from whence my Text is chosen, we find the Apostle Paul is a labouring to shew the Philippians the grand design of the Christian living in Christ, and what shall the gain be of them that live a holy life. The impropriety of those who neglect so great a privilege; he himself felt the sweet working of the spirit, which drew him both ways: So that he was willing to leave this body, and saw in the clearest light what he should gain in so doing. Yet, seemed to have a sympathising feeling for those of his fellow-creatures, who has their face Zion forward.

I shall stop here with the Introduction, and in discoursing from the words of my text, and endeavour to shew you first, in what sense we may take the words "For me to live, is Christ; and to die, is gain."

Secondly, what the faithful Ministers of Christ, and all real Christians gain by their death, and

Thirdly, that it is the duty of all the Ministers of Christ to maintain a clear evidence of their gain by death.

Death has late been walking round us, and makes breaches upon breach upon us, and now has carried away the head of this family, with a sudden stroke. So that he whom you saw a week ago singing the praises of God with you below, is now laid in the dust. But he still lives in the presence of that God, whom he long breathed out his wishes to be with. And I think it would be no unreasonable thing to entertain you a little with that which is the end of all the living. Happy are we if we lay it to heart. We have death set out in the proceeding verse, with much pomp, in many lofty figures, and that in all its approaches, in all the steps it makes towards us. And you who are the near relatives to the deceased, may God grant that you may gain at your last hour, what your son whom we hope now enjoys. So that you might leave a lively testimony that you have lived to gain eternal life. And I hope that it may be the case of all of you, my friends, to consider for what end you are made in this world, to obtain a clear evidence of your acceptance with God, in the hour of death. A reconciled peace through the atoning blood of Christ.

The object now before us is a loud call for you, that death will pass upon all men. Turn the question within you, and ask yourself, am I living to gain eternal life? He that has the faith of God's elect, shews it by a correspondent practice, and so he adorns the doctrines of God, our Saviour, though he has still the remainders of in-dwelling sin, and many comings short of spirituality, and perfection of the law; yet he proposes to himself in the governing views of his life, to be found in the constant practice of all Christian duties. What God commands, he esteems his honour to obey; and what he forbids, to refuse and abhor himself for all his sinful defects and imperfections. The Apostle, in my text, implicitly says, now Christ has gained me over from my state of Pharisai[s]m, to himself, shall he not do what he will with his own? Lo! Here I am, let him dispose of me, and all my circumstances, but let him appoint how all my time and talents shall be employed. Surely, he that hath opened my eyes, and called me by his efficacious grace, has a perfect right to me to serve himself of me, in the highest and lowest offices of life, his interest in me, authorises him to effect his own ends by me, with all that I am and have, as he shall direct. Lord, here I am, to be disposed of by thy wisdom, and good pleasure, in a more noble or ignoble service, not only in some cases at some times, but as long as I live in the world.

3dly, For me to live, is Christ; that is, his glory, is the grand design of my living. Christ is the most admirable personage, in a complex view, that men or angels ever behold, and the rich blessing of his purchase, held up in the covenant of grace, flow through him to the glory of God, and the happiness of believers. He is the living fountain from whence his servants, of every station, and denomination, draw up the waters of life. Hence all the blessings that come down upon a guilty world, are to be reduced to him as their original. And all we do is to be done for him, as the end, the Redeemer's glory, and his Father's glory, in him is to be proposed and pursued, in every undertaking; if the name of Christ may be exalted, by our poor services, we may be satisfied by being destitute of the praise of man: as Christ is superlatively excellent, in the view of his servants, they would gladly contribute what they can, to render him amiable unto all others, and are grieved when they treat his name, his word, or his image, with contempt: Yea, they ascribe all the praise, of all their gifts, and graces, the praise of all their blessings, and benefits, to him, as the purchaser. If they feel themselves accepted of God, in their persons, they fall down before God and confess it, through his perfect and atoning sacrifice, and righteousness. "Yea, doubtless." And I count all things but loss, for the excellency of the knowledge of Christ Jesus my Lord, whom I humbly claim, as my Lord and Saviour. I utterly renounce every duty, that I have done, both before my conversion, and since, in point of justification, that I may be found in him, not having mine own righteousness, but that which is of God by faith. Philippians iii. 9. or if they have done any thing that has a gracious effect, they ascribe all to God, that formed their souls, into holy dispositions. And propensions, directed and strengthened them in their word, and give the blessing to their labours. Ardent desire of them is to be the glory of Christ, not that they expect to make him more glorious in himself than he is, but that his glory may shine forth, in a more illustrious manner, and in more instances, that they might discover it to brothers in their Christian course, particularly that the beauty of his character may, as in a mirror, shine brighter in their temper, labours, and conduct.

4thly, For me to live, is Christ; that is, the interest of his kingdom, is the chief business of my life; indeed the doctrines of Christ and his interest, are not calculated to gratify the pride, and carnal reasonings of the polite world, in the present age; the instances of the great, and noble that are called are very rare, blessed be God, those of high birth and parentage, are not excluded "two or three in the top of the uppermost boughs, four or five in the outmost fruitful branches;" a remnant, according to the purpose of God are called, but whether the wise men of the world, value the interest of Christ or not, it is certainly the most honourable and important, of any interest, that the greatest and most learned can pursue. And this is the interest, that lays nearest the heart, of every real Christian. Even when it is despised, and set at nought by others, those of high degree, as well as low, are attached to this cause, and will not deny his name for fear of the greatest sufferings. The Apostle Paul, though warned of the terrible things that would befall him, could not be disuaded from his journey. "What mean ye to weep and break mine heart, for I am ready not to be bound only, but to die at Jerusalem, for the name of the Lord Jesus. Acts xxi. 13. every faithful Minister of Christ; yea, every real Christian, has the spirit of Martyrdom. We are not to let drop the interest of Christ, though its defence requires the greatest application of mind, the severest self-denial, and the most evident danger, of parting with dear friends, or feeling the resentment of cruel enemies, such as Christ has redeemed, by the price of his blood, and the power of his graces, owe him all they have, and are. Therefore to neglect his interest, because of temptations thrown in their way, to stagger their courage, must be interpreted, a defrauding him of his due. Instead of such base ingratitude, they will rather submit to the severest tryals, and even put their life in their hands, for the honour of their Lord and Saviour. Not in a vain glorious way, but relying upon the strength of divine grace, to do and suffer any thing, and every thing, to be witnesses for Christ and his Gospel. "Ye are my witnesses, saith the Lord.["] Isaiah xxiii. 10. But can any be faithful witnesses for Christ, and attest from their own experience, the power of his grace, the kindness of his providence, and the truth of his promises, and yet desert his cause? Surely no Ministers, nor others, can in a proper sense, be witnesses for Christ and his Gospel, if they could desert his cause, for the hope of the favours, or fear of the displeasure of any man. The interest of Christ is too dear to his true Ministers, and all his faithful followers, to give up through fear, or flattery, how meanly soever many people of rank, and figure in the world, may think of his gospel and interest. And what reproach soever they may suffer, for espousing and publishing it, yet they are so sensible of the grand design, carried on for the discovery of the glory of the divine character, in the salvation of sinners, that they account it their highest honour, to own and profess, preach and defend it.

5thly, For me to live is Christ; that is, I am satisfied that all my outward circumstances, should be at the disposal of Christ. Our Lord Jesus Christ is invested with uncontroulable dominion, over all things, and over every person, dignity, and authority, of what character soever, he disposes all, agreeable to his infinite wisdom, in the best manner, and uses the best means, to accomplish the best end. Now not only the Apostles, and all the faithful Ministers of Christ, but all real Christians refer themselves to him, to chuse their lot for them, and they have a Christian acquiescence, in his allwise, righteous, and faithful determination, what condition, office, station, or work soever he assigns them, that they submit to, without repining, and endeavour to answer the ends of their designation. They are for improving the advantages, watching against the temptations, performing the duties, and exercising the graces, proper to the particular lot assigned them. Some men have such an opinion of their goodness, and excellent endowments, as to despise others in higher stations, and to be dissatisfied that they are not promoted. Wise in their own eyes, and yet nothing but hypocrites, this is far from the Christian temper, when God called for a prophet to deliver messages in his name. Isaiah, who was eminently qualified for this service, dare not undertake, without a Commission from Christ; "here am I, send me." Isaiah vi. 8. those that are real Christians, will not rush into the Ministry, but wait till Christ gives them a commission, to go for him, they dare not attempt to change their station, but under the divine conduct, they are more solicitous to approve themselves to God, in their present station, than to have it changed for a higher.

6thly, For me to live, is Christ; that is, I am determined to live in all Christian exercises, of heart, and life, so as to maintain the clear evidences of my title to life eternal. It is readily granted, that the righteousness of Christ, received by faith, is the only title to eternal life; and new covenant blessings are bestowed upon them, in this right, but the evidence of their interest is "Christ in them." Coll. i. 27. and he fills not only their heads with this doctrine, but their hearts and affections with his spirit, they derive virtue from Christ, to cure their spiritual diseases, to purify their hearts, and to bring forth fruits unto God. Deeply sensible, that without

Christ, they can do nothing. "The spirit has indited a certain rule of tryal," he is the author of those gracious habits and acts, in which our conformity to the rules consists; "he shines in upon his own works, and sometimes comments upon it, so as to make it understood, with much satisfaction, that we can determine in our favour." Our Apostle lived the whole of his time after his conversion (for ought appears) with the clear, and satisfying evidences, that "Christ lived in him;" he was sensibly redeemed from the power of all sin, to bring the living fruits of right-eousness to God, and therefore knew that Christ, freely give himself, to make a complete atonement for his sins. And so considering, an unin-terrupted assurance of pardon and acceptance, is the greater favour, next to a saving interest in Christ. We ought to "give all diligence, to make our calling, and election sure." 2 Pet. i. 10. how peaceful is the reflection, on past engagements to Christ, if we can say, "I know whom I have believed, and am persuaded that he is able to keep that, I have committed to him, against that day." 2 Tim. i. 12. and how transporting, when we view that day at hand, if we can adopt the graceful language of the Apostle, who anticipated the triumphs of the day of judgment; saying, "I am now ready to be offered, and the time of my departure is at hand, I have fought a good fight, I have finished my course, I have kept the faith." 2 Tim. iv. 6, 7. the rich experiences, that such have had, of the grace of God, which has been with them to the close of life, will raise their joyful expectation, that henceforth there is laid up for them a crown of righteousness, which the Lord, the righteous judge, "will give them at that day." This is a glorious crown in reversion! not merely for faithful Ministers, but for all the faithful followers of Christ, who long, and hope for his appearing.

But let us consider what the Ministers of Christ, and other Christians, gain by their death. The Apostle knew that when he had served his generation with fidelity, and he fell asleep, he should be a gainer by it. And all others, high and low, Ministers and people, who are made alive to God, and have surrendered themselves up to Christ, to serve him, seek his glory, in all their services, endeavour to promote the interest of his kingdom, in all they do, are willing that all their outward circumstances should be at his disposal. I say, all such as these, will be great gainers, at their death. For death will put an end to all the weakness and miseries they have groaned under in this life; in these houses of clay, the best are not exempted from tryals, that cannot but be distressing to flesh and blood. And especially, the remainders of in-dwelling corruption, which is their most grievous burden, as it is offensive and dishonourable to God, and a great hindrance to them in his service; this costs them many a groan in their serious reflection upon it. "O wicked man that I am! who shall deliver me from the body of this death?" Rom. vii. 24. In-dwelling sin excites a spirit of murmuring, under outward troubles; it often hedges up the path of duty, under a sense of the need of guidance, David prayed, "make me to go in the path of thy commandments." Psalm cxix. 35. though true Christians have grace in their hearts, and have the love of Christ to direct them, yet they have so much remaining ignorance, and there are so many perplexities in their way, that they need guidance, upon all occasions; it is for lack of divine teaching, and help in this dark world, that they wander from the divine rule, loose their evidences for heaven, disturb their peace, and their minds are catched away from true and substantial pleasures. In such a condition was Heman, the wise man next after Solomon, which made him cry, "Lord, why casteth thou off my soul; why hidest thou thy face from me." Psalm xxxviii. 14. God often hides the sensible signs of his favour from his dearest friends, and leaves them in such inextricable windings, that they know not what course to steer. But death puts an end to all those evils, there is nothing in the flesh or spirit, to give the least uneasiness to saints in glory, no pain to indispose them for the holy services of God, and his Son Jesus Christ; no distress to unfit them for any of the delightful enjoyments with which heaven is furnished. "Blessed are the dead which die in the Lord, from henceforth; yea, saith the spirit, that they may rest from their labours, and their works do follow them." Rev. xiv. 13. there is nothing to break the thread of their peace, and intense pleasure to endless ages. "God shall wipe away all tears from their eyes." Rev. xxi. 4. not only relieve their sorrows, but entirely remove them, absolutely and eternally banish all things uncomfortable, and sin the cause of them, to the remotest distances.

2d. Death opens the door to the accomplishments of their hopes. Real Christians, whilst they are among fiery serpents, are waiting with desire, and holy expectation, for the good of the promise, which is yet behind. And the more they live under a lively conviction, of the sublime delights to be enjoyed, in the presence of Christ, in heaven, the more they are influenced to attain all possible purity of heart and life. Sometimes they have such evident impresses of the holy images of God, upon their hearts, as it becomes a security and earnest of the glorious inheritance of the saints in light, and gives them establishing satisfaction of their right and title to it. They have such a relish of those divine provisions, the complement of which are reserved for a state of future blessedness, as to have no doubts but they shall soon be advanced to the full possession; but still they are in the body exposed to many evils, sinful imperfections cleaving to their best services, and storms beating upon them, while the tempestuous winds below are blowing, yet hope in Christ, as trusted in by faith, is as an anchor to their souls. Heb. vi. 19. as it enters into the glorious world, which lies hid from the sight of the eyes of the body, there it fastens upon Christ, and the Father through him, as exhibited in the promises. Hence they wait patiently for the good in the promise, which is yet unaccomplished, and who can imagine the greatness of that gain, which consists in possession and full enjoyment of all the promised good, surely the eye has never seen any thing so grand, nor the ear ever heard any thing so delightful, neither has it entered into the thoughts of any man to conceive of any thing so entertaining as the blessings of salvation, which are reserved in heaven, for the servants of Christ; "there they shall be entertained with uninterrupted views of God, in his several glories." This I apprehend, is agreeable to the promise made by him, that is faithful and true, "blessed are the pure in heart, for they shall see God." Matt. v. 8. this intends not only that God will manifest himself to them here, so as he doth not to the world, but that they shall have the benedictive vision of him for ever in glory. To the same purpose our

Apostle says, "now we see through a glass darkly, but then face to face; now I know in part, but then shall I know, even as I also am known." I Cor. xiii. 12. the grand sublime mysteries of the kingdom of God, and God in the glory of his true character, are conceived with great obscurity, through the medium of his word, and holy ordinances, compared with what they will appear in open vision. Here we have but an imperfect insight into the glory of God, and the profound truths of the Gospel, but there we shall have a certain familiar knowledge of them, by a sort of immediate inspection, the open vision of glory in eternal day, must needs support, and increase holy wonder and pleasure, and bring us prostrate before the throne; saying, with the profoundest reverence, "Holy, holy, holy, Lord God Almighty, which was, and is, and is to come;" and engage them in solemn ascriptions of "glory, and honour, and thanks, to him that sitteth upon the throne, who liveth for ever, and ever." Rev. iv. 8, 9. let us only imagine the glory of the divine character, in creation and providence, if we can argue his existence, and supreme divinity, from the aspectable heavens, and this earth, and also from the works of providence, how will these great and marvellous works display the glory of God, when we come to see him as he is? His self-existence, and supreme excellency, which he has eternally, and unchangeably of himself, his transcendent wisdom and goodness, and his other perfections, will more amasingly open, and brings more intelligible characters of his glory in heaven, than is possible to been seen, though the same things, while here in the body. What magnificence and variety, beauty and order, will then open, to be the display of the infinite perfections of God, which we have but a faint idea of through glasses in this imperfect state? There is so much of God to be seen in this world, by the works of his hands, that disobedience and opposition to him, are against such light, as leaves the very heathen without excuse. How overwhelming then must the open views of these perfections be, in the vision of glory? Saints in heaven, have the clearest discoveries of the Almighty power, and other perfections of God, legible in his great and marvellous works, his divine all-sufficiency, to supply every character, with all it can need or desire, such clear and full discoveries as are not comparable with this mortal state. In heaven, all intricate dispensations are cleared up, and the inhabitants are perfectly satisfied with the various administrations of God, and feel themselves for ever under the blessings of his hands, they have a clear sight and sense of the perfect purity of his nature, attended with a sacred abhorrence of all sin, and an everlasting preservative against the admission of any one unholy thought, and divine love and grace shine in their brightest glories, to kindle a flame of everlasting joy. Again, "let us imagine, the glory of being" entertained with the clearest, and perfectly uninterrupted views, of the harmony of the Divine perfections, in the dispensations of God, towards his church, in its militant state, which to us, are inexplicable, though there is perfect order and fitness, perfect agreement, and proportion of one dispensation with another, in the divine government. Yet, we are such poor short-sighted creatures, that the beauty and harmony of the divine perfections, seem to be in a great measure hid from us. The dispensations are so mysterious, that we are ready to say with Nichodemus, in another case, "How can these things be?" What do these dispensations mean? where is the harmony and correspondence of them? how can we open the agreeableness of one dispensation with another? sometimes things are so variable, or mixed in providence, that we are ready to say, "wherein does the holiness and glory of God appear in them?" Doth infinite wisdom, and righteousness, truth, and goodness, sit at the helm and steer the ship, we may acknowledge that the judge of all the earth does right, in what he is now doing in his church, and in what he will do in the time to come. And yet the divine harmony and connection of the whole be out of sight; but when believers come to "walk through the valley of the shadow of death," all darkness will be scattered before the meridian sun, and the beauty and harmony of the divine perfections, will be seen in the clearest light. This is reserved for heaven, where they shall see unclouded glory, have dark scriptures made plain, seeming contradictions cleared up, and reconciled[.] The lowest saints in heaven, has a clearer understanding of the mysteries of redemption and salvation, and of the wisdom and goodness of God, in the kingdom of his providence, than the greatest divine upon earth. The light of heaven leaves no place for darkness, for the glory of

God does lighten it, "and the Lamb is the light thereof." Rev. xxi. 23. hence there can be no more mistakes, no more stumbling blocks, no more disquietude, no more unhallowed fire, no more implacable enemies, to darken council by words without knowledge, and turn man aside from the right ways of the Lord Jesus Christ.

Again, let us imagine "what it will be everlastingly to be assured of God's love to our souls." Christians may in this life, have "the full assurance of hope," which will never turn to their confusion, or disappointment, beauty rests not upon any merit in themselves, but upon the free grace of God, in Christ, towards them, which abundantly fills their souls with its lovely manifestations, and distinguishing fruits. They may have some foretaste of heaven, some glympse of glory, which produce these holy transports, that are better felt than expressed; but in heaven they are surrounded with divine love, and rejoice in the everlasting assurance of it, with the most intense joy, they dwell in the immediate sensation of being beloved of God for ever, and ever. Otherwise it could not with any propriety be said "in thy presence is fullness of joy, and at thy right-hand there are pleasures for evermore." Psalm xiv. 11. for the perfections of God's immediate presence, could not yield unspeakable and everlasting joy, if they were not assured of his everlasting love; the highest uninterrupted assurance of this is a spring of their blessedness, and an endless security of joy everlasting.

Again, let us imagine, "what transcendent love they have to the Lord Jesus Christ, and to God the judge of all." The first and comprehensive commandment is, "thou shalt love the Lord thy God, with all thy heart, and with all thy strength." Mark xii. 3. And "where there is effectual faith given, it worketh by love." Gal. v. 6. to its object, if a man pretends to faith, and it does not engage his supreme love to God, in Christ, it is but a dead worthless name or form of faith; but the object is seen by having faith, only through a glass darkly, whilst we are in the body, and our love bears an exact proportion to the excellency seen in the object. Besides, how often does some temptation catch our thoughts and hearts away from God, and our Saviour; how sadly true is it, that when iniquity, corrupt principles, and practices abound, "the love of many waxes cold," they grow in a great measure indifferent in their affection towards Christ and his cause, the fervent love, which they had in the day of their espousals, is decayed; but when they die, their spirit ascends to the centre of light, and are placed in such a situation to Christ, as to feel the everlasting beams of his love, let out upon the spirits of just men made perfect, will constrain them with one heart, to sing a new song, in everlasting raptures of love saying, "Worthy is the Lamb that was slain, to receive power, and riches, and wisdom, and strength, honour, and glory, and blessing."

Again, let us imagine what love they feel to one another. Believers are never entirely destitute of love to Christ, and the brethren; "he that loveth not his brother, abideth in death." I John iii. 14. that is, he continues under the power of spiritual death, and lies exposed to everlasting destruction; but real Christians, have their hearts formed unto an affectionate love to all their brethren, in the faith, hope, and fellowship of the Gospel. Some of them have had such love to their fellow Christians, that they could readily part with any worldly good, if they might be so far conformed to the image of Christ, as many seem to be round about them. But when death let them out of these dark cottages of flesh, they have such clear views of the glories and grace and of the Lord Jesus Christ, exemplified in the saints in light, and at the same time are divested of self, as to be entirely united in one indissoluble bond of love, without any mixtures of envy, or shadows of ill will, they have one heart and one soul, and are entirely as well pleased with the blessings conferred upon each other, as upon themselves.

Thirdly, it is the duty and priviledge of believers to live, as to maintain a clear evidence of their gain by death, thus the Apostle Paul, lived under all his sufferings for Christ, and the gospel[.] The men of hi[gh] rank and figure in the world, generally thought meanly of the gospel and its author. The sublimity of the duties, and the artlessness of the dress, the contrariety of the whole to the pride of man, and the poverty of Christ's followers, methinks would have shocked and humbled any man; and the firmest mind, and greatest abilities, but Paul was carried quite above all these things, because he knew, that the Gospel of Christ, "was the power of God unto salvation," Rom. i. 16. It was cloathed with divine authority to him, and was the means which Almighty power wrought by, and rendered effectual for this salvation, he knew that it was an excellent scheme, to illustrate the glory, and harmony, of the divine perfection, and to recover fallen man. He knew that the spirit of truth had sealed him, and applied the promises with light and power to his soul, for the establishment of his faith and hope in Christ; nothing more invigorates his mind, and heart, to resist unto blood, striving against sin. Nothing made him live resisting principalities, and powers, and vigorously serving God, in the Gospel of his son, with sacred firmness, more than his consciousness of serving Christ, in life, and the gain of death. Should we not, therefore, follow his worthy example? Is it not meet to be resigned to his will, living and dying under a readiness to live, if we may serve Christ thereby, and a sense of our own gain by death. How can we speak for Christ with confidence, or leave a full testimony for him, when we die, unless we can say with Christ himself, "Father into thy hands I commit my Spirit." Luke xxiii. 46. Surely Christians ought to live, offering up themselves, and all they have to Christ. They ought to make the service and the interest of his kingdom, the governing motive, and end of all they do. They ought to employ their life, and time, and talent, for him; and to value their powers, and all they have, only or chiefly as they are serviceable to his interest. All this is evident, for supreme love to God, inclines the heart to such a dedication from the best motives. Besides God has an absolute propriety in us, and all we have, and are, and Christ Jesus has an additional right by purchase, and has appointed us to his service.

Now if it is the duty, and priviledge of believers to live so devoted to God, in Christ, then it is a duty and a priviledge, by consequence so to live as to maintain the clear and full evidence of their great gain by death; for living in the full exercises of strong faith, working by love, they have the living evidence of their gain by death before them. Self dedication to God, in Christ, is an evidence of our fitness to die; and a sense of this dedication is a plain evidence of meekness for the inheritance of the saints in light.

I might have enlarged upon this divine subject, and have inferred many useful instructions, but instead of all other things, I shall turn my discourse to the very melancholy and affecting occasion, the sudden, and surprizing death of our friend, Mr. John Locke, who died with the small-pox, on the twenty-sixth day of March, in the year of our Lord, one thousand seven hundred and eighty-six, at ten o'clock in the forenoon. When I came among them first, to preach the gospel of our Lord Jesus Christ, I found many precious souls, that never knew what I meant, by telling them, that they must repent, for the kingdom of heaven is at hand; and after preaching, I had an opportunity to sit down, and speak, with Mr. Locke, about his soul, and finding that he had a family, a wife and three small children, I then began to speak about the day of judgment, and asked him what account could he give to the Great Judge in that day, for his soul, and the soul[s] of his wife and children, in the day of Judgment; and the Lord was pleased to send the word to his heart, and he began to cry out, the Lord have mercy upon me, and save me; and tears ran down his face, and he kept so for three weeks, and two days; and by this time, I came back to see him on my way home, I called in to see my friend, and found him in the same state, and I went to pray with him, and the Lord came down, with his mighty power upon our souls. And at this time the Lord was pleased to set his soul at liberty, and filled his soul with glory. Then there was joy indeed in heaven; and the next day many people came together to hear the word of God; and after preaching was over, he desired to be baptized, he and his wife and children; and I baptized them, in the name of the Father, of the Son, and of the Holy Ghost, and the Lord was pleased to give them a second blessing on that day, and filled his soul with love to God, and to all men. So the next day, after prayers, I left him in the hands of God, encouraging him to keep close to God in prayer, and I then took my leave of them.—I went home to see the church, and finding them all well, I staid with them two weeks, and then sat off for a journey in the country, and to Jordan river.—I came where my friend was, and found him rejoicing in the Lord, and I stopt with them two days, and then left them all in the hands of God.

Mr. Lock went with me over to the Ragged Island, and then I took my leave of him, and he returned home to his family, and I went on my journey, and I saw him no more in this world.

At my return home, I was informed of Mr. John Lock's death, and they gave me his dying words, which I shall give you in my journal, and I hope you will be enabled to rejoice with me, in all my troubles in this country, for the sake of the Lord Jesus Christ. But one thing must be remarked and observed, in the growth of Grace in Mr. Lock's soul, after he met with the change of heart, he was always by himself; and when he was in the field, or in the wood at home, or sea a fishing, he was heard to say, that he hoped God would be so kind as to take him out of this sinful world. So the Lord was pleased to hear his prayer, and soon took him away from it. He left three small children behind him, and the last day that he lived in this world, he called for his children to come to him, and his wife also, but they were gone to their grandfather, for fear they should take the small-pox of him. So he did not see them; but he said I leave them in the hands of that God whom I hope to see soon, and before the sun goes down to day. So he bid us all farewell, and saying, Lord Jesus Christ, into thy hands I commit my spirit; and so gave up his soul into the hands of that God who gave it.

I shall give a full account of him in my Journal, and in an affecting manner the triumph and glory of the blessed; and particularly of the Martyrs that shall have suffered for Christ; the joys that they shall have after their labours, and the felicity which God reserves for them to this purpose. St. John tells us, that they shall be before the throne of God, and shall serve him day and night in temples, and God shall wipe away all tears from their eyes, and everlasting felicity is appointed not only for Martyrs, but is reserved by God for all those that shall keep themselves pure in this world, and shall glorify him by their patience and obedience. Therefore these words of St. John ought to fill all Christians with joy and consolation, and raise in them an ardent desire, and a firm expectation of that great glory, and excite in them more and more to holiness, and the love of God——To whom be glory, now, and for evermore. Amen, and Amen.

An Account of the life of Mr. DAVID GEORGE,
from Sierra Leone in Africa;
given by himself in a Conversation
with Brother RIPPON of London, and Brother
PEARCE of Birmingham.

I WAS BORN in Essex County, Virginia, about 50 or 60 miles from Williamsburg, on Nottaway river, of parents who were brought from Africa, but who had not the fear of God before their eyes. The first work I did was fetching water, and carding of cotton; afterwards I was sent into the field to work about the Indian corn and tobacco, till I was about 19 years old. My father's name was John, and my mother's Judith. I had four brothers, and four sisters, who, with myself, were all born in slavery: our master's name was Chapel—a very bad man to the Negroes. My older sister was called Patty; I have seen her several times so whipped that her back has been all corruption, as though it would rot. My brother Dick ran away, but they caught him, and brought him home; and as they were going to tie him up, he broke away again, and they hunted him with horses and dogs, till they took him; then they hung him up to a cherry-tree in the yard, by his two hands, quite naked, except his breeches, with his feet about half a yard from the ground. They tied his legs close together, and put a pole between them, at one end of which one of the owner's sons sat, to keep him down, and another son at the other. After he had received 500 lashes, or more, they washed his back with salt water, and whipped it in, as well as rubbed it in with a rag; and then directly sent him to work in pulling off the suckers of tobacco. I also have been whipped many a time on my naked skin, and sometimes till the blood has run down over my waistband; but the greatest grief I then had was to see them whip my mother, and to hear her, on her knees, begging for mercy. She was master's cook, and if they only thought she might do any thing better than she did, instead of speaking to her as to a servant, they would strip her directly, and cut away. I believe she was on her death-bed when I got off, but I have never heard since. Master's rough and cruel usage was the reason of my running-away. Before this time I used to drink, but not steal; did not fear hell, was without knowledge; though I went sometimes to Nottaway, the English church, about eight or nine miles off. I left the plantation about midnight, walked all night, got into Brunswick county, then over Roanoak river, and soon met with some White travelling people, who helped me on to Pedee river. When I had been at work there two or three weeks, a hue and cry found me out, and the master said to me, there are 30 guineas offered for you, but I will have no hand in it: I would advise you to make your way towards Savannah river. I hearkened to him, but was several weeks going. I worked there, I suppose, as long as two years, with John Green, a white man, before they came after me again. Then I ran away up among the Creek Indians. As I travelled from Sava[n]nah river, I came to Okemulgee River, near which the Indians observed my track. They can tell the Black people's track from their own, because they are hollow in the midst of their feet, and the Black's feet are flatter than theirs. They followed my track down to the river, where I was making a long raft to cross over with. One of these Indians was a king, called Blue Salt; he could talk a little broken English. He took and carried me away about 17 or 18 miles into the woods to his camp, where they had bear meat, deer meat, turkies, and wild potatoes. I was his prize, and lived with him from the Christmas month till April, when he went into his town Augusta, in the Creek nation. I made fences, dug the ground, planted corn, and worked hard; but the people were kind to me. S. C.[,] my master's son, came there for me, from Virginia, I suppose 800 miles, and paid king Blue Salt for me in rum, linnen, and a gun; but before he could take me out of the Creek nation, I escaped and went to the Nautchee Indians, and got to live with their king, Jack, who employed me a few weeks. S. C. was waiting this while in hopes to have me. Mr. Gaulfin, who lived on Savannah river, at Silver Bluff, and who was afterwards my master, traded in these parts among the Indians in deer skins. He had a manager here, whose name was John Miller. Mr. Miller knew king Jack, and agreed with him and S. C. as to the price Mr. Gaulfin was to pay for me. So I came away from king Jack, who gave me into the hands of John Miller. Now I mended deer skins, and kept their horses together, that they might not wander too far and be lost. I used also once a year to go down with the horses, carrying deer skins, to Mr. Gaulfins', at Silver Bluff. The distance, I think, was 400 miles, over five or six rivers, which we crossed in leather boats. After three years, when I came down, I told Mr. Gaulfin, that I wished to live with him at Silver Bluff. He told me I should: so he took me to wait upon him, and was very kind to me. I was with him about four years, I t[h]ink, before I was married. Here I lived a bad life, and had no serious thoughts about my soul; but after my wife was delivered of our first child, a man of my own color, named Cyrus, who came from Charlestown, South Carolina, to Silver Bluff, told me one day in the woods, That if I lived so, I should never see the face of God in glory (Whether he himself was a converted man or not, I do not know.) This was the first thing that disturbed me, and gave me much concern. I thought then that I must be saved by prayer. I used to say the Lord's prayer, that it might make me better, but I feared that I grew worse; and I continued worse and worse, as long as I thought I would do some thing to make be better; till at last it seemed as if there was no possibility of relief, and that I must go to hell. I saw myself a mass of sin. I could not read, and had no scriptures. I did not think of Adam and Eve's sin, but *I* was sin. I felt my *own* plague; and I was so overcome that I could not wait upon my master. I told him *I was ill.* I felt myself at the disposal of Sovereign mercy. At last in prayer to God I began to think that he would deliver me, but I did not know how. Soon after I saw that I could not be saved by any of my own doings, but that it must be by God's mercy—that my sins had crucified Christ; and now the Lord took away my distress. I was sure that the Lord took it away, because I had such pleasure and joy in my soul, that no man could give me. Soon after I heard brother George Liele preach, who, as you both know, is at Kingston in Jamaica*¹. I knew him ever since he was a boy. I am older than he; I am about fifty. His sermon was very suitable, on *Come unto me all ye that labour, and are heavy laden, and I will give you rest.* When it was ended, I went to him and told him I was so; That I was weary and heavy laden, and that the grace of God had given me rest. Indeed his whole discourse seemed for me. Afterwards brother Palmer, who was pastor at some distance from Silver Bluff, came and preached to a large congregation at a mill of Mr. Gaulfin's; he was a very powerful preacher; and as he was returning home Lord's-day evening, I went with him two or three miles, and told him how it was with me. About this time more of my fellow-creatures began to seek the Lord. Afterwards Brother Palmer came again and wished us to beg Master to let him preach to us; and he had leave, and came frequently. There were eight of us now who had found the great blessing and mercy from the Lord, and my wife was one of them, and brother Jesse Gaulfin that you mention in the History of us poor slaves, was another.*² Brother Palmer appointed a Saturday evening to hear what the Lord had done for us, and the next day he baptized us in the Mill-stream. Some time afterwards, when Brother George Liele came again, and preached in a corn field, I had a great desire to pray with the people myself, but I was ashamed, and went to a swamp and poured out my heart before the Lord. I then came back to Brother George Liele, and told him my case. He said, In the intervals of service you should engage in prayer with the friends. At another time, when he was preaching, I felt the same desire, and after he had done, I began in prayer—it gave me great relief, and I went home with a desire for nothing else but to talk to the brothers and sisters about the Lord. Brother Palmer formed us into a church, and gave us the Lord's supper at Silver Bluff. Then I began to exhort in the church, and learned to sing hymns. The first I learned out of book was a hymn of that great writing man, Watts, which begins with "Thus saith the wisdom of the Lord." Afterwards the church advised with Brother Palmer about my speaking to them, and keeping them together; I refused, and felt I was unfit for all that, but Brother Palmer said this word to me, "Take care that you don't offend the Lord." Then I thought that he knew best, and I agreed that I would do as well as I could. So I was appointed to the office of an Elder and received instruction from Brother Palmer how to conduct myself. I proceeded in this way till the American war was coming on, when the Ministers were not allowed to come amongst us lest they should furnish us with too much knowledge. The Black people all around attended with us, and as Brother Palmer must not come, I had the whole management, and used to preach among them myself. Then I got a spelling book and began to read. As Master was a great man, he kept a White school-master to teach the White children to read. I used to go to the little children to teach me a, b, c. They would give me a lesson, which I tried to learn, and then I would go to them again, and ask them if I was right? The reading so ran in my mind, that I think I learned in my sleep as really as when I was awake; and I can now read the Bible, so that what I have in my heart, I can see again in the Scriptures. I continued preaching at Silver Bluff, till the church, constituted with eight, encreased to thirty or more, and till the British came to the city Savannah and took it. My Master was an Antiloyalist; and being afraid, he now retired from home and left the Slaves behind. My wife and I, and the two children we then had, and fifty or more of my Master's people, went to Ebenezer, about twenty miles from Savannah, where the King's forces were. The General sent us over the big Ogeechee river to Savages' Plantation, where the White people, who were Loyalists, reported that I was planning to carry the Black people back again to their slavery; and I was thrown into prison, and laid there about a month, when Colonel Brown, belonging to the British, took me out. I staid some time in Savannah, and at Yamacraw a little distance from it, preaching with brother George Liele. He and I worked together also a month or two: he used to plow, and I to weed Indian-corn. I and my family went into Savannah, at the beginning of the siege. A ball came through the roof of the stable where we lived, and much shattered it, which made us remove to Yamacraw, where we sheltered ourselves under the floor of a house on the ground. Not long after the siege was raised, I caught the small pox, in the fall of the year, and thought I should have died, nor could I do any more than just walk in the spring. My wife used to wash for General Clinton, and out of the little she got maintained us. I was then about a mile from Savannah, when the Americans were coming towards it a second time. I wished my wife to escape, and to take care of herself and of the children, and let me die there. She went: I had about two quarts of Indian corn, which I boiled; I ate a little, and a dog came in and devoured the rest; but it pleased God some people who came along the road gave me a little rice: I grew better, and as the troops did not come so near as was expected, I went into Savannah, where I met my family, and tarried there about two years, in a hut belonging to Lawyer Gibbons, where I kept a butcher's stall. My wife had a brother, who was half an Indian by his mother's side, and half a Negro. He sent us a steer, which I sold, and had now in all 13 dollars and about three guineas besides, with which I designed to pay our passage, and set off for Charlestown; but the British light horse came in, and took it all away. However as it was a good time for the sale of meat, I borrowed money from some of the Black people to buy hogs, and soon re-paid them, and agreed for a passage to Charlestown, where Major P. the British commander, was very kind to me. When the English were going to evacuate Charlestown, they advised me to go to Halifax, in Nova Scotia, and gave the few Black people, and it may be as many as 500 White people, their passage for nothing. We were 22 days on the passage, and used very ill on board. When we came off Halifax, I got leave to go ashore. On shewing my papers to General Patterson, he sent orders, by a Serjeant, for my wife and children to follow me. This was before Christmas, and we staid there till June; but as no way was open for me to preach to my own color, I got leave to go to Shelburne (150 miles, or more, I suppose, by sea), in the suit of General Patterson, leaving my wife and children for a while behind. Numbers of my own color were here, but I found the White people were against me. I began to sing the first night, in the woods, at a camp, for there were no houses then built; they were just clearing and preparing to erect a town. The Black people came far and near, it was so new to them: I kept on so every night in the week, and appointed a meeting for the first Lord's-day, in a valley between two hills, close by the river; and a great number of White and Black people came, and I was so overjoyed with having an opportunity once more of preaching the word of God, that after I had given out the hymn, I could not speak for tears. In the afternoon we met again, in the same place, and I had great liberty from the Lord. We had a meeting now every evening, and those poor creatures who had never heard the gospel before, listened to me very attentively: but the White people, the justices, and all, were in an uproar, and said that I might go out into the woods, for I should not stay there. I ought to except one White man, who knew me at Savannah, and who said I should have his lot to live upon as long as I would, and build a house if I pleased. I then cut down poles, stripped bark, and made a smart hut, and the people came flocking to the preaching every evening for a month, as though they had come for their supper. Then Governor Parr came from Halifax, brought my wife and children, gave me six months pro-visions for my family, and a quarter of an acre of land to cultivate for our subsistence. It was a spot where there was plenty of water, and which I had before secretly wished for, as I knew it would be convenient for baptizing at any time. The weather being severe, and the ground covered with snow, we raised a platform of poles for the hearers to stand upon, but there was nothing over their heads. Continuing to attend, they desired to have a Meeting house built. We had then a day of hearing what the Lord had done; and I and my wife heard their experiences, and I received four of my own color; brother Sampson, brother John, sister Offee, and sister Dinah; these all wear well, at Sierra Leone, except brother Sampson, an excellent man, who died on his voyage to that place. The first time I baptized here was a little before Christmas, in the creek which ran through my lot. I preached to a great number of people on the occasion, who behaved very well. I now formed the church with us six, and ad-ministered the Lord's supper in the Meeting-house before it was finished. They went on with the building, and we appointed a time every other week to hear experiences. A few months after I baptized nine more, and the congregation very much increased. The worldly Blacks, as well as the members of the church, assisted in cutting timber in the woods, and in getting shingles; and we used to give a few coppers to buy nails. We were increasing all the winter, and baptized almost every month, and administered the Lord's supper first of all once in two months; but the frame of the Meeting was not all up, nor had we covered it with shingles till about the middle of the summer, and then it had no pulpit, seats, nor flooring. About this time, Mr. William Taylor and his wife, two Baptists, who came from London to Shelburn, heard of me. She came to my house when I was so poor that I had no money to buy any potatoes for feed, and was so good as to give my children somewhat, and me money enough to buy a bushel of potatoes; which one produced thirty-five bushels. The church was now grown to about fifty members. At this time a White person, William Holmes, who, with Deborah his wife, had been converted by reading the scriptures, and lived at Jones's Harbour, about twenty miles down the river, came up for me, and would have me go with him in his schooner to his house. I went with him, first to his own house, and then to a town they called Liverpool, inhabited by White people. Many had been baptized there by Mr. Chippenham, of Annapolis, in Nova Scotia. Mr. Jesse Dexter preached to them, but was not their pastor. It is a mixed communion church. I preached there; the Christians were all alive, and we had a little heaven together. We then returned to brother Holmes's, and he and his wife came up with me to Shelburn, and gave their experiences to the church on Thursday, and were baptized on Lord's-day. Their relations who lived in the town were very angry; raised a mob, and endeavoured to hinder their being baptized. Mrs. Holmes's sister especially laid hold of her hair to keep her from going down into the water; but the justices commanded peace, and said that she should be baptized, as she herself desired it. Then they were all quiet. Soon after this the persecution increased, and became so great, that it did not seem possible to preach, and I thought I must leave Shelburn. Several of the Black people had houses upon my lot; but forty or fifty disbanded soldiers were employed, who came with the tackle of ships, and turned my dwelling house, and every one of their houses, quite over; and the Meeting house they would have burned down, had not the ring-leader of the mob himself prevented it. But I continued preaching in it till they came one night, and stood before the pulpit, and swore how they would treat me if I preached again. But I stayed and preached, and the next day they came and beat me with sticks, and drove me into a swamp. I returned in the evening, and took my wife and children over the river to Birch town, where some Black people were settled, and there seemed a greater prospect of doing good than at Shelburn, I preached at Birch Town from the fall till about the middle of December, and was frequently hearing experiences, and baptized about twenty there. Those who desired to hear the word of God, invited me from house to house, and so I preached. A little before Christmas, as my own color persecuted me there, I set off with my family, to return to Shelburn; and coming down the river the boat was frozen, but we took whip-saws and cut away the ice till we came to Shelburn. In my absence the Meeting house was occupied by a sort of tavern-keeper, who said, "The old Negro wanted to make a heaven of this place, but I'll make a hell of it." Then I preached in it as before, and as my house was pulled down, lived in it also. The people began to attend again, and in the summer there was a considerable revival of religion. Now I went down about twenty miles to a place called Ragged Island, among some White people, who desired to hear the word. One White sister was converted there while I was preaching concerning the disciples, who left all and followed Christ. She came up afterwards, gave her experience to our church, and was baptized, and two Black sisters with her. Then her other sister gave in her experience; and joined us without Baptism, to which she would have submitted, had not her family cruelly hindered her; but she was the only one in our society who was not baptized.

By this time the Christians at St. John's, about 200 miles from Shelburn, over the bay of Fundy, in New Brunswick, had heard of me, and wished me to visit them. Part of the first Saturday I was there was spent in hearing the experiences of the Black people; four were approved, some of whom had been converted in Virginia: a fortnight after I baptized them in the river, on the Lord's-day. Numerous spectators, White and Black, were present, who behaved very well. But on Monday many of the inhabitants made a disturbance, declaring that nobody should preach there again without a licence from the Governor. He lived at Frederick town, about an hundred miles from thence up St. John's river. I went off in the packet to him. Colonel Allen, who knew me in Charlestown, lived but a few miles from the Governor, and introduced me to him; upon which his secretary gave me a licence*.[3] I returned then to St. John's, and preached again, and left brother Peter Richards to exhort among them. He afterwards died on the passage, just going into Sierra Leone, and we buried him there. When I got back to Shelburn, I sent Brother Sampson Colbert, one of my Elders, to St. John's, to stay there. He was a loving brother, and the Lord had endowed him with great gifts.— When the experiences of nine or ten had been related there, they sent for me to come and baptize them. I went by water to Halifax, and walked from thence to Haughton about 80 miles from Annapolis, and not far from New Brunswick. There is a large church at Haughton, I think the largest in Nova Scotia. They are all Baptists; Mr. Scott is their minister. We spent one Sabbath together, and all day long was a day to be remembered. When I was landing at St. John's, some of the people who intended to be baptized were so full of joy that they ran out from waiting at table on their masters, with the knives and forks in their hands, to meet me at the water side. This second time of my being at St. John's I staid preaching about a fortnight, and baptized ten people. Our going down into the water seemed to be a pleasing sight to the whole town, White people and Black. I had now to go to Frederick Town again, from whence I obtained the licence before; for one of our brethren had been there, and heard the experiences of three of the people, and they sent to me, intreating that I would not return until I had been and baptized them. Two brethren took me to Frederick Town in a boat. I baptized on the Lord's-day, about 12 o'clock: a great number of people attended. The Governor said he was sorry that he could not come down to see it; but he had a great deal of company that day, which also hindered one of his servants from being baptized. I came back to St. John's, and home to Shelburn. Then I was sent for to Preston, it may be four miles from Halifax, over against it, on the other side of the river. Five converted persons who lived there, desired to be baptized and join the church. I baptized them, and administered the Lord's supper to them at Preston, and left brother Hector Peters, one of my Elders, with them. In returning to Shelburn, with about 30 passengers, we were blown off into the sea, and lost our course. I had no blanket to cover me, and got frost-bitten in both my legs up to my knees, and was so ill when I came towards land, that I could not walk. The church met me at the river side, and carried me home. Afterwards, when I could walk a little, I wanted to speak of the Lord's goodness, and the brethren made a wooden sledge, and drew me to Meeting. In the spring of the year I could walk again, but have never been strong since.

The next fall, Agent (afterwards Governor) Clarkson came to Halifax, about settling the new colony at Sierra Leone. The White people in Nova Scotia were very unwilling that we should go, though they had been very cruel to us, and treated many of us as bad as though we had been slaves.*⁴ They attempted to persuade us that if we went away we should be made slaves again. The brethren and sisters all round at St. John's, Halifax, and other places, Mr. Wesley's people and all, consulted what was best to do, and sent in their names to me, to give to Mr. Clarkson, and I was to tell him that they were willing to go. I carried him their names, and he appointed to meet us at Birch Town the next day. We gathered together there, in the Meeting-house of brother Moses, a blind man, one of Mr. Wesley's preachers. Then the Governor read the proclamation, which contained what was offered, in case we had a mind willingly to go, and the greatest part of us were pleased and agreed to go. We appointed a day over at Shelburn, when the names were to be given to the Governor. Almost all the Baptists went, except a few of the sisters whose husbands were inclined to go back to New York; and sister Lizze, a Quebec Indian, and brother Lewis, her husband, who was an half Indian, both of whom were converted under my ministry, and had been baptized by me. There are a few scattered Baptists yet at Shelburn, St. John's, Jones's Harbour, and Ragged Island, beside the congregations at the other places I mentioned before. The meeting-house lot, and all our land at Shelburn, it may be half an acre, was sold to merchant Black for about 7£.

We departed and called at Liverpool, a place I mentioned before. I preached a farewel sermon there; I longed to do it. Before I left the town, Major Collins, who with his wife used to hear me at this place, was very kind to me, and gave me some salted herrings, which were very acceptable all the way to Sierra Leone. We sailed from Liverpool to Halifax, where we tarried three or four weeks, and I preached from house to house, and my farewel sermon in Mr. Marchington's Methodist Meeting-house. There is also a Mr. William Black, at Halifax, a smart preacher, one of Mr Wesley's, who baptizes those Christians who desire it by immersion.†⁵

Our passage from Halifax to Sierra Leone was seven weeks, in which we had very stormy weather. Several persons died on the voyage, of a catching fever, among whom were three of my Elders, Sampson Colwell, a loving man, Peter Richards, and John Williams.

There was great joy to see the land. The high mountain, at some distance from Free-town, where we now live, appeared like a cloud to us. I preached the first Lord's day, it was a blessed time, under a sail, and so I did for several weeks after. We then erected a hovel for a Meeting-house, which is made of posts put into the ground, and poles over our heads, which are covered with grass. While I was preaching under the sails, sisters Patty Webb and Lucy Lawrence were converted, and they, with old sister Peggy, brother Bill Taylor, and brother Sampson Haywood, three who were awakened before they came this voyage, have since been baptized in the river.

On the voyage from Halifax to Sierra Leone, I asked the Governor if I might not hereafter go to England? and some time after we arrived there, I told him I wished to see the Baptist brethren who live in his country. He was a very kind man to me and to every body; he is very free and good natured, and used to come to hear me preach, and would sometimes sit down at our private meetings; and he liked that I should call my last child by his name. And I sent to Mr. Henry Thornton, O what a blessed man is that! he is brother, father, every thing. He ordered me five guineas, and I had leave to come over. When I came away from Sierra Leone, I preached a farewel sermon to the church, and encouraged them to look to the Lord, and submit to one another, and regard what is said to them by my three Elders, brethren Hector Peters, and John Colbert, who are two exhorters, and brother John Ramsey.

A FEW, from NUMEROUS, TESTIMONIALS to the CHARACTER
of Mr. DAVID GEORGE.

Shelburn, Nova Scotia, Oct. 22, 1790.

I HAVE known the bearer, Mr[.] David George, above five years in this settlement, and know that he hath conducted himself like a good christian; and he is a very industrious good citizen.

GEO. WHITE, *Justice of Peace.*

THESE are to certify, that David George, a Baptist preacher, is an inhabitant of the town of Shelburn, and province of Nova Scotia; That he bears a good character, is charitable, sober, honest, and industrious, and is entitled to the attention of all well-disposed people. Witness my hand this second day of December, 1791.

STEPHEN SKINNER, *Agent for the District of Shelburn.*

Ship York, Sierra Leone, 10th Dec. 1792.
My Dear Friends,

I BEG leave to recommend to your brotherly love and Christian kindness, the bearer of this letter, Mr. David George, as a sincere Christian, and an humble, diligent, and faithful minister of the word of God, which has ever been blessed from his lips, as it has always been exemplified in his conversation. He is connected with Christians of the Baptist profession, but his heart embraces, with ingenuous love, all who love God and our Saviour Jesus Christ. His intention, in visiting England, is to see and converse with Christians of all denominations, and particularly to acquaint himself with the Baptist ministers; hoping by these means to increase in Christian knowledge, and to be still better qualified for administering the word of God. I earnestly request you, for Christ's sake, to shew him all kind offices, particularly to introduce him to the most humble, pious, experienced Christians of your acquaintance; not much among those who move in the circle of fashionable christianity. I remain, your affectionate Friend and servant,

MELVILL HORNE*.[6]

TO REV. JOHN NEWTON,
REV. RICH. CECIL,
REV. HENRY FOSTER,
REV. MR. SCOTT.

GOVERNOR Clarkson, in the most unreserved manner, assured me that he esteemed David George as his brother, and that he believes him to be the best man, without exception, in the colony at Sierra Leone.

EDITOR.

A

CHARGE

Delivered to the Brethren of the

AFRICAN LODGE

On the 25th of June, 1792.

At the Hall of Brother WILLIAM SMITH,

IN CHARLESTOWN.

By the Right Worshipful Master

PRINCE HALL.

Printed at the Request of the Lodge.

Printed and Sold at the Bible and Heart, Cornhill,
Boston.

A CHARGE, &C.

DEARLY and well beloved Brethren of the African Lodge, as through the goodness and mercy of God, we are once more met together, in order to celebrate the Festival of St. John the Baptist; it is requisite that we should on these public days, and when we appear in form, give some reason as a foundation for our so doing, but as this has been already done, in a discourse delivered in substance by our late Reverend Brother *John Marrant*, and now in print,

I shall at this time endeavour to raise part of the superstructure, for howsoever good the foundation may be, yet without this it will only prove a Babel. I shall therefore endeavour to shew the duty of a Mason; and the first thing is, that he believes in one supreme Being, that he is the great Architect of this visible world, and that he governs all things here below by his almighty power, and his watchful eye is over all our works. Again we must be good subjects to the laws of the land in which we dwell, giving honour to our lawful Governors and Magistrates, giving honour to whom honour is due; and that we have no hand in any plots or conspiracies or rebellion, or side or assist in them: for when we consider the bloodshed, the devastation of towns and cities that hath been done by them, what heart can be so hard as not to pity those our distrest brethren, and keep at the greatest distance from them. However just it may be on the side of the opprest, yet it doth not in the least, or rather ought not, abate that love and fellow-feeling which we ought to have for our brother fellow men.

The next thing is love and benevolence to all the whole family of mankind, as God's make and creation, therefore we ought to love them all, for love or hatred is of the whole kind, for if I love a man for the sake of the image of God which is on him, I must love all, for he made all, and upholds all, and we are dependant upon him for all we do enjoy and expect to enjoy in this world and that which is to come.—Therefore he will help and assist all his fellow-men in distress, let them be of what colour or nation they may, yea even our very enemies, much more a brother Mason. I shall therefore give you a few instances of this from

Holy Writ, and first, how did Abraham prevent the storm, or rebellion that was rising between Lot's servants and his? Saith Abraham to Lot, let there be no strife I pray thee between me and thee, for the land is before us, if you will go to the left, then I will go to the right, and if you will go to the right, then I will go to the left. They divided and peace was restored. I will mention the compassion of a blackman to a Prophet of the Lord, Ebedmelech, when he heard that Jeremiah was cast into the dungeon, he made intercession for him to the King, and got liberty to take him out from the jaws of death. See Jer. xxxviii 7–13.

Also the prophet Elisha after he had led the army of the Eramites blindfold into Samaria, when the King in a deriding manner said, my *Father* (not considering that he was as much their Father as his) shall I smite, or rather kill them out of the way, as not worthy to live on the same earth, or draw the same air with himself; so eager was he to shed his brethren's blood, that he repeats his blood-thirsty demand, but the Prophet after reproaching him therefor, answers him no, but set bread and water before them; or in other words, give them a feast and let them go home in peace. See 2 Kings, vi. 22.23.

I shall just mention the good deeds of the Samaritan, though at that time they were looked upon as unworthy to eat, drink or trade with their fellow-men, at least by the Jews; see the pity and compassion he had on a poor distrest and half dead stranger, see Luke x. from 30 to 37. See that you endeavour to do so likewise.—But when we consider the amazing condescending love and pity our blessed Lord had on such poor worms as we are, as not only to call us his friends, but his brothers, we are lost and can go no further in holy writ for examples to excite us to the love of our fellow-men.—But I am aware of an objection that may arise (for some men will catch at any thing) that is that they were not all Masons, we allow it, and I say that they were not all Christians, and their benevolence to strangers ought to shame us both, that there is so little, so very little of it to be seen in these enlightened days.

Another thing which is the duty of a Mason is, that he pays a strict regard to the stated meetings of the Lodge, for masonry is of a progressive nature, and must be attended to if ever he intends to be a good

Mason; for the man that thinks that because he hath been made a Mason, and is called so, and at the same time will willfully neglect to attend his Lodge, he may be assured he will never make a good Mason, nor ought he to be looked upon as a good member of the craft. For if his example was followed, where would be the Lodge; and besides what a disgrace is it, when we are at our set meetings, to hear that one of our members is at a drinking house, or at a card table, or in some worse company, this brings disgrace on the Craft: Again there are some that attend the Lodge in such a manner that sometimes their absence would be better than their Company (I would not here be understood a brother in disguise, for such an one hath no business on a level floor) for if he hath been displeased abroad or at home, the least thing that is spoken that he thinks not right, or in the least offends him, he will raise his temper to such a height as to destroy the harmony of the whole Lodge; but we have a remedy and every officer ought to see it put in execution.— Another thing a Mason ought to observe, is that he should lend his helping hand to a brother in distress, and relieve him, this we may do various ways; for we may sometimes help him to a cup of cold water, and it may be better to him than a cup of wine. Good advice may be sometimes better than feeding his body, helping him to some lawful employment, better than giving him money; so defending his case and standing by him when wrongfully accused, may be better than cloathing him; better to save a brother's house when on fire, than to give him one. Thus much may suffice.

I shall now cite some of our fore-fathers, for our imitation: and the first shall be Tertullian, who defended the Christians against their heathen false accusations, whom they charged with treason against the empire and Emperor, because of their silent meetings: he proved that to be false for this reason, for in their meetings, they were wont to pray for the prosperity of the Empire of Rome, and him also; and they were accused of being enemies to mankind, how can that be, said he, when their office is to love and pray for all mankind. When they were charged with worshipping the Sun, because they looked towards the East when they prayed; he defended them against this slander also, and proved that they were slandered, slighted and ill-treated, not for any desert of theirs, but only out of hatred of them and their profession.—This friend of the distrest was born in Carthage in Africa, and died Anno Christi, 202.

Take another of the same city, Cyprian, for his fidelity to his profession was such, that he would rather suffer death than betray his trust and the truth of the gospel, or approve of the impious worship of the Gentiles: He was not only Bishop of Carthage, but of Spain and the east, west and northern churches, who died anno Christi, 259.

But I have not time to cite but one more (out of hundreds that I could count of our Fathers, who were not only examples to us, but to many of their nobles and learned,) that is Augustine, who had engraven on his table these words[:]

> He that doth love an absent Friend to jeer,
> May hence depart, no room is for him here.

His saying was that sincere and upright Prayer pierceth heaven, and returns not empty. That it was a shelter to the soul. A sacrifice to God and a scourge to the Devil. There is nothing, said he, more abateth pride and sin than the frequent meditation on death he cannot die ill, that lives well; and seldom doth he die well, that lives ill: Again, if men want wealth, it is not to be unjustly gotten, if they have it they ought by good works to lay it up in heaven: And again, he that hath tasted the sweetness of divine love, will not care for temporal sweetness. The reasonable soul made in the likeness of God, may here find much distraction, but no full satisfaction; not to be without afflictions, but to overcome them is blessedness. Love is as strong as death; as death kills the body, so love of eternal life kills worldly desires and affections. He called Ingratitude the Devil's spunge, wherewith he wipes out all the favours of the Almighty. His prayer was, Lord give first what thou requirest, and then require of me what thou wilt.—This good man died anno Christi, 430.—

The next is Fulgentius, his speech was, why travel I in the world which can yield me no future, nor durable reward, answerable to my pains. Thought it better to weep well, than to rejoice ill, yet if joy be our desire, how much more excellent is their joy, who have a good conscience before God, who dread nothing but sin, study to do nothing but to accomplish the precepts of Christ. Now therefore let me change my course, and as before I endeavoured amongst my noble friends, to prove more noble, so now let my care and employment be among the humble and poor servants of Christ, and become more humble that I may help and instruct my poor and distrest brethren.

Thus my brethren I have quoted a few of your reverend fathers, for your imitation, which I hope you will endeavour to follow, so far as your abilities will permit in your present situation and the disadvantages you labour under on account of your being deprived of the means of education in your younger days, as you see it is at this day with our children, for we see notwithstanding we are rated for that, and other Town charges, we are deprived of that blessing. But be not discouraged, have patience, and look forward to a better day; Hear what the great Architect of the universal world saith, *Æthiopia shall stretch forth her hands unto me.* Hear also the strange, but bold and confident language of *J. Husk*, who just before the Executioner gave the last stroke, said, *I challenge you to meet me an hundred years hence.* But in the mean time let us lay by our recreations, and all superfluities, so that we may have that to educate our rising generation, which was spent in those follies. Make you this beginning, and who knows but God may raise up some friend or body of friends, as he did in *Philadelphia*, to open a School for the blacks here, as that friendly city has done there.

I shall now shew you what progress Masonry hath made since the siege and taking of Jerusalem in the year 70, by Titus Vespasian, after a long and bloody siege, a million of souls having been slain, or had perished in the city, it was taken by storm and the city set on fire. There was an order of men called the order of St. John, who besides their other engagements, subscribed to another, by which they bound themselves to keep up the war against the Turks, these men defended the temple when on fire, in order to save it, so long, that Titus was amazed and went to see the reason of it; but when he came so near as to behold the *Sanctum Sanctorum*, he was amazed, and shed tears, and said, no wonder these men should so long to save it. He honored them with many honors, and large contributions were made to that order from many kingdoms; and were also knighted. They continued 88 years in Jerusalem, till that city was again retaken by the Turks, after which they resided 104 years in the Cyrean city of Ptolemy, till the remains of the Holy Conquest were lost. Whereupon they settled on the Island of Cyprus, where they continued 18 years, till they found an opportunity to take the Island Rhodes, being masters of that they maintained it for 213 years, and from thence they were called knights of Rhodes, till the year 1530, they took their residence in the Island of Malta, where they have continued to this day, and are distinguished by the name of the knights of Malta. Their first Master was Villaret in the year 1099. Fulco Villaret in the year 1322, took the Island of Rhodes, and was after that distinguished by the title of Grand-Master, which hath devolved to his Successors to this day.

Query, Whether at that day, when there was an African church, and perhaps the largest Christian church on earth, whether there was no African of that order; or whether, if they were all whites, they would refuse to accept them as their fellow Christians and brother Masons; or whether there were any so weak, or rather so foolish, as to say, because they were Blacks, that would make their lodge or army too common or too cheap? Sure this was not our conduct in the late war; for then they marched shoulder to shoulder, brother soldier and brother soldier, to the field of battle; let who will answer; he that despises a black man for the sake of his colour, reproacheth his Maker, and he hath resented it, in the case of Aaron and Miriam. See for this Numbers xii.—

But to return: In the year 1787 (the year in which we received our charter) there were 489 lodges under charge of his late Royal Highness the Duke of Cumberland; whose memory will always be esteemed by every good Mason.

And now, my African brethren, you see what a noble order you are members of. My charge to you is, that you make it your study to live up to the precepts of it, as you know that they are all good; and let it be known this day to the spectators, that you have not been to a feast of Bacchus, but to a refreshment with Masons; and see to it that you behave as such, as well at home as abroad; always to keep in your minds the obligations you are under, both to God and your fellow men. And more so, you my dear brethren of Providence, who are at a distance from, and cannot attend the Lodge here but seldom; yet I hope you will endeavour to communicate to us by letters of your welfare; and remember your obligations to each other, and live in peace and love as brethren.— We thank you for your attendance with us this day, and wish you a safe return.

If thus, we by the grace of God, live up to this our Profession; we may cheerfully go the rounds of the compass of this life. Having lived according to the plumb line of uprightness, the square of justice, the level of truth and sincerity. And when we are come to the end of time, we may then bid farewell to that delightful Sun and Moon, and the other planets, that move so beautifully round her in their orbits, and all things here below, and ascend to that new Jerusalem, where we shall not want these tapers, for God is the Light thereof; where the Wicked cease from troubling, and where the weary are at rest.

> Then shall we hear and see and know,
> All we desir'd and wish'd below,
> And every power find sweet employ,
> In that eternal world of joy.
> Our flesh shall slumber in the ground,
> Till the last trumpet's joyful sound,
> Then burst the chains with sweet surprize,
> And in our Saviour's image rise.

A

CHARGE,

DELIVERED TO THE

AFRICAN LODGE

JUNE 24, 1797

AT MENOTOMY.

BY THE RIGHT WORSHIPFUL

PRINCE HALL.

Published by the Desire of the Members of said Lodge.

—1797—

A
CHARGE

Beloved Brethren of the African Lodge,

'TIS now five years since I deliver'd a Charge to you on some parts and points of Masonry. As one branch or superstructure on the foundation; when I endeavoured to shew you the duty of a Mason to a Mason, and charity or love to all mankind, as the mark and image of the great God, and the Father of the human race.

I shall now attempt to shew you, that it is our duty to sympathise with our fellow men under their troubles: the families of our brethren who are gone: we hope to the Grand Lodge above, here to return no more. But the cheerfulness that you have ever had to relieve them, and ease their burdens, under their sorrows, will never be forgotten by them; and in this manner you will never be weary in doing good.

But my brethren, although we are to begin here, we must not end here; for only look around you and you will see and hear of numbers of our fellow men crying out with holy Job, Have pity on me, O my friends, for the hand of the Lord hath touched me. And this is not to be confined to parties or colours; not to towns or states; not to a kingdom, but to the kingdoms of the whole earth, over whom Christ the king is head and grand master.

Among these numerous sons and daughters of distress, I shall begin with our friends and brethren; and first, let us see them dragg'd from their native country, by the iron hand of tyranny and oppression, from their dear friends and connections, with weeping eyes and aching hearts, to a strange land and strange people, whose tender mercies are cruel; and there to bear the iron yoke of slavery & cruelty till death as a friend shall relieve them. And must not the unhappy condition of these our fellow men draw forth our hearty prayer and wishes for their deliverance from these merchants and traders, whose characters you have in the xviii chap. of the Revelations, 11, 12, & 13 verses, and who knows but these same sort of traders may in a short time, in the like manner, bewail the loss of the African traffick, to their shame and confusion: and if I mistake not, it now begins to dawn in some of the West-India islands; which puts me in mind of a nation (that I have somewhere read of) called Ethiopeans, that cannot change their skin: But God can and will change their conditions, and their hearts too; and let Boston and the world know, that He hath no respect of persons; and that that bulwark of envy, pride, scorn, and contempt, which is so visible to be seen in some and felt, shall fall, to rise no more.

When we hear of the bloody wars which are now in the world, and thousands of our fellow men slain; fathers and mothers bewailing the loss of their sons; wives for the loss of their husbands; towns and cities burnt and destroy'd; what must be the heart-felt sorrow and distress of these poor and unhappy people! Though we cannot help them, the distance being so great, yet we may sympathize with them in their troubles, and mingle a tear of sorrow with them, and do as we are exhorted to— weep with those that weep.

Thus my brethren we see what a chequered world we live in. Sometimes happy in having our wives and children like olive branches about our tables; receiving the bounties of our great Benefactor. The next year, or month, or week, we may be deprived of some of them, and we go mourning about the streets: so in societies; we are this day to celebrate this Feast of St. John's, and the next week we might be called upon to attend a funeral of some one here, as we have experienced since our last in this Lodge. So in the common affairs of life we sometimes enjoy health and prosperity; at another time sickness and adversity, crosses and disappointments.

So in states and kingdoms; sometimes in tranquility; then wars and tumults; rich to-day, and poor to-morrow; which shews that there is not an independent mortal on earth; but dependent one upon the other, from the king to the beggar.

The great law-giver, Moses, who instructed by his father-in-law, Jethro, an Ethiopean, how to regulate his courts of justice, and what sort of men to choose for the different offices; hear now my words, said he, I will give you counsel, and God shall be with you; be thou for the people to Godward, that thou mayest bring the causes unto God, and thou shall teach them ordinances and laws, and shall shew the way wherein they must walk; and the work that they must do: moreover thou shall provide out of all the people, able men, such as fear God, men of truth, hating covetousness, and place such over them, to be rulers of thousands, of hundreds and of tens.

So Moses hearkened to the voice of his father-in-law, and did all that he said.—Exodus xviii. 22–24.

This is the first and grandest lecture that Moses ever received from the mouth of man; for Jethro understood geometry as well as laws, *that* a Mason may plainly see: so a little captive servant maid by whose advice Nomen, the great general of Syria's army, was healed of his leprosy; and by a servant his proud spirit was brought down: 2 Kings v. 3–14. The feelings of this little captive, for this great man, her captor, was so great, that she forgot her state of captivity, and felt for the distress of her enemy. Would to God (said she to her mistress) my lord were with the prophets in Samaria, he should be healed of his leprosy: So after he went to the prophet, his proud host was so haughty that he not only disdain'd the prophet's direction, but derided the good old prophet; and had it not been for his servant, he would have gone to his grave, with a double leprosy, the outward and the inward, in the heart, which is the worst of leprosies; a black heart is worse than a white leprosy.

How unlike was this great general's behaviour to that of as grand a character, and as well beloved by his prince as he was; I mean Obadiah, to a like prophet. See for this 1st Kings xviii. from 7 to the 16th.

And as Obadiah was in the way, behold Elijah met him, and he knew him, and fell on his face, and said, Art not thou, my Lord, Elijah, and he told him, Yea, go and tell thy Lord, behold Elijah is here: and so on to the 16th verse. Thus we see, that great and good men have, and always will have, a respect for ministers and servants of God. Another instance of this is in Acts viii. 27 to 31, of the [Ethiopian] Eunuch, a man of great authority, to Philip, the apostle: here is mutual love and friendship between them. This minister of Jesus Christ did not think himself too good to receive the hand, and ride in a chariot with a black man in the face of day; neither did this great monarch (for so he was) think it beneath him to take a poor servant of the Lord by the hand, and invite him into his carriage, though but with a staff, one coat and no money in his pocket. So our Grand Master, Solomon, was not asham'd to take the Queen of Sheba by the hand, and lead her into his court, at the hour of high twelve, and there converse with her on points of masonry (for if ever there was a female mason in the world she was one) and other curious matters; and gratified her, by shewing her all his riches and curious pieces of architecture in the temple, and in his house: After some time staying with her, he loaded her with much rich presents: he gave her the right hand of affection and parted in love.

I hope that no one will dare openly (tho' in fact the behaviour of some implies as much) to say, as our Lord said on another occasion. Behold a greater than Solomon is here. But yet let them consider that our Grand Master Solomon did not divide the living child, whatever he might do with the dead one, neither did he pretend to make a law to forbid the parties from having free intercourse with one another without the fear of censure, or be turned out of the synagogue.

Now my brethren, as we see and experience, that all things hear are frail and changeable and nothing here to be depended upon: Let us seek those things which are above, which are sure, and stedfast, and unchangeable, and at the same time let us pray to Almighty God, while we remain in the tabernacle, that he would give us the grace of patience and strength to bear up under all our troubles, which at this day God knows we have our share. Patience I say, for were we not possess'd of a great measure of it you could not bear up under the daily insults you meet with in the streets of Boston; much more on public days of recreation, how are you shamefully abus'd, and that at such a degree, that you may truly be said to carry your lives in your hands; and the arrows of death are flying about your heads; helpless old women have their clothes torn off their backs, even to the exposing of their nakedness; and by whom are these disgraceful and abusive actions committed, not by the men born and bred in Boston, for they are better bred; but by a mob or horde of shameless, low-lived, envious, spiteful persons, some of them not long since, servants in gentlemen's kitchings, scouring knives, tending horses, and driving chaise. 'Twas said by a gentleman who saw that filthy behaviour in the common, that in all the places he had been in, he never saw so cruel behaviour in all his life, and that a slave in the West-Indies, on Sunday or holidays enjoys himself and friends without any molestation. Not only this man, but many in town who hath seen their behaviour to you, and that without any provocations, twenty or thirty cowards fall upon one man, have wonder'd at the patience of the Blacks: 'tis not for want of courage in you, for they know that they dare not face you man for man, but in a mob, which we despise, and had rather suffer wrong than to do wrong, to the disturbance of the community and the disgrace of our reputation: for every good citizen doth honor to the laws of the State where he resides.

My brethren, let us not be cast down under these and many other abuses we at present labour under: for the darkest is before the break of day: My brethren, let us remember what a dark day it was with our African brethren six years ago, in the French West-Indies. Nothing but the snap of the whip was heard from morning to evening; hanging, broken on the wheel, burning, and all manner of tortures inflicted on those unhappy people, for nothing else but to gratify their masters pride, wantonness and cruelty: but blessed be God, the scene is changed; they now confess that God hath no respect of persons, and therefore receive them as their friends, and treat them as brothers. Thus doth Ethiopia begin to stretch forth her hand, from a sink of slavery to freedom and equality.

Although you are deprived of the means of education; yet you are not deprived of the means of meditation; by which I mean thinking, hearing and weighing matters, men, and things in your own mind, and making that judgment of them as you think reasonable to satisfy your minds and give an answer to those who may ask you a question. This nature hath furnished you with, without letter learning; and some have made great progress therein, some of those I have heard repeat psalms and hymns, and a great part of a sermon, only by hearing it read or preached and why not in other things in nature: how many of this class of our brethren that follow the seas can foretell a storm some days before it comes; whether it will be a heavy or light, a long or short one; foretell a hurricane, whether it will be destructive or moderate, without any other means than observation and consideration.

So in the observation of the heavenly bodies, this same class without a telescope or other apparatus have through a smoak'd glass observed the eclipse of the sun: One being ask'd what he saw through his smoaked glass? said, Saw, saw, de clipsey, or de clipseys;—and what do you think of it?—stop, dere be two;—right, and what do they look like?—Look like, why if I tell you, they look like two ships sailing one bigger than tother; so they sail by one another, and make no noise. As simple as the answers are they have a meaning, and shew, that God can out of the mouth of babes and Africans shew forth his glory; let us then love and adore him as the God who defends us and supports us and will support us under our pressures, let them be ever so heavy and pressing. Let us by the blessing of God, in whatsoever state we are, or may be in, to be content; for clouds and darkness are about him; but justice and truth is his habitation; who hath said, Vengeance is mine and I will repay it, therefore let us kiss the rod and be still, and see the works of the Lord.

Another thing I would warn you against, is the slavish fear of man, which bringest a snare, saith Solomon. This passion of fear, like pride and envy, hath slain its thousands.—What but this makes so many per-jure themselves; for fear of offending them at home they are a little depending on, for some trifles: A man that is under a panic of fear, is affraid to be alone; you cannot hear of a robbery or house broke open or set on fire, but he hath an accomplice with him, who must share the spoil with him; whereas if he was truly bold, and void of fear, he would keep the whole plunder to himself: so when either of them is detected and not the other, he may be call'd to oath to keep it secret, but through fear, (and that passion is so strong) he will not confess, till the fatal cord is put on his neck; then death will deliver him from the fear of man, and he will confess the truth when it will not be of any good to himself or the community: nor is this passion of fear only to be found in this class of men, but among the great.

What was the reason that our African kings and princes have plunged themselves and their peaceable kingdoms into bloody wars, to the destroying of towns and kingdoms, but the fear of the report of a great gun or the glittering of arms and swords, which struck these kings near the seaports with such a panic of fear, as not only to destroy the peace and happiness of their inland brethren, but plung'd millions of their fellow countrymen into slavery and cruel bondage.

So in other countries; see Felix trembling on his throne. How many Emperors and kings have left their kingdoms and best friends, at the sight of a handful of men in arms: how many have we seen that have left their estates and their friends and ran over to the stronger side as they thought: all through the fear of m[a]n; who is but a worm, and hath no more power to hurt his fellow worm, without the permission of God, than a real worm.

Thus we see my brethren, what a miserable condition it is to be under the slavish fear of men; it is of such a destructive nature to mankind, that the scriptures every where from Genesis to the Revelations warns us against it; and even our blessed Saviour himself forbids us from this slavish fear of man, in his sermon on the mount; and the only way to avoid it is to be in the fear of God: let a man consider the greatness of his power, as the maker and upholder of all things here below, and that in Him we live, and move, and have our being, the giver of the mercies we enjoy here from day to day, and that our lives are in his hands, and that he made the heavens, the sun, moon and stars to move in their various orders; let us thus view the greatness of God, and then turn our eyes on mortal man, a worm, a shade, a wafer, and see whether he is an object of fear or not; on the contrary, you will think him in his best estate, to be but vanity, feeble and a dependent mortal, and stands in need of your help, and cannot do without your assistance, in some way or other; and yet some of these poor mortals will try to make you believe they are Gods, but worship them not. My brethren, let us pay all due respect to all whom God hath put in places of honor over us: do justly and be faithful to them that hire you, and treat them with that respect they may deserve; but worship no man. Worship God, this much is your duty as christians and as masons.

We see then how becoming and necessary it is to have a fellow feeling for our distress'd brethren of the human race, in their troubles, both spiritual and temporal—How refreshing it is to a sick man, to see his sympathising friends around his bed, ready to administer all the relief in their power; although they can't relieve his bodily pain yet they may ease his mind by good instructions and cheer his heart by their company.

How doth it cheer up the heart of a man when his house is on fire, to see a number of friends coming to his relief; he is so transported that he almost forgets his loss and his danger, and fills him with love and gratitude; and their joys and sorrows are mutual.

So a man wreck'd at sea, how must it revive his drooping heart to see a ship bearing down for his relief.

How doth it rejoice the heart of a stranger in a strange land to see the people cheerful and pleasant and are ready to help him.

How did it, think you, cheer the heart of those our poor unhappy African brethren, to see a ship commissioned from God, and from a nation that without flattery saith, that all men are free and are brethren; I say to see them in an instant deliver such a number from their cruel bolts and galling chains, and to be fed like men, and treated like brethren. Where is the man that has the least spark of humanity, that will not rejoice with them; and bless a righteous God who knows how and when to relieve the oppressed, as we see he did in the deliverance of the captives among the Algerines; how sudden were they delivered by the sympathising members of the Congress of the United States, who now enjoy the free air of peace and liberty, to their great joy and surprize, to them and their friends. Here we see the hand of God in various ways, bringing about his own glory for the good of mankind, by the mutual help of their fellow men; which ought to teach us in all our straits, be they what they may, to put our trust in Him, firmly believing, that he is able and will deliver us and defend us against all our enemies; and that no weapon form'd against us shall prosper; only let us be steady and uniform in our walks, speech and behaviour; always doing to all men as we wish and desire they would do to us in the like cases and circumstances.

Live and act as Masons, that you may die as Masons; let those de-

spisers see, altho' many of us cannot read, yet by our searches and re-
searches into men and things, we have supplied that defect, and if they
will let us we shall call ourselves a charter'd lodge, of just and lawful
Masons; be always ready to give an answer to those that ask you a
question; give the right hand of affection and fellowship to whom it
justly belongs let their colour and complexion be what it will: let their
nation be what it may, for they are your brethren, and it is your indispensable duty so to do; let them as Masons deny this, and we & the
world know what to think of them be they ever so grand: for we know
this was Solomon's creed, Solomon's creed did I say, it is the decree of
the Almighty, and all Masons have learnt it: tis plain market language,
and plain and true facts need no apologies.

I shall now conclude with an old p[o]em which I found among some
papers:—

> Let blind admirers handsome faces praise,
> And graceful features to great honor raise,
> The glories of the red and white express,
> I know no beauty but in holiness;
> If God of beauty be the uncreate
> Perfect idea, in this lower state,
> The greatest beauties of an human mould
> Who most resemble Him we justly hold;
> Whom we resemble not in flesh and blood,
> But being pure and holy, just and good:
> May such a beauty fall but to my share,
> For curious shape or face I'll never care.

MEMOIRS of the LIFE of BOSTON KING,
a Black Preacher.
Written by Himself, during his Residence
at Kingswood-School.

IT is by no means an agreeable task to write an account of my Life, yet my gratitude to Almighty GOD, who considered my affliction, and looked upon me in my low estate, who delivered me from the hand of the oppressor, and established my goings, impels me to acknowledge his goodness: And the importunity of many respectable friends, whom I highly esteem, have induced me to set down, as they occurred to my memory, a few of the most striking incidents I have met with in my pilgrimage. I am well aware of my inability for such an undertaking, having only a slight acquaintance with the language in which I write, and being obliged to snatch a few hours, now and then, from pursuits, which to me, perhaps, are more profitable. However, such as it is, I present it to the Friends of Religion and Humanity, hoping that it will be of some use to mankind.

I was born in the Province of South Carolina, 28 miles from Charles-Town. My father was stolen away from Africa when he was young. I have reason to believe that he lived in the fear and love of GOD. He attended to that true Light which lighteth every man that cometh into world. He lost no opportunity of hearing the Gospel, and never omitted praying with his family every night. He likewise read to them, and to as many as were inclined to hear. On the Lord's-Day he rose very early, and met his family: After which he worked in the field till about three in the afternoon, and then went into the woods and read till sun-set: The slaves being obliged to work on the Lord's-Day to procure such things as were not allowed by their masters. He was beloved by his master, and had the charge of the Plantation as a driver for many years. In his old age he was employed as a mill-cutter. Those who knew him, say, that they never heard him swear an oath, but on the contrary, he reproved all who spoke improper words in his hearing. To the utmost of his power he endeavored to make his family happy, and his death was a very great loss to us all. My mother was employed chiefly in attending upon those that were sick, having some knowledge of the virtue of herbs, which she learned from the Indians. She likewise had the care of making the people's clothes, and on these accounts was indulged with many privileges which the rest of the slaves were not.

When I was six years old I waited in the house upon my master. In my 9th year I was put to mind the cattle. Here I learnt from my comrades the horrible sin of Swearing and Cursing. When 12 years old, it pleased GOD to alarm me by a remarkable dream. At mid-day, when the cattle went under the shade of the trees, I dreamt that the world was on fire, and that I saw the supreme Judge defend on his great white Throne! I saw millions of millions of souls; some of whom ascended up to heaven; while others were rejected, and fell into the greatest confusion and despair. This dream made such an impression upon my mind, that I refrained from swearing and bad company, and from that time acknowledged that there was a GOD; but how to serve GOD I knew not. Being obliged to travel in different parts of America with race-horses, I suffered many hardships. Happening one time to lose a boot belonging to the Groom, he would not suffer me to have any shoes all that Winter, which was a great punishment to me. When 16 years old, I was bound apprentice to a trade. After being in the shop about two years, I had the charge of my master's tools, which being very good, were often used by the men, if I happened to be out of the way: When this was the case, or any of them were lost, or misplaced, my master beat me severely, striking me upon the head, or any other part without mercy. One time in the holy-days, my master and the men being from home, and the care of the house devolving upon me and the younger apprentices, the house was broke open, and robbed of many valuable articles, thro' the negligence of the apprentice who had then the charge of it. When I came home in the evening, and saw what had happened, my consternation was inconceivable, as all that we had in the world could not make good the loss. The week following, when the master came to town, I was beat in a most unmerciful manner, so that I was not able to do any thing for a fortnight. About eight months after, we were employed in building a store-house, and nails were very dear at that time, it being in the American war, so that the work-men had their nails weighed out to them; on this account they made the younger apprentices watch the nails while they were at dinner. It being my lot one day to take care of them, which I did till an apprentice returned to his work, and then I went to dine.

In the mean time he took away all the nails belonging to one of the journeymen, and he being of very violent temper, accused me to the master with stealing of them. For this offence I was beat and tortured most cruelly, and was laid up three weeks before I was able to do any work. My proprietor, hearing of the bad usage I received, came to town, and severely reprimanded my master for beating me in such a manner, threatening him, that if he ever heard the like again, he would take me away and put me to another master to finish my time, and make him pay for it. This had a good effect, and he behaved much better to me, the two succeeding years, and I began to acquire a proper knowledge of my trade. My master being apprehensive that Charles-Town was in danger on account of the war, removed into the country, about 38 miles off. Here we built a large house for Mr. Waters, during which time the English took Charles-Town. Having obtained leave one day to see my parents, who lived about 12 miles off, and it being late before I could go, I was obliged to borrow one of Mr. Waters's horses; but a servant of my master's, took the horse from me to go a little journey, and stayed two or three days longer than he ought. This involved me in the greatest perplexity, and I expected the severest punishment, because the gentleman to whom the horse belonged was a very bad man, and knew not how to shew mercy. To escape his cruelty, I determined to go to Charles-Town, and throw myself into the hands of the English. They received me readily, and I began to feel the happiness of liberty, of which I knew nothing before, altho' I was much grieved at first, to be obliged to leave my friends, and reside among strangers. In this situation I was seized with the small-pox, and suffered great hardships; for all the Blacks affected with that disease, were ordered to be carried a mile from the camp, lest the soldiers should be infected, and disabled from marching. This was a grievous circumstance to me and many others. We lay sometimes a whole day without any thing to eat or drink; but Providence sent a man, who belonged to the York volunteers whom I was acquainted with, to my relief. He brought me such things as I stood in need of; and by the blessing of the Lord I began to recover.

By this time, the English left the place; but as I was unable to march with the army, I expected to be taken by the enemy. However when they came, and understood that we were ill of the small-pox, they precipitately left us for fear of the infection. Two days after, the waggons were sent to convey us to the English Army, and we were put into a little cottage, (being 25 in number) about a quarter of a mile from the Hospital.

Being recovered, I marched with the army to Chamblem. When we came to the head-quarters, our regiment was 35 miles off. I stayed at the head-quarters three weeks, during which time our regiment had an engagement with the Americans, and the man who relieved me when I was ill of the small-pox, was wounded in the battle, and brought to the hospital. As soon as I heard of his misfortune, I went to see him, and tarried with him in the hospital six weeks, till he recovered; rejoicing that it was in my power to return him the kindness he had shewed me. From thence I went to a place about 35 miles off, where we stayed two months: at the expiration of which, a express came to the Colonel to decamp in fifteen minutes. When these orders arrived I was at a distance from the camp, catching some fish for the captain that I waited upon; upon returning to the camp, to my great astonishment, I found all the English were gone, and had left only a few militia. I felt my mind greatly alarmed, but Captain Lewes, who commanded the militia, said, "You need not be uneasy, for you will see your regiment before 7 o'clock to-night." This satisfied me for the present, and in two hours we set off. As we were on the march, the Captain asked, "How will you like me to be your master?" I answered that I was Captain Grey's servant. "Yes," said he; "but I expect they are all taken prisoners before now; and I have been long enough in the English service, and am determined to leave them." These words roused my indignation, and I spoke some sharp things to him. But he calmly replied, "If you do not behave well, I will put you in irons, and give you a dozen stripes every morning." I now perceived that my case was desperate, and that I had nothing to trust to, but to wait the first opportunity for making my escape. The next morning, I was sent with a little boy over the river to an island to fetch the Captain some horses. When we came to the Island we found about fifty of the English horses, that Captain Lewes had stolen from them at different times while they were at Rockmount. Upon our return to the Captain with the horses we were sent for, he immediately set off by himself. I stayed till about 10 o'clock, and then resolved to go to the English army. After traveling 24 miles, I came to a farmer's house, where I tarried all night, and was well used. Early in the morning I continued my journey till I came to the ferry, and found all the boats were on the other side of the river: After anxiously waiting some hours, Major Dial crossed the river, and asked me many questions concerning the regiment to which I belonged. I gave him satisfactory answers, and he ordered the boat to put me over. Being arrived at the head-quarters, I informed my Captain that Mr. Lewes had deserted. I also told him of the horses which Lewes had conveyed to the Island. Three weeks after, our Light-horse went to the Island and burnt his house; they likewise brought back forty of the horses, but he escaped. I tarried with Captain Grey about a year, and then left him, and came to Nelson's-ferry. Here I entered into the service of the commanding officer of that place. But our situation was very precarious, and we expected to be made prisoners every day; for the Americans had 1600 men, not far off; whereas our whole number amounted only to 250: But here were 1200 English about 30 miles off; only we knew not how to inform them of our danger, as the Americans were in possession of the country. Our commander at length determined to send me with a letter, promising me great rewards, if I was successful in the business. I refused going on horse-back, and set off on foot about 3 o'clock in the afternoon; I expected every moment to fall in with the enemy, whom I well knew would shew me no mercy. I went on without interruption, till I got within six miles of my journey's end, and then was alarmed with a great noise a little before me. But I stepped out of the road, and fell flat upon my face till they were gone by. I then arose, and praised the Name of the Lord for his great mercy, and again pursued my journey, till I came to Mums-corner tavern. I knocked at the door, but they blew out the candle. I knocked again, and entreated the master to open the door. At last he came with a frightful countenance, and said, "I thought it was the Americans; for they were here about an hour ago, and I thought they were returned again." I asked, How many were there?

he answered, "about one hundred." I desired him to saddle his horse for me, which he did, and went with me himself. When we had gone about two miles, we were stopped by the picket-guard, till the Captain came out with 30 men: As soon as he knew that I had brought an express from Nelson's-ferry, he received me with great kindness, and expressed his approbation of my courage and conduct in this dangerous business. Next morning, Colonel Small gave me three shillings, and many fine promises, which were all that I ever received for this service from him. However he sent 600 men to relieve the troops at Nelson's-ferry.

Soon after I went to Charles-Town, and entered on board a man of war. As we were going to Chesepeak-bay, we were at the taking of a rich prize. We stayed in the bay two days, and then sailed for New-York, where I went on shore. Here I endeavoured to follow my trade, but for want of tools was obliged to relinquish it, and enter into service. But the wages were so low that I was not able to keep myself in clothes, so that I was under the necessity of leaving my master and going to another. I stayed with him four months, but he never paid me, and I was obliged to leave him also, and work about the town until I was married. A year after I was taken very ill, but the Lord raised me up again in about five weeks. I then went out in a pilot-boat. We were at sea eight days, and had only provisions for five, so that we were in danger of starving. On the 9th day we were taken by an American whale-boat. I went on board them with a chearful countenance, and asked for bread and water, and made very free with them. They carried me to Brunswick, and used me well. Notwithstanding which, my mind was sorely distressed at the thought of being again reduced to slavery, and separated from my wife and family; and at the same time it was exceeding difficult to escape from my bondage, because the river at Amboy was above a mile over, and likewise another to cross at Staten-Island. I called to remembrance the many great deliverances the Lord had wrought for me, and besought him to save me this once, and I would serve him all the days of my life. While my mind was thus exercised, I went into the jail to see a lad whom I was acquainted with at New-York. He had been taken prisoner, and attempted to make his escape, but was caught 12 miles off: They tied him to the tail of a horse, and in this manner brought him back to Brunswick. When I saw him, his feet were fastened in the stocks, and at night both his hands. This was a terrifying sight to me, as I expected to meet with the same kind of treatment, if taken in the act of attempting to regain my liberty. I was thankful that I was not confined in a jail, and my master used me as well as I could expect; and indeed the slaves about Baltimore, Philadelphia, and New-York, have as good victuals as many of the English; for they have meat once a day, and milk for breakfast and supper; and what is better than all, many of the masters send their slaves to school at night, that they may learn to read the Scriptures. This is a privilege indeed. But alas, all these enjoyments could not satisfy me without liberty! Sometimes I thought, if it was the will of GOD that I should be a slave, I was ready to resign myself to his will; but at other times I could not find the least desire to content myself in slavery.

Being permitted to walk about when my work was done, I used to go to the ferry, and observed, that when it was low water the people waded across the river; tho' at the same time I saw there were guards posted at the place to prevent the escape of prisoners and slaves. As I was at prayer one Sunday evening, I thought the Lord heard me, and would mercifully deliver me. Therefore putting my confidence in him, about one o'clock in the morning I went down to the river side, and found the guards were either asleep or in the tavern. I instantly entered into the river, but when I was a little distance from the opposite shore, I heard the sentinels disputing among themselves: One said, "I am sure I saw a man cross the river." Another replied, "There is no such thing." It seems they were afraid to fire at me, or make an alarm, lest they should be punished for their negligence. When I had got a little distance from the shore, I fell down upon my knees, and thanked GOD for this deliverance. I travelled till about five in the morning, and then concealed myself till seven o'clock at night, when I proceeded forward, thro' bushes and marshes, near the road, for fear of being discovered. When I came to the river, opposite Staten-Island, I found a boat; and altho' it was very near a whale-boat, yet I ventured into it, and cutting the rope, got safe over. The commanding officer, when informed of my case, gave me a passport, and I proceeded to New-York.

When I arrived at New-York, my friends rejoiced to see me once more restored to liberty, and joined me in praising the Lord for his mercy and goodness. But notwithstanding this great deliverance, and the promises I had made to serve GOD, yet my good resolutions soon vanished away like the morning dew: The love of this world extinguished my good desires, and stole away my heart from GOD, so that I rested in a mere form of religion for near three years. About which time, (in 1783,) the horrors and devastation of war happily terminated, and peace was restored between America and Great Britain, which diffused universal joy among all parties, except us, who had escaped from slavery, and taken refuge in the English army; for a report prevailed at New-York, that all the slaves, in number 2000, were to be delivered up to their masters, altho' some of them had been three or four years among the English. This dreadful rumour filled us all with inexpressible anguish and terror, especially when we saw our old masters coming from Virginia, North-Carolina, and other parts, and seizing upon their slaves in the streets of New-York, or even dragging them out of their beds. Many of the slaves had very cruel masters, so that the thoughts of returning home with them embittered life to us. For some days we lost our appetite for food, and sleep departed from our eyes. The English had compassion upon us in the day of distress, and issued out a Proclamation, importing, That all slaves should be free, who had taken refuge in the British lines, and claimed the sanction and privileges of the Proclamations respecting the security and protection of Negroes. In consequence of this, each of us received a certificate from the commanding officer at New-York, which dispelled all our fears, and filled us with joy and gratitude. Soon after, ships were fitted out, and furnished with every necessary for conveying us to Nova Scotia. We arrived at Burch Town in the month of August, where we all safely landed. Every family had a lot of land, and we exerted all our strength in order to build comfortable huts before the cold weather set in.

That Winter, the work of religion began to revive among us, and many were convinced of the sinfulness of sin, and turned from the error of their ways. It pleased the Lord to awaken my wife under the preaching of Mr. Wilkinson; she was struck to the ground, and cried out for mercy: she continued in great distress for near two hours, when they sent for me. At first I was much displeased, and refused to go; but presently my mind relented, and I went to the house, and was struck with astonishment at the sight of her agony. In about six days after, the Lord spoke peace to her soul: she was filled with divine consolation, and walked in the light of GOD's countenance about nine months. But being unacquainted with the corruptions of her own heart, she again gave place to bad tempers, and fell into great darkness and distress. Indeed, I never saw any person, either before or since, so overwhelmed with anguish of spirit on account of backsliding, as she was. The trouble for her soul brought affliction upon her body, which confined her to bed a year and a half.

However, the Lord was pleased to sanctify her afflictions, and to deliver her from all her fears. He brought her out of the horrible pit, and set her soul at perfect liberty. The joy and happiness which she now experienced, were too great to be concealed, and she was enabled to testify of the goodness and loving-kindness of the Lord, with such liveliness and power, that many were convinced by her testimony, and sincerely sought the Lord. As she was the first person at Burch Town that experienced deliverance from evil tempers, and exhorted and urged others to seek and enjoy the same blessing, she was not a little opposed by some of our Black brethren. But these trials she endured with the meekness and patience becoming a christian; and when Mr. FREEBORN GARRETTSON came to Burch Town to regulate the society and form them into classes, he encouraged her to hold fast her confidence, and cleave to the Lord with her whole heart.

Soon after my wife's conversion, the Lord strove powerfully with me. I felt myself a miserable wretched sinner, so that I could not rest night or day. I went to Mr. BROWN, one evening, and told him my case. He received me with great kindness and affection, and intreated me to seek the Lord with all my heart. The more he spoke to me, the more my distress increased; and when he went to prayer, I found myself burdened with a load of guilt too heavy for me to bear. On my return home, I had to pass thro' a little wood, where I intended to fall down on my knees and pray for mercy; but every time I attempted, I was so terrified, that I thought my hair stood upright, and that the earth moved beneath my feet. I hastened home in great fear and horror, and yet hoped that the Lord would bless me as well as my neighbours: for the work of the Lord prospered greatly among us, for that sometimes in our class-meetings, six or seven persons found peace, before we were dismissed.

Notwithstanding I was a witness of the great change which many experienced, yet I suffered the enemy, through unbelief, to gain such advantage over me, that instead of rejoicing with them, and laying hold of the same blessing, I was tempted to envy their happiness, and sunk deeper into darkness and misery. I thought I was not worthy to be among the people of GOD, nor even to dwell in my own house; but was fit only to reside among the beasts of the forest. This drove me out into the woods, when the snow lay upon the ground three or four feet deep, with a blanket, and a fire-brand in my hand. I cut the boughs of the spruce tree and kindled a fire. In this lonely situation I frequently intreated the Lord for mercy. Sometimes I thought that I felt a change wrought in my mind, so that I could rejoice in the Lord; but I soon fell again thro' unbelief into distracting doubts and fears, and evil-reasonings. The devil persuaded me that I was the most miserable creature upon the face of the earth, and that I was predestinated to be damned before the foundation of the world. My anguish was so great, that when night appeared, I dreaded it as much as the grave.

I laboured one year under these distressing temptations, when it pleased GOD to give me another offer of mercy. In 1784, I and sixteen persons worked for Mrs. ROBINSON; all of them were devoted to GOD, except myself and two others. The divine presence was with these men, and every night and morning they kept a prayer-meeting, and read some portion of Scripture. On the 5th of January, as one of them was reading the Parable of the Sower, the word came with power to my heart. I stood up and desired him to explain the parable; and while he was shewing me the meaning of it, I was deeply convinced that I was one of the stony-ground hearers. When I considered how many offers of mercy I had abused from day to day, and how many convictions I had trifled away, I was astonished that the Lord had bourne with me so long. I was at the same time truly thankful that he gave me a desire to return to him, and resolved by the grace of GOD to set out afresh for the kingdom of Heaven.

As my convictions increased, so did my desires after the Lord; and in order to keep them alive, I resolved to make a covenant with him in the most solemn manner I was able. For this purpose I went into the garden at midnight, and kneeled down upon the snow, lifting up my hands, eyes, and heart to Heaven; and intreated the Lord, who had called me by his Holy Spirit out of ignorance and wickedness, that he would increase and strengthen my awakenings and desires, and impress my heart with the importance of eternal things; and that I might never find rest or peace again, till I found peace with him, and received a sense of his pardoning love. The Lord mercifully looked down upon me, and gave me such a sight of my fallen state, that I plainly saw, without an interest in Christ, and an application of his atoning blood to my conscience, I should be lost to all eternity. This led me to a diligent use of all the means of Grace, and to forsake and renounce everything that I knew to be sinful.

The more convictions increased, and the more I felt the wickedness of my own heart; yet the Lord helped me to strive against evil, so that temptations instead of prevailing against me, drove me nearer to him. The first Sunday in March, as I was going to the preaching, and was engaged in prayer and meditation, I thought I heard a voice saying to me, "Peace be unto thee!" I stopped, and looked round about, to see if any one was near me. But finding myself alone, I went forward a little way, when the same words were again powerfully applied to my heart, which removed the burden of misery from it; and while I sat under the sermon, I was more abundantly blessed. Yet in the afternoon, doubts and fears again arose in my mind. Next morning I resolved like Jacob, not to let the Lord go till he blessed me indeed. As soon as my wife went out, I locked the door, and determined not to rise from my knees until the Lord fully revealed his pardoning love. I continued in prayer about half an hour, when the Lord again spoke to my heart, "Peace be unto thee." All my doubts and fears vanished away: I saw, by faith, heaven opened to my view; and Christ and his holy angels rejoicing over me. I was now enabled to believe in the name of Jesus, and my Soul was dissolved into love. Every thing appeared to me in a different light to what they did before; and loved every living creature upon the face of the earth. I could truly say, I was now become a new creature. All tormenting and slavish fear, and all the guilt and weight of sin were done away. I was so exceedingly blessed, that I could no longer conceal my happiness, but went to my brethren and told them what the Lord had done for my soul.

I continued to rejoice in a sense of the favour and love of GOD for about six weeks, and then the enemy assaulted me again; he poured in a flood of temptations and evil-reasonings; and suggested, that I was deceiving myself: The temptation alarmed and dejected me and my mind was discomposed. Then the enemy pursued his advantage, and insulted me with his cruel upbraidings, insinuating,—"What is become of all your joy, that you spoke of a few days ago? You see, there is nothing in it." But blessed be the Lord, he did not suffer the enemy to rejoice long over me; for while I heard Mr. GARRETTSON preaching from John ix. 25, "One thing I know, that whereas I was blind, now I see;" the words were so suitable to my experience that I was encouraged to exercise fresh faith upon the Lord; and he removed every doubt and fear; and re-established me in his peace and favour. I could say with the Psalmist, "the fear of the Lord is beginning of wisdom," for I had him always before my eyes, and in some measure walked in the light, as he is in the light. I found his ways were ways of pleasantness, and all his paths were peace.

Soon after, I found a great concern for the salvation of others; and was constrained to visit my poor ungodly neighbours, and exhort them to fear the Lord, and seek him while he might be found. Those that were under convictions, I prayed with them, and pointed them to the

Saviour, that they might obtain the same mercy he had bestowed upon me. In the year 1785, I began to exhort both in families and prayer-meetings, and the Lord graciously afforded me his assisting presence.

The Goodness and Mercy of GOD supported me in the various trials and exercises which I went through; nevertheless I found great reluctance to officiate as an exhorter among the people, and had many doubts and fears respecting my call to that duty, because I was conscious of my great ignorance and insufficiency for a work of such importance, and was often overwhelmed with grief and sorrow: But the Lord relieved me by impressing upon my mind these words, "I will send, by whom I will send." In the year 1787, I found my mind drawn out to commiserate my poor brethren in Africa; and especially when I considered that we who had the happiness of being brought up in a christian land, where the Gospel is preached, were notwithstanding our great privileges, involved in gross darkness and wickedness; I thought, what a wretched condition then must those poor creatures be in, who never heard the Name of GOD or of CHRIST; nor had any instruction afforded them with respect to a future judgment. As I had not the least prospect at that time of ever seeing Africa, I contented myself with pitying and praying for the poor benighted inhabitants of that country which gave birth to my forefathers. I laboured in Burchtown and Shelwin two years, and the word was blessed to the conversion of many, most of whom continued stedfast in the good way to the heavenly kingdom.

About this time the country was visited with a dreadful famine, which not only prevailed at Burchtown, but likewise at Chebucto, Annapolis, Digby, and other places. Many of the poor people were compelled to sell their best gowns for five pounds of flour, in order to support life. When they had parted with all their clothes, even to their blankets, several of them fell down dead in the streets, thro' hunger. Some killed and eat their dogs and cats; and poverty and distress prevailed on every side; so that to my great grief I was obliged to leave Burchtown, because I could get no employment. I traveled from place to place, to procure the necessaries of life, but in vain. At last I came to Shelwin on the 20th of January. After walking from one street to the other, I met with Capt.

Selex, and he engaged me to make him a chest. I rejoiced at the offer, and returning home, set about it immediately. I worked all night, and by eight o'clock next morning finished the chest, which I carried to the Captain's house, thro' the snow which was three feet deep. But to my great disappointment he rejected it. However he gave me directions to make another. On my way home, being pinched with hunger and cold, I fell down several times, thro' weakness, and expected to die upon the spot. But even in this situation, I found my mind resigned to the divine will, and rejoiced in the midst of tribulation; for the Lord delivered me from all murmurings and discontent, altho' I had but one pint of Indian meal left for the support of myself and wife. Having finished another chest, I took it to my employer the next day; but being afraid he would serve me as he had done before, I took a saw along with me in order to sell it. On the way, I prayed that the Lord would give me a prosperous journey, and was answered to the joy of my heart, for Capt. Selex paid me for the chest in Indian-corn; and the other chest I sold for 2s. 6d. and the saw for 3s. 9d. altho' it cost me a guinea; yet I was exceeding thankful to procure a reprieve from the dreadful anguish of perishing by famine. O what a wonderful deliverance did GOD work for me that day! And he taught me to live by faith, and to put my trust in him, more than I ever had done before.

While I was admiring the goodness of GOD, and praising him for the help he afforded me in the day of trouble, a gentleman sent for me, and engaged me to make three flat-bottomed boats for the salmon-fishery, at 1£. each. The gentleman advanced two baskets of Indian-corn, and found nails and tar for the boats. I was enabled to finish the work by the time appointed, and he paid me honestly. Thus did the kind hand of Providence interpose in my preservation; which appeared still greater, upon viewing the wretched circumstances of many of my black brethren at that time, who were obliged to sell themselves to the merchants, some for two or three years; and others for five or six years. The circumstances of the white inhabitants were likewise very distressing, owing to their great imprudence in building large houses, and striving to excel one another in this piece of vanity. When their money was almost expended, they began to build small fishing vessels; but alas, it was too late to repair their error. Had they been wise enough at first to have turned their attention to the fishery, instead of the fine houses, the place would soon have been in a flourishing condition; whereas it was reduced in a short time to a heap of ruins, and its inhabitants were compelled to flee to other parts of the continent for sustenance.

Next Winter, the same gentleman employed me to build him some more boats. When they were finished he engaged me to go with him to Chebucto, to build a house, to which place he intended to remove his family. He agreed to give me 2£. per month, and a barrel of mackrel, and another of herrings, for my next Winter's provision. I was glad to embrace this offer, altho' it gave me much pain to leave the people of GOD. On the 20th of April I left my wife and friends, and sailed for Chebucto. When we arrived at that place, my employer had not all the men necessary for the fishing voyage; he therefore solicited me to go with him; to which I objected, that I was engaged to build a house for him. He answered, that he could purchase a house for less money than build one, and that if I would go with him to Bayshallow, I should greatly oblige him; to which I at length consented. During our stay at Chebucto, perceiving that the people were exceeding ignorant of religious duties, and given up to all manner of wickedness, I endeavoured to exhort them to flee from the wrath to come, and to turn unto the Lord Jesus. My feeble labours were attended with a blessing to several of them, and they began to seek the Lord in sincerity and truth, altho' we met with some persecution from the baser sort.

On the 2d of June we sailed for Bayshallow; but in the Gulph of St. Lawrence we met with a great storm, and expected every moment would be our last. In about 24 hours the tempest abated, and was succeeded by a great fog, in which we lost the company of one of our vessels, which had all our provisions on board for the fishing season. July 18, we arrived at the River Pisguar, and made all necessary preparations for taking the salmon; but were greatly alarmed on account of the absence of the vessel belonging to us; but on the 29th, to our great joy, she arrived safe; which was four days before the salmon made their appearance. We now entered upon our business with alacrity, and Providence favoured us with good success.

My employer, unhappy for himself as well as others, was as horrible a swearer as I ever met with. Sometimes he would stamp and rage at the men, when they did not please him, in so dreadful a manner, that I was stupified like a drunken man, and knew not what I was doing. My soul was exceedingly grieved at his ungodly language; I repented that I ever entered into his service, and was even tempted to murmur against the good Providence of GOD. But the case of righteous Lot, whose soul was vexed day by day with the ungodly deeds of the people of Sodom, occurred to my mind; and I was resolved to reprove my master when a proper opportunity offered. I said to him, "Dear sir, don't you know that the Lord hath declared, that he will not hold them guiltless who take his Name in vain? And that all profane swearers shall have their portion in the lake that burneth with fire and brimstone?" He bore the reproof with patience, and scarce ever gave me an unkind word; not-withstanding which, he persisted in his impiety, and the men, encouraged by his example, imitated him to the utmost of their ability. Being much grieved with their sinful deeds, I retired into the woods for meditation and prayer. One day when I was alone, and recollecting the patient sufferings of the servants of GOD for the Truth's sake, I was ashamed of myself, on account of the displeasure I felt at my ship-mates, because they would not be persuaded by me to forsake their sins. I saw my folly in imagining that it was in my power to turn them from their evil ways. The Lord shewed me, that this was his prerogative; and that my duty consisted in intreating them, and bearing patiently their insults, as GOD for Christ's sake had borne with me. And he gave me a resolution to reprove in a right spirit, all that swore in my presence.

Next day my master began to curse and swear in his usual manner. When I saw him a little calm, I intreated him not to come into the boat any more, but give me orders how to proceed; assuring him, that I would do every thing according to his pleasure to the utmost of my power; but that if he persisted in his horrible language, I should not be able to discharge my duty. From that time he troubled me no more, and I found myself very comfortable, having no one to disturb me. On the 11th of August we sailed for home; and my master thanked me for my fidelity and diligence, and said, "I believe if you had not been with me, I should not have made half a voyage this season." On the 16th we arrived at Chebucto, and unloaded the vessels. When this business was finished, we prepared for the herring-fishery in Pope's Harbour, at which place we arrived on the 27th of August, and began to set the nets and watch for the herrings. One day as we were attending our net at the mouth of the harbour, we dropped one of the oars, and could not recover it; and having a strong west wind, it drove us out to sea. Our alarm was very great, but the kind hand of Providence interposed and saved us; for when we were driven about two miles from our station, the people on shore saw our danger, and immediately sent two boats to our assistance, which came up with us about sun-set, and brought us safe into the harbour.

October 24, we left Pope's Harbour, and came to Halifax, where we were paid off, each man receiving 15£. for his wages; and my master gave me two barrels of fish agreeable to his promise. When I returned home, I was enabled to clothe my wife and myself; and my Winter's store consisted of one barrel of flour, three bushels of corn, nine gallons of treacle, 20 bushels of potatoes which my wife had set in my absence, and the two barrels of fish; so that this was the best Winter I ever saw in Burchtown.

In 1791, I removed to Prestent, where I had the care of the Society by the appointment of Mr. William Black, almost three years. We were in all 34 persons, 24 of whom professed faith in Christ. Sometimes I had a tolerable congregation. But alas, I preached a whole year in that place without seeing any fruit of my labours. On the 24th of Jan. 1792, after preaching in the morning I was greatly distressed, and said to the Lord, "How long shall I be with this people before thy work prospers among them! O Lord GOD! if thou hast called me to preach to my Black Brethren, answer me this day from heaven by converting one sinner, that I may know that thou hast sent me. In the afternoon I preached from James ii. 19. "Thou believest that there is one God; thou doest well. The devils also believe, and tremble." Towards the conclusion of the meeting, the divine presence seemed to descend upon the congregation: Some fell flat upon the ground, as if they were dead; and others cried out aloud for mercy. After prayer, I dismissed the public congregation; but many went away with great reluctance. While the Society was meeting, Miss F—— knocked at the door, and said, "This people is the people of GOD; and their GOD shall be my GOD." She then desired to be admitted among us, that she might declare what the Lord had done for her soul. We opened the door, and she said, "Blessed be the Name of the Lord forever, for I know he hath pardoned my sins for the sake of his Son Jesus Christ. My mind has been so greatly distressed for these three weeks, that I could scarcely sleep; and particularly the last night I did not close mine eyes; but while I was under the preaching all my grief vanished away, and such light broke in upon my soul, that I was enabled to believe unto salvation. O praise the Lord with me, all ye that love his Name; for he hath done great things for my soul." All the Society were melted into tears of joy, when they heard her declarations: and she immediately entered into connexion with us, and many others in a few weeks after. From this time the work of the Lord prospered among us in a wonderful manner. I blessed GOD for answering my petition, and was greatly encouraged to persevere in my labours.

The Blacks attended the preaching regularly; but when any of the White inhabitants were present, I was greatly embarrassed, because I had no learning, and I knew that they had. But one day Mr. Ferguson, and several other gentlemen came to hear me; the Lord graciously assisted me, and gave me much liberty in speaking the Truth in my simple manner. The gentlemen afterwards told our Preachers, that they liked my discourse very well; and the Preachers encouraged me to use the talent which the Lord had entrusted me with.

I continued to labour among the people at Prestent with great satisfaction, and the Society increased both in number and love, till the beginning of the year 1792, when an opportunity was afforded us of removing from Nova Scotia to Sierra Leone. The advantages held out to the Blacks were considered by them as valuable. Every married man was promised 30 acres of land, and every male child under 15 years of age, was entitled to five acres. We were likewise to have a free passage to Africa, and upon our arrival, to be furnished with provisions till we could clear a sufficient portion of land necessary for our subsistence. The Company likewise engaged to furnish us with all necessaries, and to take in return the produce of the new plantations. Their intention being, as far as possible in their power, to put a stop to the abominable slave-trade. With respect to myself, I was just got into a comfortable way, being employed by a gentleman, who gave me two shillings per day, with victuals and lodging; so that I was enabled to clothe myself and family, and provide other necessaries of life: But recollecting the concern I had felt in years past, for the conversion of the Africans, I resolved to embrace the opportunity of visiting that country; and therefore went to one of the Agents employed in this business, and acquainted him with my intention. The gentleman informed Mr. Clarkson, that I was under no necessity of leaving Nova Scotia, because I was comfortably provided for: But when I told them, that it was not for the sake of the advantages I hoped to reap in Africa, which induced me to undertake the voyage, but from a desire that had long possessed my mind, of contributing to the best of my poor ability, in spreading the knowledge of Christianity in that country. Upon which they approved of my intention, and encouraged me to persevere in it. The Preachers likewise gave us the Rules of the Society, and many other little books which they judged might be useful to us: they also exhorted us to cleave to the Lord with our whole heart, and treated us with the tenderness and affection of parents to their children. After praying with us, we parted with tears, as we never expected to meet again in this world.

January 16, we sailed for Africa; and on the 22d, we met with a dreadful storm which continued sixteen days. Some of the men who had been engaged in a sea-faring life for 30 or 40 years, declared, that they never saw such a storm before. Our fleet, consisting of 15 ships, were dispersed, and only five of us kept together. We lost one man, who was washed overboard; he left a wife and four children; but what most affected me was, that he died as he had lived, without any appearance of religion. I was upon deck at the same time that he met with this misfortune, but the Lord wonderfully preserved me. After the storm abated, we had a very pleasant passage. But the situation of my wife greatly distressed me. She was exceeding ill most of the voyage; sometimes, for half a day together, she was not able to speak a word. I expected to see her die before we could reach land, and had an unaccountable aversion to bury her in the sea. In the simplicity of my heart, I intreated the Lord to spare her, at least till we reached the shore, that I might give her a decent burial, which was the last kind office I could perform for her. The Lord looked upon my sincerity, and restored her to perfect health.

March 6, we arrived safe at Sierra Leone; and on the 27th, my wife caught a putrid fever. For several days she lost her senses, and was as helpless as an infant. When I enquired into the state of her mind, she could give me no satisfactory answer, which greatly heightened my distress. On Friday, while we were at prayer with her, the Lord mercifully manifested his love and power to her soul; she suddenly rose up, and said, "I am well: I only wait for the coming of the Lord. Glory be to his Name, I am prepared to meet him, and that will be in a short time." On Sunday, while several of our friends were with her, she lay still; but as soon as they began singing this hymn, "Lo! he comes, with clouds descending, Once for favour'd sinners slain," &c. She joined with us, till we came to the last verse, when she began to rejoice aloud, and expired in a rapture of love. She had lived in the fear of GOD, and walked in the light of his countenance for above eight years.

About two months after the death of my wife, I was likewise taken ill of the putrid fever. It was an universal complaint, and the people died so fast, that it was difficult to procure a burial for them. This affliction continued among us for three months, when it pleased the Lord to remove the plague from the place. It was a happy circumstance, that before the rainy season commenced, most of us had built little huts to dwell in; but as we had no house sufficient to hold the congregation, we preached under a large tree when the weather would permit. The people regularly attended the means of Grace, and the work of the Lord prospered. When the rains were over, we erected a small chapel, and went on our way comfortably. I worked for the Company, for 3s. per day, and preached in my turn. I likewise found my mind drawn out to pity the native inhabitants, and preached to them several times, but laboured under great inconveniences to make them understand the Word of GOD, as I could only visit them on the Lord's-Day. I therefore went to the Governor, and solicited him to give me employment in the Company's Plantation on Bullam Shore, in order that I might have frequent opportunities of conversing with the Africans. He kindly approved of my intention, and sent me to the Plantation to get ship-timber in company with several others. The gentleman who superintended the Plantation, treated me with the utmost kindness, and allowed six men to help me to build a house for myself, which we finished in 12 days. When a sufficient quantity of timber was procured, and other business for the Company in this place compleated, I was sent to the African town to teach the children to read, but found it difficult to procure scholars, as the parents shewed no great inclination to send their children. I therefore said to them, on the Lord's-Day after preaching, "It is a good thing that GOD has made the White People, and that he has inclined their hearts to bring us into this country, to teach you his ways, and to tell you that he gave his Son to die for you; and if you will obey his commandments he will make you happy in this world, and in that which is to come; where you will live with him in heaven;—and all pain and wretchedness will be at an end;—and you shall enjoy peace without interruption, joy without bitterness, and happiness to all eternity. The Almighty not only invites you to come unto him, but also points out the way whereby you may find his favour, viz. turn from your wicked ways, cease to do evil, and learn to do well. He now affords you a means which you never had before; he gives you his Word to be a light to your feet, and a lantern to your paths; and he likewise gives you an opportunity of having your children instructed in the Christian Religion. But if you neglect to send them, you must be answerable to GOD for it."

The poor Africans appeared attentive to the exhortation, altho' I laboured under the disadvantage of using an interpreter. My scholars soon increased from four to twenty; fifteen of whom continued with me five months. I taught them the Alphabet, and to spell words of two syllables;

and likewise the Lord's-Prayer. And I found them as apt to learn as any children I have known. But with regard to the old people, I am doubtful whether they will ever abandon the evil habits in which they were educated, unless the Lord visits them in some extraordinary manner.

In the year 1793, the gentlemen belonging to the Company told me, that if I would consent to go to England with the Governor, he would procure me two or three years schooling, that I might be better qualified to teach the natives. When this proposal was first mentioned to me, it seemed like an idle tale; but upon the further conversation on the subject, difficulties were removed, and I consented. On the 26th of March 1794, we embarked for England, and arrived at Plymouth, after a pleasant voyage, on the 16th of May. On the 1st of June we got into the Thames, and soon after, Mrs. Paul, whom I was acquainted with in America, came to Wapping, and invited me to the New Chapel in the City-Road, where I was kindly received.

When I first arrived in England, I considered my great ignorance and inability, and that I was among a wise and judicious people, who were greatly my superiors in knowledge and understanding; these reflections had such an effect upon me, that I formed a resolution never to attempt to preach while I stayed in the country; but the kind importunity of the Preachers and others removed my objections, and I found it profitable to my own soul, to be exercised in inviting sinners to Christ; particularly one Sunday, while I was preaching at Snowsfields-Chapel, the Lord blessed me abundantly, and I found a more cordial love to the White People than I had ever experienced before. In the former part of my life I had suffered greatly from the cruelty and injustice of the Whites, which induced me to look upon them, in general, as our enemies: And even after the Lord had manifested his forgiving mercy to me, I still felt at times an uneasy distrust and shyness towards them; but on that day the Lord removed all my prejudices; for which I bless his holy Name.

In the month of August 1794, I went to Bristol; and from thence Dr. Coke took me with him to Kingswood-School, where I continued to the present time, and have endeavoured to acquire all the knowledge I possibly could, in order to be useful in that sphere which the blessed hand of Providence may conduct me into, if my life is spared. I have great cause to be thankful that I came to England, for I am now fully convinced, that many of the White People, instead of being enemies and oppressors of us poor Blacks, are our friends, and deliverers from slavery, as far as their ability and circumstances will admit. I have met with the most affectionate treatment from the Methodists of London, Bristol, and other places which I have had an opportunity of visiting. And I must confess, that I did not believe there were upon the face of the earth a people so friendly and humane as I have proved them to be. I beg leave to acknowledge the obligations I am under to Dr. Coke, Mr. Bradford, and all the Preachers and people; and I pray GOD to reward them a thousand fold for all the favours they have shewn to me in a strange land.

BOSTON KING

Kingswood-School, June 4, 1796

+About the latter end of September, 1796, Boston King embarked for Sierra Leone; where he arrived safe, and resumed the employment of a school-master in that Colony; the number of scholars under his care are about forty; and we hope to hear that they will not only learn the English Language, but also attain some knowledge of the way of salvation thro' faith in the Lord Jesus Christ.

Notes

❧❧❧

INTRODUCTION

1. Paul Gilroy, *The Black Atlantic: Modernity and Double Consciousness* (Cambridge: Harvard University Press, 1993). Gilroy's formulation of the black Atlantic as a "counterculture of modernity" extends Cedric Robinson's "black radical tradition," Robert Farris Thompson's "black Atlantic tradition," and other modern concepts of the black diaspora. See Robinson, *Black Marxism: The Making of the Black Radical Tradition* (1983; reprint, Chapel Hill: University of North Carolina Press, 2000), and Thompson, *Flash of the Spirit: African and Afro-American Art and Philosophy* (New York: Vintage, 1983).

2. Paul E. Lovejoy, *Transformations in Slavery: A History of Slavery in Africa*, African Studies Series, no. 36 (New York: Cambridge University Press, 1983), pp. 88–107, 135–40; Robert J. Allison, *The Crescent Obscured: The United States and the Muslim World, 1776–1815* (New York: Oxford University Press, 1995), pp. 3–126; David Eltis, "The Volume and Structure of the Transatlantic Slave Trade: A Reassessment," *William and Mary Quarterly*, 3d ser., 58 (2001): 33–34; David Richardson, "Shipboard Revolts, African Authority, and the Atlantic Slave Trade," *William and Mary Quarterly*, 3d ser., 58 (2001): 83.

3. A useful guide to legislation restricting the world's various slave trades and the rights of slaveowners worldwide is David Ziskind, *Emancipation Acts: Quintessential Labor Laws* (Los Angeles: Litlaw Foundation, 1993). An "internal" slave trade remained legal in many parts of the United States, of course, until the Civil War.

4. Christopher Fyfe, *A History of Sierra Leone* (New York: Oxford University

Press, 1962), pp. 14–73; James W. St. George Walker, *The Black Loyalists: The Search for a Promised Land in Nova Scotia and Sierra Leone*, Dalhousie African Studies Series (New York: Africana Press and Dalhousie University Press, 1976), pp. 97–132.

5. For two of the many examples of abolitionism joined with anti-Islam sentiments at the end of the eighteenth century and beginning of the nineteenth, see the following: Quobna Ottobah Cugoano, "Thoughts and Sentiments on the Evil and Wicked Traffic of the Slavery and Commerce of the Human Species, Humbly Submitted to the Inhabitants of Great-Britain, by Ottobah Cugoano, a Native of Africa" (1787), in Cugoano, *Thoughts and Sentiments on the Evil of Slavery and Other Writings*, ed. Vincent Carretta (New York: Penguin Books, 1999), pp. 67, 92–93; Jedediah Morse, *A Discourse Delivered at the African Meeting-House, in Boston, July 14, 1808, in Grateful Celebration of the Abolition of the African Slave-trade, by the Governments of the United States, Great Britain and Denmark* (Boston: Lincoln and Edmands, 1808), pp. 9, 18.

6. Boucabar Barry, *Senegambia and the Atlantic Slave Trade*, trans. Ayi Kwei Armah, African Studies Series, no. 92 (New York: Cambridge University Press, 1998), pp. 94–125; Sylviane A. Diouf, *Servants of Allah: African Muslims Enslaved in the Americas* (New York: New York University Press, 1998), pp. 18–29.

7. Gilroy, *Black Atlantic*, pp. 1–40.

8. David Brion Davis, *The Problem of Slavery in the Age of Revolution, 1770–1823* (Ithaca, N.Y.: Cornell University Press, 1975), pp. 141–52.

9. A. Leon Higginbotham, Jr., *In the Matter of Color: Race and the American Legal Process, the Colonial Period* (New York: Oxford University Press, 1978), pp. 333–55; James Walvin, *Black Ivory: A History of British Slavery* (Washington, D.C.: Howard University Press, 1994), pp. 14–15.

10. Sylvia R. Frey, *Water from the Rock: Black Resistance in a Revolutionary Age* (Princeton: Princeton University Press, 1991), pp. 87–89, 106, 144–45, 173–93.

11. *The Book of Negroes* has been published on-line by the Government of Canada, Canada's Digital Collections office: <http://collections.ic.gc.ca/blackloyalists/documents/official/book_of_negroes.htm>. Physical copies are housed at the Public Records Office, Kew, England; the Nova Scotia Archives, Halifax, Nova Scotia; and the National Archives, Washington, D.C. See also D. G. Bell, "African-American Refugees to Annapolis Royal and Saint John, 1783: A Ship Passenger List," *Nova Scotia Historical Review* 16 (1996): 71–81.

12. Prospects for farming and fishing at Birchtown are described in a diary entry written by Shelburne resident William Booth on March 14, 1787: "They

have given no proof of their judgment in Farming about this spot ... 'tis a Valley with much stones, and a little Swampy.... Fishing is the chief and most profitable employment for these Poor, but really Spirited People." Captain William Booth Diary, 1787–1789, volume 11, Shelburne County Genealogical Society, Shelburne, Nova Scotia. A 1788 Birchtown visitor echoed Booth's assessment: "The place is beyond description wretched, situated on the coast in the middle of barren rocks, and partly surround by thick impenetrable wood. Their huts miserable to guard against the inclemency of a Nova Scotia winter, and their existence almost depending on what they could lay up in summer." Mary Louise Clifford, *From Slavery to Freetown: Black Loyalists after the American Revolution* (Jefferson, N.C.: McFarland, 1999), p. 46. On Shelburne, see also Charles Wetherell and Robert Roetger, "Another Look at the Loyalists of Shelburne, Nova Scotia, 1783–1795," *Canadian Historical Review* 70 (1989): 76–91; Mary Archibald, "The Shelburne Loyalists," *Nova Scotia Historical Review* 3 (1983): 5–20; and W. O. Raymond, "The Founding of Shelburne," in *Collections of the New Brunswick Historical Society, No. 8* (Saint John, New Brunswick: Barnes and Co., 1909), pp. 227–33, 268–71.

13. Conditions at Birchtown are described in Clifford, *From Slavery to Freetown*, pp. 43–49; Walker, *The Black Loyalists*, pp. 18–87; Ellen Gibson Wilson, *The Loyal Blacks* (New York: G. P. Putnam's Sons, 1976), pp. 92–101; and Phyllis R. Blakeley and John N. Grant, eds., *Eleven Exiles: Accounts of Loyalists in the American Revolution* (Toronto: Dundurn Press, 1982), pp. 274–76.

14. On the economic difficulties of Nova Scotia in the decades before the arrival of the Loyalists, see Lewis R. Fischer, "Revolution without Independence: The Canadian Colonies, 1749–1775," in *The Economy of Early America: The Revolutionary Period, 1763–1790*, ed. Ronald Hoffman, John J. McCusker, Russell R. Menard, and Peter J. Albert (Charlottesville: University Press of Virginia, 1988), pp. 94–108.

15. Walker, *The Black Loyalists*, p. 49; Wilson, *The Loyal Blacks*, p. 92; Anthony Kirk-Greene, "David George: The Nova Scotian Experience," *Sierra Leone Studies* 14 (1960): 104. Benjamin Marston, the surveyor who apportioned Loyalist land grants at Shelburne and Birchtown, chronicled the antiblack riot in his journal: "Monday, 26. Great Riot today. The disbanded soldiers have risen against the Free negroes to drive them out of Town, because they labour cheaper than they—the soldiers." "Tuesday, 27. Riot continues. The soldiers force the free negroes to quit the Town—pulled down about 20 of their houses." Marston

himself was "threatened by the Rioters" and consequently fled Shelburne for Halifax. See Raymond, "The Founding of Shelburne," p. 265. Simeon Perkins, a resident of nearby Liverpool, Nova Scotia, recorded in his diary that "some thousands of People Assembled with Clubbs & Drove the Negroes out of the Town." Simeon Perkins, *The Diary of Simeon Perkins, 1780–1789,* ed. D. C. Harvey and Bruce Fergusson (Toronto: Publications of the Champlain Society, 1958), p. 93.

16. Clifford, *From Slavery to Freetown,* pp. 53–57; Kirk-Greene, "David George," pp. 112–13; A. F. Walls, "The Nova Scotian Settlers and Their Religion," *Sierra Leone Bulletin of Religion* 1 (1959): 19–25; Christopher Fyfe, "The Countess of Huntingdon's Connection in Nineteenth Century Sierra Leone," *Sierra Leone Bulletin of Religion* 4 (1962): 53–61.

17. Walker, *The Black Loyalists,* pp. 68, 82; Wilson, *The Loyal Blacks,* pp. 121–29.

18. Wesley's letter appears in Blakeley and Grant, *Eleven Exiles,* p. 278. See also Wilson, *The Loyal Blacks,* p. 96; Nathan Bangs, ed., *The Life of the Rev. Freeborn Garrettson* (New York: T. Mason and G. Lane, 1839), pp. 152, 158, 161; and Robert Drew Simpson, ed., *American Methodist Pioneer: The Life and Journals of the Rev. Freeborn Garrettson, 1752–1827* (Rutland, Vt.: Academy Books, 1984), pp. 246, 249–51.

19. On water baptism, see Melville Herskovits, *The Myth of the Negro Past* (Boston: Beacon Press, 1958), pp. 233–35; Michael Gomez, *Exchanging Our Country Marks: The Transformation of African Identities in the Colonial and Antebellum South* (Chapel Hill: University of North Carolina Press, 1998), pp. 244–90; and Arthur Charles Dayfoot, *The Shaping of the West Indian Church, 1492–1962* (Kingston, Jamaica: Press University of the West Indies, 1999), pp. 128–30, 184–85. On the Nova Scotian black Baptists, see P. E. McKerrow, *A Brief History of the Coloured Baptists of Nova Scotia, 1783–1895* (Halifax: Afro Nova Scotian Enterprises, 1976).

20. The Huntingdon Connexion, its evangelical activity in the Americas, and the Countess of Huntingdon's interest in proselytizing among nonwhite people are discussed in the following works: A. C. H. Seymour, *The Life and Times of Selina, Countess of Huntingdon, by a Member of the House of Shirley and Hastings* (London: William Edward Painter, 1840), 2:441–44; Helen C. Knight, *Lady Huntington [sic] and Her Friends; Or, the Revival of the Work of God in the Days of Wesley, Whitefield, Romaine, Venn, and Others in the Last Century* (New York: American Tract Society, 1853), pp. 39, 54–56, 147–48; T. Watson Smith, *History of the Methodist Church within the Territories Embraced in the Late Conference of Eastern British America, including Nova Scotia, New Brunswick, Prince Edward Island and Bermuda* (Halifax: Methodist Book

Room, 1877), 1:32–34, 174; Horton Davies, *The English Free Churches* (New York: Oxford University Press, 1952), pp. 136–44. The predestinarianism of "traditional African philosophy," which suggests an affinity between Calvinism and blacks in the era of the slave trade, is emphasized in Paget Henry, *Caliban's Reason: Introducing Afro-Caribbean Philosophy*, Books in Africana Thought (New York: Routledge, 2000), pp. 27–37.

21. J. B. Elliott, *Lady Huntingdon's Connexion in Sierra Leone, A Narrative of Its History and Its Present State* (London: Society for the Spread of the Gospel at Home and Abroad, 1851), pp. 14–18; "Governor Clarkson's Diary," in *Sierra Leone after a Hundred Years*, ed. E. G. Ingham (London: Seeley and Co., 1894), p. 36; E. P. Nicol, *A Brief History of St. Mark's Church, (Countess of Huntingdon's Connexion), Waterloo, Sierra Leone* (Aberdeen: Scottish Institute of Missionary Studies, 1970); S. E. Boyd Smith, "The Effective Countess: Lady Huntingdon and the 1780 Edition of a Select Collection of Hymns," *The Hymn* 44 (1993): 27.

22. One of the fifteen points of doctrine affirmed in 1783 by the Huntingdonians read, "Although the whole world is . . . guilty before God, it hath pleased him to predestine some unto everlasting life. Predestination therefore to life is the everlasting purpose of God, whereby (before the foundations of the world were laid) he hath constantly decreed by his counsel, secrets to us, to deliver from curse and damnation those whom he hath chosen in Christ out of mankind, and to bring them by Christ to everlasting salvation." Seymour, *The Life and Times of Selina, Countess of Huntingdon*, 2:441. Free-will Christianity, or Arminianism, posited that men and women could effect their own salvation through faith and good works, neither of which was predetermined by God but was rather each individual's to choose or not. As late as 1851 there were black Huntingdonians in Sierra Leone claiming to adhere to the fifteen points. Elliott, *Lady Huntingdon's Connexion in Sierra Leone*, p. 18. The authoritative study of Coke is John Vickers, *Thomas Coke: Apostle of Methodism* (Nashville: Abingdon Press, 1969).

23. Sylvia Frey and Betty Wood detail the contiguous development of these black religious movements in *Come Shouting to Zion: African American Protestantism in the American South and British Caribbean to 1830* (Chapel Hill: University of North Carolina Press, 1998).

24. On the "black poor" of London, see James Walvin, *England, Slaves and Freedom, 1776–1838* (Jackson: University Press of Mississippi, 1986), pp. 62–65. On their removal to Sierra Leone, see Stephen J. Braidwood, *Black Poor and White Philanthropists: London's Blacks and the Foundations of the Sierra Leone Settlement, 1786–1791*

(Liverpool: Liverpool University Press, 1994). Thomas Peters had served as a sergeant in the War of Independence under Sir Henry Clinton and almost certainly had the British promises of freedom of the 1770s on his mind when he sailed to England. Betty Fladeland, *Men and Brothers: Anglo-American Antislavery Cooperation* (Urbana: University of Illinois Press, 1972), p. 84.

25. Antonio McDaniel, *Swing Low, Sweet Chariot: The Mortality Cost of Colonizing Liberia in the Nineteenth Century* (Chicago: University of Chicago Press, 1995), pp. 24–34. McDaniel reports that Sierra Leone was "thought to have the highest death rate in the British colonial world" (p. 34).

26. David Eltis, *Economic Growth and the Ending of the Atlantic Slave Trade* (New York: Oxford University Press, 1987), pp. 20–23; Robin Law, "The Historiography of the Commercial Transition in Nineteenth-Century West Africa," in *African Historiography: Essays in Honor of Jacob Ade Ajayi*, ed. Toyin Falola (Essex, Eng.: Longman, 1993), pp. 91–115.

27. After an initial migration of about 1,200, at least 500 New World blacks joined the settlers of Sierra Leone. Fladeland, *Men and Brothers*, pp. 83–84. In 1815, a figure of 2,000 was offered as a count of all black settlers in the area. Robert Thorpe, *A Letter to William Wilberforce, Esq., M.P. . . . Containing Remarks on the Reports of the Sierra Leone Company, and African Institute* (London: F. C. and J. Rivington, 1815), p. 3. An estimate of "nearly 2000" by 1800 appears in Christopher Fyfe, ed., introduction to *"Our Children Free and Happy": Letters from Black Settlers in Africa in the 1790s*, with a contribution by Charles Jones (Edinburgh: Edinburgh University Press, 1991), p. 1.

28. Election days are described in William Piersen, *Black Yankees: The Development of an Afro-American Subculture in Eighteenth-Century New England* (Amherst: University of Massachusetts Press, 1988), pp. 117–28, and Joseph P. Reidy, " 'Negro Election Day' and Black Community Life in New England, 1750–1860," *Marxist Perspectives* 1 (1978): 102–17. Pinkster celebrations are described in Shane White, *Somewhat More Independent: The End of Slavery in New York City, 1770–1810* (Athens: University of Georgia Press, 1991), pp. 95–106; Graham Russell Hodges, introduction to *Black Itinerants of the Gospel: The Narratives of John Jea and George White* (Madison, Wis.: Madison House, 1993), pp. 20–21; and Linda Pershing, "Negotiating History and Memory: Racial Representations at Pinkster, an Annual New York Celebration," *New York Folklore* 24 (1998): 77–95.

29. Harry E. Davis, "Documents Relating to Negro Masonry in America," *Journal of Negro History* 21 (1936): 411–32. On black Masonic history, see Joseph

A. Walkes, Jr., *Black Square and Compass: 200 Years of Prince Hall Freemasonry* (Richmond: Macoy Publishing and Masonic Supply, 1979), and Charles H. Wesley, *Prince Hall. Life and Legacy* (Philadelphia: Afro-American Historical and Cultural Museum, and Washington, D.C.: United Supreme Council, Prince Hall Affiliation, 1977).

30. On the lampooning of the African Lodge, see Gary Nash, *Forging Freedom: The Formation of Philadelphia's Black Community, 1720–1840* (Cambridge: Harvard University Press, 1988), pp. 255–57. Antebellum conflicts over race and public space are chronicled in Emma Jones Lapsansky, " 'Since They Got Those Separate Churches': Afro-Americans and Racism in Jacksonian Philadelphia," *American Quarterly* 32 (1980): 54–78; Leonard P. Curry, *The Free Black in Urban America, 1800–1850: The Shadow of the Dream* (Chicago: University of Chicago Press, 1981); and Joanne Pope Melish, *Disowning Slavery: Gradual Emancipation and "Race" in New England, 1780–1860* (Ithaca, N.Y.: Cornell University Press, 1998).

31. Some of the attraction of Freemasonry for Marrant is described in James Horton and Lois Horton, *In Hope of Liberty: Culture, Community, and Protest among Northern Free Blacks, 1700–1860* (New York: Oxford University Press, 1997), pp. 125–27, and Sandra M. Gustafson, *Eloquence Is Power: Oratory and Performance in Early America* (Chapel Hill: University of North Carolina Press, 2000), pp. 108–10. See also Joanna Brooks, "Prince Hall, Freemasonry, and Genealogy," *African-American Review* 34 (2000): 197–216, and Maurice Wallace, " 'Are We Men?': Prince Hall, Martin Delaney, and the Masculine Ideal in Black Freemasonry, 1775–1865," *American Literary History* 9 (1997): 396–424.

32. Literary critics have often undervalued the authority of early black writers and underestimated the complexity of early black texts. For example, Vernon Loggins dismissed *A Journal of the Rev. John Marrant* in his book *The Negro Author: His Development in America to 1900* (New York: Kennikat, 1964), pp. 33–34: "The *Journal*, supposedly written by Marrant without aid, is scarcely more than an adaptation of the *Narrative*. . . . Even though Marrant had evidently by 1789 become something of a racial leader, neither the *Journal* nor the *Sermon* contains the slightest allusion to the pitiable condition of his people in American life."

33. "Art. 52. A Narrative of the Lord's Dealings with John Marrant" [review], *Monthly Review* (November 1785): 399. Similarly, Thomas Jefferson believed that the imagination of blacks was so extravagant that it was incapable of guiding the composition of noble and rational literary works. See Thomas F. Gossett, *Race: The History of an Idea in America* (New York: Schocken Books, 1965), pp. 42–44.

34. For a parallel, see Angelo Costanzo, *Surprizing Narrative: Olaudah Equiano and the Beginnings of Black Autobiography* (Westport, Conn.: Greenwood Press, 1987), pp. 96–104.

35. Vincent Carretta, ed., *Unchained Voices: An Anthology of Black Authors in the English-Speaking World of the 18th Century* (Lexington: University Press of Kentucky, 1996), p. 129, n. 9; Margaret Washington Creel, *"A Peculiar People": Slave Religion and Community-Culture among the Gullahs* (New York: New York University Press, 1988), p. 376, n. 12.

36. The Mayrant family is enumerated in the United States Census, State of South Carolina, Claremont County, Camden District, 1790, p. 228. The digitized census record may be viewed at <http://www.rootsweb.com/~usgenweb/sc/census/1790/227-228.gif>. John Marrant's name is transcribed "Morant" in letters by Freeborn Garrettson; see Bangs, *The Life of the Rev. Freeborn Garrettson*, pp. 152, 158, and Simpson, *American Methodist Pioneer*, pp. 246, 249. On the subject of African American slaveholders more generally, see Larry Koger, *Black Slaveowners: Free Black Slave Masters in South Carolina, 1790–1860* (Jefferson, N.C.: McFarland and Co., 1985).

37. Register of Marriages in the Parish of St. George and St. Patrick, in the County of Shelburne, in the Province of Nova Scotia (1788), Shelburne Historical Society, Shelburne, Nova Scotia, n.p.

38. For a parallel, see Rosemary Fithian Guruswamy, " 'Thou Has the Holy Word': Jupiter Hammon's 'Regards' to Phillis Wheatley," in *Genius in Bondage: Literature of the Early Black Atlantic*, ed. Vincent Carretta and Philip Gould (Lexington: University Press of Kentucky, 2001), pp. 190–98. Despite Marrant's use of scriptural references to convey an unspoken message to blacks, he relied on texts and incidents familiar to whites. Conversion accounts and captivity narratives are obvious examples. Less well known in the twenty-first century, perhaps, are incidents of South Carolina settler history that were echoed in Marrant's narrative. See, for example, *Calendar of State Papers, Colonial: North America and the West Indies, 1574–1739*, CD-ROM edition, consultant editors Karen Ordahl Kupperman, John C. Appleby, and Mandy Banton (London: Routledge, in association with the Public Record Office, 2000); George Rodd to his Employer in London, May 8, 1715, Charlestown, 28:166–69; Abel Kettleby and other planters and merchants trading to Carolina to the Council of Trade and Plantations, July 18, 1715, n.p., 28:236–38; Governor Johnson to the Council of Trade and Plantations, September 28, 1732, Charles Town, 39:217–20.

39. Mark Valeri, "The New Divinity and the American Revolution," *William and Mary Quarterly*, 3d ser., 46 (1989): 741–69.

40. Fyfe, *"Our Children Free and Happy,"* p. 37.

41. A. M. Falconridge, *Narrative of Two Voyages to the River Sierra Leone during the Years 1791–1793*, 2d ed. (1802; reprint, London: Frank Cass, 1967), p. 277; John Peterson, *Province of Freedom: A History of Sierra Leone, 1787–1870* (Evanston: Northwestern University Press, 1969), pp. 48, 52–53.

42. Arthur Zilversmit, *The First Emancipation: The Abolition of Slavery in the North* (Chicago: University of Chicago Press, 1967), pp. 109–229; Melish, *Disowning Slavery*, pp. 84–118.

JOHN MARRANT, *A Narrative of the Lord's Wonderful Dealings*

1. Marrant's note: "Mr. HART, a Baptist Minister at Charles-Town." All subsequent notes are John Marrant's.

2. "These Pegs were to be kindled at the opposite end from the Body."

3. "The Office of Executioner there, in many respects resembles that of a High Sheriff in this country."

4. "Or what those parts were which seemed to affect me so much, not knowing what I read, as he did not understand the English language."

5. "I had been absent from them near twenty-three months."

6. "Though it is unusual for Indians to have a horse, yet the king accompanied the general on the present successful occasion riding on horse-back.—If the king wished to serve me, there was no opportunity; the Town being taken on Friday afternoon, Saturday an express arrived from the commander in chief at New York, for a large detachment, or the town would fall into the hands of the Americans, which hurried us away on Sunday morning."

7. "This action was on the 5th of August, 1781."

JOHN MARRANT, *A Sermon Preached*

1. "Such as Tertullian, Cyprian, Origen, Augustine, Chrysostom, Gregory Nazianen, Arnobius, and many others."

JOHN MARRANT, *A Funeral Sermon Preached*

1. "This is to inform my Friends and the Public in general, that the report which Mr. Platt of Holywell Mount Chapel, made in public concerning this sermon, he could not prove, and therefore is false in saying it was taken from

Dr. Dodderidge's [Philip Doddridge, 1702–51, a British commentator on Calvin, a patron of George Whitefield, and an author of popular hymns]. I hope the public will prove both sermons together, and they will see the falsity of it, and let the prejudice be removed from their minds, which was hurt so much by it. It was done out of revenge and envy, and when he was convinced, would not submit nor lie open to conviction; nor was he able to prove his assertion. So we leave him in the hands of God, being not willing to go to law with our brethren."

DAVID GEORGE, *AN ACCOUNT OF THE LIFE*

1. *Baptist Annual Register* editor John Rippon's note: "See an account of him in the *Register*, p. 332." All subsequent notes are John Rippon's.

2. "The account to which he refers is in p. 336 of the *Register*."

3. "Secretary's Office, Frederick-town, 17th July, 1792. I do hereby certify, that David George, a free Negro man, has permission from his Excellency the Lieutenant Governor, to instruct the Black people in the knowledge, and exhort them to the practice of, the Christian religion. Jon. Odell, Secretary."

4. "This Governor Clarkson also has confirmed to the EDITOR."

5. "Baptism by immersion, in an occasional way, not only obtains in Mr. Wesley's connexions, as above, but also in some of the West India islands, as well as in Kentuckey, and other parts of North America; and it is said to be done, even under the permission of Dr. Coke himself."

6. "Rev. Mr. Melvill Horne was curate to Mr. Fletcher of Medley, and is now the much-loved officiating clergyman at Sierra Leone. EDITOR."